T0288623

The Story of God Bible Commentary Series Endorsements

"Getting a story is about more than merely enjoying it. It means hearing it, understanding it, and above all, being impacted by it. This commentary series hopes that its readers not only hear and understand the story, but are impacted by it to live in as Christian a way as possible. The editors and contributors set that table very well and open up the biblical story in ways that move us to act with sensitivity and understanding. That makes hearing the story as these authors tell it well worth the time. Well done."

Darrell L. Bock
Dallas Theological Seminary

"The Story of God Bible Commentary series invites readers to probe how the message of the text relates to our situations today. Engagingly readable, it not only explores the biblical text but offers a range of applications and interesting illustrations."

Craig S. Keener
Asbury Theological Seminary

"I love The Story of God Bible Commentary series. It makes the text sing, and helps us hear the story afresh."

John Ortberg
Senior Pastor of Menlo Park Presbyterian Church

"In this promising new series of commentaries, believing biblical scholars bring not only their expertise but their own commitment to Jesus and insights into today's culture to the Scriptures. The result is a commentary series that is anchored in the text but lives and breathes in the world of today's church with its variegated pattern of socioeconomic, ethnic, and national diversity. Pastors, Bible study leaders, and Christians of all types who are looking for a substantive and practical guide through the Scriptures will find these volumes helpful."

Frank Thielman
Beeson Divinity School

"The Story of God Bible Commentary series is unique in its approach to exploring the Bible. Its easy-to-use format and practical guidance brings God's grand story to modern-day life so anyone can understand how it applies today."

Andy Stanley
North Point Ministries

"I'm a storyteller. Through writing and speaking I talk and teach about understanding the Story of God throughout Scripture and about letting God reveal more of His story as I live it out. Thus I am thrilled to have a commentary series based on the Story of God—a commentary that helps me to Listen to the Story, that Explains the Story, and then encourages me to probe how to Live the Story. A perfect tool for helping every follower of Jesus to walk in the story that God is writing for them."

Judy Douglass
Director of Women's Resources, Cru

"The Bible is the story of God and his dealings with humanity from creation to new creation. The Bible is made up more of stories than of any other literary genre. Even the psalms, proverbs, prophecies, letters, and the Apocalypse make complete sense only when set in the context of the grand narrative of the entire Bible. This commentary series breaks new ground by taking all these observations seriously. It asks commentators to listen to the text, to explain the text, and to live the text. Some of the material in these sections overlaps with introduction, detailed textual analysis and application, respectively, but only some. The most riveting and valuable part of the commentaries are the stories that can appear in any of these sections, from any part of the globe and any part of church history, illustrating the text in any of these areas. Ideal for preaching and teaching."

Craig L. Blomberg
Denver Seminary

"Pastors and lay people will welcome this new series, which seeks to make the message of the Scriptures clear and to guide readers in appropriating biblical texts for life today."

Daniel I. Block
Wheaton College and Graduate School

"An extremely valuable, and long overdue series that includes comment on the cultural context of the text, careful exegesis, and guidance on reading the whole Bible as a unity that testifies to Christ as our Savior and Lord."

Graeme Goldsworthy
author of *According to Plan*

1, 2 & 3 JOHN

Editorial Board
of
The Story of God Bible Commentary

Old Testament general editor
Tremper Longman III

Old Testament associate editors
George Athas
Mark J. Boda
Myrto Theocharous

New Testament general editor
Scot McKnight

New Testament associate editors
Lynn H. Cohick
Michael F. Bird
Joel L. Willitts

Zondervan editors

Senior acquisitions editor
Katya Covrett

Senior production editor, Old Testament
Nancy L. Erickson

Senior production editor, New Testament
Christopher A. Beetham

The
Story of God
Bible Commentary

1, 2 & 3 JOHN

Constantine R. Campbell
Tremper Longman III & Scot McKnight
General Editors

ZONDERVAN

1, 2, and 3 John
Copyright © 2017 by Constantine R. Campbell

This title is also available as a Zondervan ebook.

Requests for information should be addressed to:
Zondervan, 3900 *Sparks Dr. SE, Grand Rapids, Michigan 49546*

ISBN 978-0-310-32732-5

Excerpts from *1, 2, and 3 John*, ZECNT (Grand Rapids: Zondervan, 2014) by Karen H. Jobes, ©2014. Used with permission.

All Scripture quotations, unless otherwise indicated, are taken from the Holy Bible, New International Version®, NIV®. Copyright © 1973, 1978, 1984, 2011 by Biblica, Inc.® Used by permission of Zondervan. All rights reserved worldwide. www.Zondervan.com. The "NIV" and "New International Version" are trademarks registered in the United States Patent and Trademark Office by Biblica, Inc.®

Any Internet addresses (websites, blogs, etc.) and telephone numbers in this book are offered as a resource. They are not intended in any way to be or imply an endorsement by Zondervan, nor does Zondervan vouch for the content of these sites and numbers for the life of this book.

All rights reserved. No part of this publication may be reproduced, stored in a retrieval system, or transmitted in any form or by any means—electronic, mechanical, photocopy, recording, or any other—except for brief quotations in printed reviews, without the prior permission of the publisher.

Cover design: *Ron Huizinga*
Cover image: *iStockphoto®*
Interior composition: *Matthew Van Zomeren*

Printed in the United States of America

17 18 19 20 21 22 23 24 /DHV/ 20 19 18 17 16 15 14 13 12 11 10 9 8 7 6 5 4 3 2 1

For Maria, Eleni, and Dimitra

Sisters by water and blood

Old Testament series

1 ▪ Genesis — *Tremper Longman III*
2 ▪ Exodus — *Christopher J. H. Wright*
3 ▪ Leviticus — *Jerry E. Shepherd*
4 ▪ Numbers — *Jay A. Sklar*
5 ▪ Deuteronomy — *Myrto Theocharous*
6 ▪ Joshua — *Lissa M. Wray Beal*
7 ▪ Judges — *Athena E. Gorospe*
8 ▪ Ruth/Esther — *Marion Taylor*
9 ▪ 1–2 Samuel — *Paul S. Evans*
10 ▪ 1–2 Kings — *David T. Lamb*
11 ▪ 1–2 Chronicles — *Carol M. Kaminski and Christine Palmer*
12 ▪ Ezra/Nehemiah — *Douglas J. Green*
13 ▪ Job — *Martin A. Shields*
14 ▪ Psalms — *Elizabeth R. Hayes*
15 ▪ Proverbs — *Ryan P. O'Dowd*
16 ▪ Ecclesiastes/Song of Songs — *George Athas*
17 ▪ Isaiah — *Mark J. Boda*
18 ▪ Jeremiah/Lamentations — *Andrew G. Shead*
19 ▪ Ezekiel — *D. Nathan Phinney*
20 ▪ Daniel — *Wendy L. Widder*
21 ▪ Minor Prophets I — *Beth M. Stovell*
22 ▪ Minor Prophets II — *Beth M. Stovell*

New Testament series

1 ▪ Matthew — *Rodney Reeves*
2 ▪ Mark — *Timothy G. Gombis*
3 ▪ Luke — *Kindalee Pfremmer DeLong*
4 ▪ John — *Nicholas Perrin*
5 ▪ Acts — *Dean Pinter*
6 ▪ Romans — *Michael F. Bird*
7 ▪ 1 Corinthians — *Justin K. Hardin*
8 ▪ 2 Corinthians — *Judith A. Diehl*
9 ▪ Galatians — *Nijay K. Gupta*
10 ▪ Ephesians — *Mark D. Roberts*
11 ▪ Philippians — *Lynn H. Cohick*
12 ▪ Colossians/Philemon — *Todd Wilson*
13 ▪ 1, 2 Thessalonians — *John Byron*
14 ▪ 1, 2 Timothy, Titus — *Marius Nel*
15 ▪ Hebrews — *Radu Gheorghita*
16 ▪ James — *Mariam J. Kamell*
17 ▪ 1 Peter — *Dennis R. Edwards*
18 ▪ 2 Peter, Jude — *C. Rosalee Velloso Ewell*
19 ▪ 1–3 John — *Constantine R. Campbell*
20 ▪ Revelation — *Jonathan A. Moo*
21 ▪ Sermon on the Mount — *Scot McKnight*

Contents

The Story of God Bible Commentary Series

The Word of God may not change, but culture does. Think of what we have seen in the last twenty years: we now communicate predominantly through the internet and email; we read our news on iPads and computers; we can talk on the phone to our friends while we are driving, while we are playing golf, while we are taking long walks; and we can get in touch with others from the middle of nowhere. We carry in our hands small devices that connect us to the world and to a myriad of sources of information. Churches have changed; the "Nones" are rising in numbers and volume, and atheists are bold to assert their views in public forums. The days of home Bible studies are waning; there is a marked rise in activist missional groups in churches, and pastors are more and more preaching topical sermons, some of which are not directly connected to the Bible. Divorce rates are not going down, marriages are more stressed, rearing children is more demanding, and civil unions and same-sex marriages are knocking at the door of the church.

Progress can be found in many directions. While church attendance numbers are waning in Europe and North America, churches are growing in the South and the East. More and more women are finding a voice in churches; the plea of the former generation of leaders that Christians be concerned not just with evangelism but with justice is being answered today in new and vigorous ways. Resources for studying the Bible are more available today than ever before, and preachers and pastors are meeting the challenge of speaking a sure Word of God into shifting cultures.

Readers of the Bible change, too. These cultural shifts, our own personal developments, the progress in intellectual questions, as well as growth in biblical studies and theology and discoveries of new texts and new paradigms for understanding the contexts of the Bible—each of these elements works on an interpreter so that the person who reads the Bible today asks different questions from different angles.

Culture shifts, but the Word of God remains. That is why we as editors of The Story of God Bible Commentary series, a commentary based on the New International Version 2011 (NIV 2011), are excited to participate in this new series of commentaries on the Bible. This series is designed to address this generation with the same Word of God. We are asking the authors to explain what the Bible says to the sorts of readers who pick up commentaries so they can understand not only what Scripture says but what it means for today. The Bible does not change, but relating it to our culture changes constantly and in differing ways in different contexts.

When we, the New Testament editors, sat down in prayer and discussion to choose authors for this series, we realized we had found fertile ground. Our list of potential authors staggered in length and quality. We wanted the authors to be exceptional scholars, faithful Christians, committed evangelicals, and theologically diverse, and we wanted this series to represent the changing face of both American and world evangelicalism: ethnic and gender diversity. I believe this series has a wider diversity of authors than any commentary series in evangelical history.

The title of this series, emphasizing as it does the "Story" of the Bible, reveals the intent of the series. We want to explain each passage of the Bible in light of the Bible's grand Story. The Bible's grand Story, of course, connects this series to the classic expression *regula fidei*, the "rule of faith," which was the Bible's story coming to fulfillment in Jesus as the Messiah, Lord, and Savior of all. In brief, we see the narrative built around the following biblical themes: creation and fall, covenant and redemption, law and prophets, and especially God's charge to humans as his image-bearers to rule under God. The theme of God as King and God's kingdom guides us to see the importance of Israel's kings as they come to fulfillment in Jesus, Lord and King over all, and the direction of history toward the new heavens and new earth, where God will be all in all. With these guiding themes, each passage is examined from three angles.

Listen to the Story. We believe that if the Bible is God speaking, then the most important posture of the Christian before the Bible is to listen. So our first section cites the text of Scripture and lists a selection of important biblical and sometimes noncanonical parallels; then each author introduces that passage. The introductions to the passages sometimes open up discussion to the theme of the passage while other times they tie this passage to its context in the specific book. But since the focus of this series is the Story of God in the Bible, the introduction leads the reader into reading this text in light of the Bible's Story.

Explain the Story. The authors follow up listening to the text by explaining each passage in light of the Bible's grand Story. This is not an academic series, so the footnotes are limited to the kinds of texts typical Bible readers and preachers readily will have on hand. Authors are given the freedom to explain the text as they read it, though you should not be surprised to find occasional listings of other options for reading the text. Authors explore biblical backgrounds, historical context, cultural codes, and theological interpretations. Authors engage in word studies and interpret unique phrases and clauses as they attempt to build a sound and living reading of the text in light of the Story of God in the Bible.

Authors will not shy away from problems in the texts. Whether one is examining the meaning of "perfect" in Matthew 5:48, the problems with Christology in the hymn of Philippians 2:6–11, the challenge of understanding Paul in light of the swirling debates about the old, new, and post-new perspectives, the endless debates about eschatology, or the vagaries of atonement theories, the authors will dive in, discuss evidence, and do their best to sort out a reasonable and living reading of those issues for the church today.

Live the Story. Reading the Bible is not just about discovering what it meant back then; the intent of The Story of God Bible Commentary series is to probe how this text might be lived out today as that story continues to march on in the life of the church. At times our authors will tell stories about what this looks like; at other times they may offer some suggestions for living it out; but always you will discover the struggle involved as we seek to live out the Bible's grand Story in our world.

We are not offering suggestions for "application" so much as digging deeper; we are concerned in this section with seeking out how this text, in light of the Story of God in the Bible, compels us to live in our world so that our own story lines up with the Bible's Story.

> Scot McKnight, general editor New Testament
> Lynn Cohick, Joel Willitts, and Michael Bird, editors

Abbreviations

AB	Anchor Bible
ANTC	Abingdon New Testament Commentary
BDAG	Danker, Frederick W., Walter Bauer, William F. Arndt, and F. Wilbur Gingrich. *Greek-English Lexicon of the New Testament and Other Early Christian Literature.* 3rd ed. Chicago: University of Chicago Press, 2000.
BECNT	Baker Exegetical Commentary on the New Testament
BETL	Bibliotheca Ephemeridum Theologicarum Lovaniensium
Bib	*Biblica*
BN	*Biblische Notizen*
BSac	*Bibliotheca Sacra*
BTNT	Biblical Theology of the New Testament series
BZNW	Beihefte zur Zeitschrift für die neutestamentliche Wissenschaft
CBET	Contributions to Biblical Exegesis and Theology
CSB	Christian Standard Bible (2017)
DNTB	*Dictionary of New Testament Background*
ESV	English Standard Version
EvQ	*Evangelical Quarterly*
HCSB	Holman Christian Standard Bible (2009)
IVPNTC	IVP New Testament Commentary
JBL	*Journal of Biblical Literature*
JGRChJ	*Journal of Greco-Roman Christianity and Judaism*
JSNTSup	Journal for the Study of the New Testament Supplement Series
LXX	Septuagint (the Greek Old Testament)
MNTC	Moffatt New Testament Commentary
NICNT	New International Commentary on the New Testament
NIV	New International Version
NIVAC	The NIV Application Commentary
NovT	*Novum Testamentum*

NRSV	New Revised Standard Version
NTL	New Testament Library
NTS	*New Testament Studies*
PG	Patrologia Graeca. Edited by J.-P. Migne. 162 vols. Paris, 1857–86.
PL	Patrologia Latina. Edited by J.-P. Migne. 217 vols. Paris, 1844–64.
PNTC	Pillar New Testament Commentary
RSV	Revised Standard Version
RTR	*Reformed Theological Review*
SBG	Studies in Biblical Greek
SNTSMS	Society for New Testament Studies Monograph Series
SP	Sacra Pagina
TNTC	Tyndale New Testament Commentary
TynBul	*Tyndale Bulletin*
WBC	Word Biblical Commentary
WTJ	*Westminster Theological Journal*
ZAW	*Zeitschrift für die alttestamentliche Wissenschaft*
ZECNT	Zondervan Exegetical Commentary on the New Testament
ZNW	*Zeitschrift für die neutestamentliche Wissenschaft und die Kunde der älteren Kirche*

Introduction to 1 John

First John has a special place in my heart. When I first became a Christian (or, perhaps more accurately, *while I was becoming* a Christian), I joined a small-group Bible study for the very first time. It was a ministry of the church I had been attending, and I was eager to learn more of the Bible beyond Sunday sermons. I was a young music student, freshly out of high school, and was taking "God stuff" seriously for the first time. What was the first book we studied in this small group? First John.

I remember vividly the wonder of trying to grasp what 1 John was teaching. I remember wrestling with some of the issues that have remained "wrestle worthy" to this day. But I also remember falling in love with the God who is love. The God who loves me with a profound love. The God revealed by Jesus Christ. It was truly a life-changing experience that I will always cherish.

While 1 John is ripe with immediate encouragement and profound theological insight, it certainly claims its share of challenges too. A big one is how it fits into the rest of the Bible, which is one of the major concerns of The Story of God Bible Commentary series. When we consider the story of God that runs through the entire Bible, we must ask where 1 John fits. The letter seems more detached from the biblical narrative than most other parts of the New Testament. The Gospels tell the story of Israel's Messiah coming in fulfillment of prophetic expectation to deliver God's people. Acts sees the message of Christ reach out to every place as the nations are brought into the knowledge of God. Then the letters of Paul sort out several pastoral and theological issues related to this story of God, particularly as Jewish and Gentile believers work out what it means to be God's people together in Christ.

But 1 John does not connect to the big story in the same way. There is no mention of Israel. There are no quotations from the Old Testament and few unambiguous allusions to it.[1] There is no mention of Adam. Or Abraham. Or Moses. Or David. Or any of the prophets. The only Old Testament figure mentioned is Cain, who is used as a negative example (of murder).[2] There is no mention of anything to do with the history of the kingdom of Israel. So where is the story of God in this letter?

---

1. D. A. Carson, "1–3 John," in *Commentary on the New Testament Use of the Old Testament*, ed. G. K. Beale and D. A. Carson (Grand Rapids: Baker, 2007), 1063.

2. See the commentary on 3:12 for a theory as to why Cain of all people is mentioned by name.

The answer is first addressed by appreciating 1 John's relationship to John's Gospel (discussed below). For what the letter lacks in references to the Old Testament, it makes up for in the abundance of references to the Fourth Gospel. John's Gospel is the source of *intertextuality* (i.e., one text referring to another) for 1 John in the way that the Old Testament is the source of inter-textuality for the rest of the New Testament.

Unlike 1 John, the Fourth Gospel is soaked in references to the Old Testament, albeit conceived differently when compared to the other three Gospels. As 1 John is engaged in intense "conversation" with John's Gospel, it assumes the Old Testament richness of that earlier document. Therefore, 1 John is not written in isolation from the story of God revealed in the Old Testament and in the ministry of Jesus. That story is assumed. First John expects the reader to understand its message in light of the story.

Second, the themes of 1 John resonate strongly with the themes of God's story. While the rest of the Bible tends to couch those themes within the unfolding story of God, 1 John explores its themes without explicitly doing so. But once we assume the story as John assumes it, we can see that his themes are very much the themes revealed in the unfolding story of God: love, the centrality of Jesus Christ, and fellowship with God.[3]

Love

Love is a major theme of 1 John. God is love. Love comes from God. Love is seen in Jesus's death for us. To know God is to love him. To love God is to love others. Without love, we cannot know God. Love is central. Love is what we need.

First John is a love letter from God. And it inspires love among God's children, as Augustine appreciated.

> This book is very sweet to every healthy Christian heart that savors the bread of God, and it should constantly be in the mind of God's holy church. But I choose it more particularly because what it specially commends to us is love. The person who possesses the thing which he hears about in this epistle must rejoice when he hears it. His reading will be like oil to a flame. . . . For others, the epistle should be like flame set to firewood; if it was not already burning, the touch of the word may kindle it.[4]

---

3. These themes and others are explored more fully below (see "Content of 1 John").

4. Augustine, "Ten Homilies on the First Epistle General of St. John," in *Augustine: Later Writings*, ed. John Burnaby, vol. 8 of *The Library of Christian Classics*, ed. J. Baillie et al. (Philadelphia: Westminster 1953–1966), 259.

It is impossible to walk away from 1 John without being struck by the awesome love of God in Christ. We also cannot walk away without being deeply challenged to love one another in sacrificial, costly, practical ways.

The Absolute Centrality of Jesus Christ

At the very heart of God's love for us is his Son. God sent Jesus Christ as an expression of his love to achieve for us the forgiveness of sins and to bring us into eternal fellowship with the Father and the Son. Relationship with God is only possible through Jesus. He is absolutely central.

Because of the centrality of Jesus Christ, it is a very serious problem if we get him wrong. This inspires John's pervasive warnings against christological error. False teachers have separated themselves from the church because of erroneous views about Jesus. They deny that Jesus is the Christ and that he has come in the flesh. Because they hold to these falsehoods about Jesus, John is emphatic that these false teachers are outside fellowship with God. They have not remained "in him."

Against the false teachers, John affirms the historical fact of Jesus's coming into the world as the incarnate Son of God. He purifies us from all sin and died to make atonement for our sins. To have the Son is to have the Father, and thus believing that Jesus is the Christ is essential for fellowship with God. If we remain in him, we will share eternal life with the Father and the Son.

Fellowship with God

All of this has been leading to what is arguably the ultimate concern of John's theology: fellowship with God. The centrality of Jesus is for fellowship with the Father and the Son; that is the goal of John's proclamation.[5] Since God is love, he is all about relationship.

And that is why he sent his Son into the world—that we might enjoy relationship with God. Through the forgiveness of sin and being made the children of God, believers live "in him," and he lives in us. We share in the dynamics of mutual indwelling, just as the Father and the Son so indwell one another by the Spirit. The gift of eternal life is found by remaining in the Son and in the Father. Indeed, fellowship with God is the joy of eternal life; that is what it is for.

Along with the general characteristics of John's message, we must also consider the historical elements surrounding 1 John. Who actually wrote the

---

5. See Max Turner, "The Churches of the Johannine Letters as Communities of 'Trinitarian' Koinōnia," in *The Spirit and Spirituality: Essays in Honour of Russell P. Spittler*, ed. Wonsuk Ma and Robert P Menzies (London: T&T Clark, 2004).

letter and why? What was the author's situation? Who were the original readers? Who were the author's opponents? We now turn to consider such matters.

Who Wrote 1 John and Why?

Authorship

It may surprise modern readers to realize that the letter universally known as
1 John does not claim to be written by John—or anyone else for that matter.
It is technically anonymous, a feature shared with only one other letter in the
New Testament—that written to the Hebrews.

The opening of 1 John (1:1–4) claims eyewitness testimony to Jesus's
incarnate life (and possibly his resurrection; see the commentary on these
verses). This, however, does not necessitate apostolic authorship as there were
other eyewitnesses who could make the same claim.

Moreover, some scholars challenge whether the apparent claims to eyewitness testimony really are what they seem. Schnackenburg suggests that the
author could have been a pupil of the fourth evangelist,[6] while Brown thinks
the author is a representative of a "Johannine School."[7] Bultmann takes it further by suggesting that the "we" of 1 John refers to "eschatological" contem-
poraries of Jesus—that is, the "eyewitness" testimony is "spiritual" in nature.[8]
None of these suggestions, however, do justice to the strength of language
used by the author in asserting his eyewitness credentials. Instead, Bauckham
mounts a compelling argument for the eyewitness origin of John's Gospel
and John's Letters.[9] Indeed, there is no compelling reason not to take 1 John's
claims at face value. This does not *prove* the author's claims to eyewitness
testimony, but we should not resort to hyperskepticism either.

One of the strongest indicators of the authorship of 1 John is its many
similarities in style, content, and theology to John's Gospel. The relationship
between the Gospel and 1 John will be explored below, but here we note
that the strong similarities do not necessarily solve the problem of who wrote
1 John since many scholars ask the same question of the Gospel. What we
may say with some confidence, however, is that whoever wrote John's Gospel
also wrote 1 John. As Kruse indicates, "If we are prepared to accept that the

6. Rudolph Schnackenburg, *The Johannine Epistles*, trans. Reginald and Ilse Fuller (New York: Crossroad, 2013), 41.

7. Raymond E. Brown, *The Epistles of John*, AB 30 (Garden City, NY: Doubleday, 1982), 30.

8. Rudolph Bultmann, *The Johannine Epistles*, trans. R. Philip O'Hara with Lane C. McGaughy and Robert W. Funk (Philadelphia: Fortress, 1973), 10.

9. Richard Bauckham, *Jesus and the Eyewitnesses: The Gospels as Eyewitness Testimony* (Grand Rapids: Eerdmans, 2006), 358–411. This does not mean that Bauckham regards the author to be John the son of Zebedee, as argued here; he prefers the moniker "the Beloved Disciple."

author was an eyewitness, then there exists a prima facie case for identifying the author of 1 John with the author of [. . .] the Fourth Gospel, because of the striking similarities of language and concepts."[10]

This is not the place to unpack all the arguments surrounding the authorship of John's Gospel,[11] so I will simply indicate my own preference to adhere to church tradition in ascribing authorship of the Fourth Gospel to John, the son of Zebedee, the "beloved disciple" of Jesus. Or, to put it another way, I do not find the skeptical scholarly arguments to the contrary sufficiently persuasive to overturn the tradition of the church. If tradition is correct about the Gospel, then it is also correct that 1 John was written by that same beloved disciple.

But how did this tradition begin? Early Christian tradition is unanimous in ascribing authorship of 1 John to John, the son of Zebedee and the apostle of Jesus.[12] First, there are no ancient manuscripts of John's Epistles that do not bear his name.[13] All manuscripts ascribe authorship to John.

Second, there are possible allusions to 1 John in several early patristic writings by Clement of Rome (ca. AD 92–101), the Didache (ca. AD 140), and The Epistle to Diognetus (ca. AD 130 or later). Polycarp of Smyrna (ca. AD 69–155) provides the earliest sure reference to 1 John in his letter to the Philippians, which dates to thirty or forty years before his death. But he did not attribute his quotations to John.

Third, Papias, active in the era AD 95–110 along with Ignatius and Polycarp, is said to have used 1 John. Eusebius said he saw 1 John quoted (or at least clearly alluded to) as he read Papias's *Expositions of the Oracles of the Lord* (no longer extant).[14]

Fourth, Irenaeus of Lyons (ca. AD 130–200) attributes 1 and 2 John to John the "disciple of the Lord" and author of the Fourth Gospel. He directly quotes 1 John 2:18–22; 4:1–3; 5:1; and 2 John 7, 8.[15] Clement of Alexandria, Tertullian, Origin of Alexandria, and Cyprian of Carthage (all early- to mid-third century) each made extensive use of 1 John.

Fifth, the Muratorian Canon (compiled between ca. AD 170–215) indicates Johannine authorship for the Gospel and the Letters. By the time of Eusebius (ca. AD 325), 1 John was regarded as one of the "acknowledged books."[16]

---

10. Colin G. Kruse, *The Letters of John*, PNTC (Grand Rapids: Eerdmans, 2000), 11.

11. For a concise overview of the history of critical scholarship regarding the question of authorship, see Robert W. Yarbrough, *1–3 John*, BECNT (Grand Rapids: Baker Academic, 2008), 6–11.

12. Kruse, *Letters of John*, 14.

13. Yarbrough, *1–3 John*, 12.

14. Ibid.

15. Irenaeus, *Against Heresies* 3.16.18.

16. John R. W. Stott, *The Letters of John: An Introduction and Commentary*, TNTC (Leicester: Inter-Varsity Press, 1988), 19.

So, though technically anonymous, 1 John has always been regarded as authored by John the apostle—at least, as far back as history will allow us to see and until the rise of critical scholarship in the nineteenth century. As indicated above, I do not regard the various critical arguments sufficient to overturn the weight of such tradition, nor is there any direct evidence that the letter was written by anyone else. Having said that, however, the issue of authorship does not dramatically affect the message of 1 John, notwithstanding its claims to eyewitness testimony.

John's Situation

According to tradition, John spent his later years in Asia Minor in and around Ephesus, as attested by Irenaeus (e.g., *Haer.* 3.1.2) and Eusebius (*Hist. eccl.* 3.1.1). He left Palestine after the Jewish rebellion in AD 66 and relocated to Asia Minor. Irenaeus indicates that John stayed in Ephesus until the reign of Trajan (AD 98–117), and he refers to John's ministry there.[17] According to Polycrates, John is one of the "luminaries" buried in Ephesus.[18] For these reasons, and without any evidence to the contrary, most scholars accept the Ephesus tradition.[19]

John's Reasons for Writing

John writes with pastoral intent. We see in 2:19 that some false teachers have departed from the church (or churches), leaving John's readers in a manner that has apparently grieved and confused them. The two recurring criticisms that John levels at the secessionists are that they do not love other believers and that they have denied that Jesus is the Christ. But John's first concern is not to correct the false teachers but to protect his readers, his beloved children.[20] The polemical elements of the letter serve this pastoral end, as John writes so that they would not be led astray (3:7) and would have assurance of eternal life (5:13).[21]

It is not surprising, then, that the two most significant themes in 1 John are concerned with love for other believers and holding to the truth about Jesus. It is not possible to know God without true love, nor is it possible to

---

17. Andreas J. Köstenberger, *A Theology of John's Gospel and Letters* (Grand Rapids: Zondervan, 2009), 94.

18. Eusebius, *Hist. eccl.* 3.31.3; 5.24.2.

19. Köstenberger, *A Theology of John's Gospel and Letters*, 94.

20. Stott, *Letters of John*, 44. Indeed, Hansjörg Schmid argues that the polemical nature of 1 John has been overplayed ("How To Read the First Epistle of John Non-Polemically," *Bib* 84 [2004]: 24–41).

21. See Stephen Rockwell, "Assurance as the Interpretive Key to Understanding the Message of 1 John," *Reformed Theological Review* 69 (2010): 17–33.

know him if you deny that Jesus is the Christ. On the other hand, real love comes from God, and if you have the Son you also have the Father.

In this way, love and the truth about Jesus are intertwined. You can't have one without the other. Love means that you know God through Jesus, and knowing God through Jesus means you know love. John writes to impress these two concerns on his readers and to show how to discern between genuine and false brothers and sisters. In so doing, he reassures and comforts them while also challenging them to love and fidelity.

The Composition of 1 John

Just about every part of the designation "the First Letter of John" is disputed. "John" is disputed (see above), "first" is disputed,[22] and 1 John being a letter is disputed. Only "the" and "of" are safe!

While the canonical designation of 1 John is that of a letter, there is almost universal acknowledgment that it "lacks some of the key elements of a conventional letter or epistle, and is therefore perhaps better understood as a 'treatise,' 'tractate,' or 'church order.'"[23] Certainly, 1 John does not fit the category of the typical Greco-Roman letter. It lacks an opening greeting, thanksgiving, and closing salutations.[24]

Some scholars have regarded 1 John as a tract or a paper intended for wide use within the church,[25] while others have wondered if it began its life as a homily. Brown suggested that it was written in part as a commentary on John's Gospel.[26] Kruse suggests that 1 John was intended to be a circular letter. This can account for its general tone and lack of greetings or any mention of individuals, which might have been provided in each location by a courier; yet it also accounts for the particularity of the problems addressed.[27]

In the sense that 1 John is sent to a particular readership and includes personal appeals from the author, some will remain content to understand it as a letter (most likely a circular, with Kruse). In any case, this commentary will continue the ancient convention of referring to the document as a letter while acknowledging the problems of that designation.

---

22. E.g., John Christopher Thomas thinks 1 John was last of the three letters to be composed, after 3 and 2 John, respectively ("The Order of the Composition of the Johannine Epistles," *NovT* 37 [1995]: 68–75).

23. Daniel R. Streett, *They Went Out from Us: The Identity of the Opponents in First John*, BZNW 177 (Berlin: de Gruyter, 2011), 1n1.

24. Kruse, *Letters of John*, 28.

25. E.g., Julian V. Hills, "A Genre for 1 John," in *The Future of Early Christianity: Essays in Honor of Helmut Koester*, ed. Birger A. Pearson (Minneapolis: Fortress, 1991), 367–77.

26. Brown, *Epistles of John*, 90–92.

27. Kruse, *Letters of John*, 28–29.

As for *when* 1 John was written, the question hinges entirely on its relationship to and the date of John's Gospel. The dating of the Gospel is its own controversial issue, with some scholars putting it before AD 70, some in the 80s, and most in the last decade of the first century.[28] It is also not known whether 1 John was written *before* or *after* John's Gospel, but scholarly consensus understands it as coming after the Gospel, and that is the position adopted in this commentary. If John's Gospel was composed in the mid-80s, as Carson and Moo suggest, then it seems best to date 1 John in the early 90s. It cannot be dated too much later than that because of apparent allusions to it in some early church writings.[29]

John's Opponents

A major concern of John's writing is seen in 1 John 2:18–27 where he refers to certain people as "antichrists" and "liars." These have turned away from foundational Christian beliefs and have consequently left the community to whom John writes. These people deny that Jesus is the Christ and are trying to lead John's readers astray. John writes to confirm their error and to encourage his readers to hold fast to their original faith.

The identity of John's opponents has long fascinated scholars. While dozens of solutions have been proposed over the years, Streett gathers them into five main categories, as quoted here:[30]

1. The secessionists [John's opponents who have left, or seceded, from the group] are *gnostics*, who stress their advanced knowledge, regard matter as evil, and advocate libertinism and/or perfectionism.
2. The secessionists are *docetists*, who hold that Jesus Christ was not truly a flesh-and-blood human being but only appeared to be so.
3. The secessionists hold to a *separation Christology* (commonly associated with Cerinthus) that distinguishes the human being Jesus from the Christ, a divine spirit being or power. Separation Christology teaches that the Christ descended upon Jesus at his baptism and departed sometime prior to his death. Thus, Jesus and the Christ are not to be identified.
4. The secessionists *deemphasize or devalue Jesus's historical ministry and atoning death* while emphasizing the Son's glory and preexistence as well as his roles as revealer and dispenser of the Holy

28. D. A. Carson and Douglas J. Moo, *An Introduction to the New Testament*, 2nd ed. (Grand Rapids: Zondervan, 2005), 676.
29. Carson and Moo, *Introduction*, 676.
30. Streett, *They Went Out from Us*, 7–8.

Spirit. In many cases, the secessionists display enthusiastic or pneumatic tendencies that amplify these differences.

5. The secessionists are *apostate Jews* or *Judaizers* (i.e., Judaizing Gentiles) who advocate either a lower (perhaps Ebionite) Christology or who have forsaken their confession of Jesus as the Messiah and have left the community to return to Judaism.

Streett notes exegetical and historical weaknesses of all five categories and offers his own solution.

According to 1 John 2:22–23, their identifying mark—and presumably the reason for their departure—is their denial that Jesus is the Messiah. It was the confession of Jesus as Messiah that served as the capstone of the Fourth Gospel and functioned as the primary boundary marker and most basic statement of faith for the Johannine community. It thus appears that the secessionists of 1 John 2:19 were apostates who had once confessed that Jesus was the Messiah but later reneged on their confession and left the community. There is therefore no reason to think that the secessionists left because of a christological heresy such as docetism or Cerinthianism.[31]

Streett's solution concerning the identity of John's opponents does not claim too much and rests on the two elements that are clearly discerned from 1 John itself, namely, their denial of Jesus as the Messiah and their abandoning the Johannine community of faith in Christ. In this commentary, it will not be deemed necessary to speculate further about their identity, though it is noted when possible hints against Gnosticism or docetism seem to appear in the text.[32]

Content of 1 John

The major themes of 1 John are knit together in a rich tapestry. The letter does not present a linear argument that moves from point one to point two to point three, with a conclusion that neatly brings it all together in a logical way. The content is presented more elusively, which is why 1 John has proven such an intriguing and, at times, difficult document to navigate. It may frustrate the reader looking for a straightforward argument but will fascinate the one willing to look deeply into the nature of God and his relationship with us in Christ.

However, there is a "deep logic" that runs through the letter. Everything that John writes grows out of profound theological convictions about God,

---

31. Streett, *They Went Out from Us*, 359. See also Terry Griffith, "A Non-Polemical Reading of 1 John: Sin, Christology and the Limits of Johannine Christianity," *TynBul* 49 (1998): 253‑76.

32. For a study of contemporary scholarship on Gnosticism, see Karen L. King, *What Is Gnosticism?* (New York: Belknap Press, 2003). For concise descriptions of Gnosticism, see E. M. Yamauchi, "Gnosticism," *DNTB* 414–18; Craig S. Keener, *The IVP Bible Background Commentary: New Testament*, 2nd ed. (Downers Grove, IL: InterVarsity Press, 2014), 781.

Jesus Christ, humanity, the truth, and love. Much like John's Gospel, 1 John flows forth out of a deep well of reflection about God in Christ.

Because of these characteristics, it is not possible to separate out the main themes in a detached way. They are all interrelated and fold back on each other in a recursive fashion. Nevertheless, it is worth attempting to articulate each major theme to understand John's theological and pastoral concerns. But in the end we must return to the integration of the thematic material because the rich tapestry demands that we see its woven-together, fully orbed picture of God in Christ.

Truth

Truth is a major concern of 1 John. The opening prologue affirms the author's eyewitness testimony concerning the Word of life (1:1–3) upon which his preaching of the truth about Jesus depends. Believers are to live out the truth by walking in the light rather than the darkness (1:6–7). Part of living out the truth is to acknowledge our own sinfulness; indeed, if we claim to be without sin the truth is not in us (1:8, 10).

John warns about false teachers who teach falsehoods about Jesus. Many antichrists who deny that Jesus is the Christ have come—such people are liars (2:18–22). They have separated from the faithful community, seeking to lead others astray too. But John's readers know the truth because no lie comes from the truth (2:21). The truth they have heard is to remain in them so that they remain in the Son and in the Father (2:24).

As people who belong to the truth, faithful believers may have assurance before God (3:19), including that he hears their prayers (3:22). And those who know the truth are able to "test the spirits" to discern who belongs to the truth and who does not. Any spirit that does not acknowledge that Jesus Christ has come in the flesh is the spirit of the antichrist (4:1–3). On the contrary, the Spirit of God is the Spirit of truth who testifies about the Son. To reject his testimony about the Son is to call God a liar (5:6–10).

Truth is clearly an essential theme of the letter and is intricately intertwined with its other major themes. Those who reject the truth are not able to love as God loves, nor are they able to know or love God. Rejecting the truth about Jesus therefore disqualifies them from eternal life. John's readers, rather, must reject the falsehood of the antichrists and remain in the truth they first heard. In so doing, they are assured of remaining in God, knowing and loving him, and loving fellow brothers and sisters in the truth.

Love

Love is also a major theme of 1 John. Some may even say it is the greatest theme of the letter, though it is not possible to separate it out from the other themes, especially those of truth and relationship with God. Considering its importance, it is introduced relatively late in the letter, first appearing at 2:5: love for God is made complete in the person who obeys his word.

The first major section concerning love follows immediately in 2:7–11, in which John issues an "old" command that he also calls "new," which is to love one another (2:7–8; 4:21). Anyone who hates brother or sister is in the darkness, while those who love live in the light (2:9–11).

While love and hate are contrasted in 2:7–11, love for the world is contrasted with love for the Father in 2:15–17. Anyone who loves the world and the evil things produced by it does not have love for the Father in them. The Father's love for us is explored in 3:1–3. His love has been lavished on us, calling us the children of God. While the children of the devil are recognized by failing to love others (3:10), the children of God know they have passed from death to life because of their love for one another (3:14; 5:1–2).

The model of God's love is Jesus. We know what love is because Jesus Christ laid down his life for us, and so we ought to do the same for our brothers and sisters (3:16). And this sacrificial love should be expressed in practical ways, not just with words or speech (3:17–18). Love comes from God, so that those who love know him while those who fail to love do not know him because God is love (4:7–8, 16). His love is expressed in action as he sent his Son as an atoning sacrifice for our sins (4:10). Those who love live in God, and God in them, and his perfect love drives out fear (4:19–20, 16).

For John, love is deeply theological. It all begins with the fact that God *is* love. And therefore love comes from God, seen in the sending of his Son. The Son models God's love by laying down his life for us and so demonstrates that this kind of love involves rugged commitment to others. And we are to emulate that sort of love toward one another, which is why John can say that those who know God and are born of God will love like God. In the absence of love, we neither know God nor are born of him. To love is to share in the family likeness.

Sin and Forgiveness

The way John deals with the issues of sin and God's forgiveness is a key contribution to our theology of those weighty matters. While perhaps not on the same level as the themes of truth and love, this topic is a clear concern throughout the letter, beginning immediately after the opening prologue: those who walk in the light are purified from all sin by the blood of Jesus (1:7).

Sin then becomes the focus at the end of chapter 1 as John says that anyone who claims to be sinless is a liar, while those who confess their sins will receive God's forgiveness and purification (1:8–10; 2:12). One of the purposes for writing, John says, is "so that you will not sin"; yet when we do sin Jesus Christ is our advocate with the Father and the propitiatory sacrifice for our sins and for the sins of the whole world (2:1–2; 4:10).

Jesus, in whom there is no sin, came to take away our sins. If we live in him, we will not continue to live in the realm of sin since we are born of God (3:5–6, 9; 5:18). Those living according to sin belong to the devil, but the Son of God came to destroy the devil's work (3:8–9).

The forgiveness of sins is a central feature of belonging to God and being called his children. That is why it is not possible to continue to live in the way of sin and yet claim to be God's child; the two are incompatible. This does not mean that believers will never sin, as John emphatically states in 1:8–10, but their orientation will no longer be one of open rebellion against God. Sin belongs to the devil and the world, but God's children have been taken out of the world.

John's theology of atonement makes a vital contribution to the New Testament teaching on the forgiveness of sins. Jesus is presented as the atoning sacrifice for sin (using the rare New Testament word *propitiation* in 2:2 and 4:10), taking our penalty for sin by diverting God's righteous wrath toward himself. He also takes away our sins, purifying us from all sin by his blood (*expiation*). But Jesus's death does not only achieve propitiation and expiation; he has also destroyed the devil's work. So John's conception of the atonement includes the complementary *Christus Victor* image alongside propitiation and expiation.

Fellowship with God

While we might expect the primary benefit of the forgiveness of sins to be the gift of eternal life, John sees our relationship with God as much more central. John does indeed hold out hope for life eternal (2:25; 3:14; 4:9; 5:11–13), but this is folded within the bigger reality of life in God.

From the opening prologue, we see John's focus on fellowship with God, which is the goal of his proclamation (1:3). Believers are the children of God (3:1–2, 10; 5:2, 19), who have been born of him (3:9; 4:7; 5:1, 4, 18). God's love for us is paramount (4:10–11, 16), stemming from his own nature as love. Knowing God is key to our fellowship with him (2:4, 13–14; 3:6; 4:7–8; 5:20), as is loving him (2:15; 4:20–21; 5:1–3).

But central to fellowship with God is acknowledging the Son; whoever acknowledges him "has the Father also" (2:23; 4:2, 15). And our fellowship is so profound that John can say that God lives in us, and we in him (2:24, 27–28; 3:6; 4:12–13, 15–16; 5:20). Eternal life is found by remaining in the Son and in the Father, and so is confidence at Jesus's coming (2:24–25, 28; 5:11–12). God has given us eternal life, and this life is in his Son (5:11).

It would not be claiming too much to say that, for John, the ultimate goal of believers' existence is fellowship with God. In him true life is found. In him we are beloved children. In him we have passed from death to life. Being in him is what it is all about in the end.

Outline of Contents

The structure of 1 John is a notoriously difficult issue. Several attempts to explain its structure have been attempted, but scholars have not arrived at any clear consensus on the matter.[33]

If anything, 1 John has a circular character in which the same themes appear and reappear. Rather than presenting a linear argument, such as we find in most of Paul's letters, John circles back around to his key themes in a recursive fashion. This fact presents significant challenges for the preacher seeking to expound the text in an ordered program, since the same themes recur throughout. While the natural repetition of themes helps to reinforce ideas, the preacher will need to find ways to avoid sounding repetitive in a negative sense.

Jensen's recent work offers a strategy for reading the letter in which 2:15–17 functions as "the topic paragraph for the body of 1 John."[34] This section contains two distinct parts—the "poem" of 2:12–14 sets the situation of John's audience, and 2:15–17 contains the first command in the letter: not to love the world or the things in the world.[35] The rest of the letter unfolds what it means to love God rather than the world.

With the material prior to 2:15–17 establishing the identity of John's readers as sharers in fellowship with God,[36] the topic paragraph sets up the fundamental polarity of the letter—that between God and the world. The remaining discussion takes place in the context of believers living faithfully in the world—a life of love and resisting sin and avoiding the attendant dangers of the world, such as false teachers, false brothers and sisters, and antichrists. Believers are born of God and, no longer belonging to the world, are assured of their victory over it, of their possession of God's true testimony, and of eternal life.[37]

Jensen's reading strategy offers a helpful approach to the overall shape of 1 John, with 2:15–17 as the topic paragraph of the letter. But rather than attempting any further explanation of the logic of the structure of 1 John, an outline of its contents is offered as follows.[38]

---

33. For an overview see L. Scott Kellum, "On the Semantic Structure of 1 John: A Modest Proposal," *Faith and Mission* 23.1 (2005): 34–82.

34. Matthew D. Jensen, *Affirming the Resurrection of the Incarnate Christ: A Reading of 1 John*, SNTSMS 153 (Cambridge: Cambridge University Press, 2012), 104.

35. Jensen, *Affirming the Resurrection*, 104–5.

36. Jensen, *Affirming the Resurrection*, 103.

37. Jensen, *Affirming the Resurrection*, 197.

38. With few differences, this outline resembles that proposed by Longacre through the tools of discourse analysis. See Robert E. Longacre, "Towards an Exegesis of 1 John Based on the Discourse

Outline of 1 John

1:1–4	Prologue
1:5–10	Walking in the Light vs Walking in the Darkness
2:1–6	Avoiding Sin and Keeping God's Commands
2:7–11	Love vs Hate
2:12–17	**Love of the Father vs Love of the World**
2:18–27	Remaining in the Son vs Being Led Astray
2:28–3:10	Being and Acting as the Children of God
3:11–18	Love is Expressed in Action
3:19–24	Reassurance and Confidence before God
4:1–6	Recognizing the Spirit of Truth vs the Spirit of Falsehood
4:7–21	Love One Another because Love Is from God
5:1–12	The Theological Conclusion of the Letter
5:13–21	The Pastoral Conclusion of the Letter

How 1 John Relates to the Gospel of John

As mentioned above, the relationship between 1 John and the Gospel of John is important for matters of authorship, but it is a significant issue in its own right. The reader will be struck by the similarities of language, images, themes, and theology between the two documents. And yet there are differences too due to their differing genres, purposes, and dates.

The tight relationship between Epistle and Gospel has been appreciated throughout the history of the church. An articulate example is found in the assessment of the bishop Dionysius of Alexandria, writing in the middle third century.

> The Gospel and the Epistle agree with one another. They being alike [. . .] and he deals with his whole matter by way of the same topics and terms, some of which I will briefly enumerate. Anyone who reads attentively will find in each writing, life largely, light largely, and the repudiation of darkness; truth continually, grace, joy, the flesh and blood of the Lord, judgment, the forgiveness of sin, God's love for us, and the mutual love enjoined upon us; that we must keep all the commandments; the condemnation of the world, the devil, the Antichrist; the promise of the Holy Spirit; God's adoption of us as sons; the absolute faith demanded of us; the Father and the Son everywhere. To characterize them generally all through, one may observe one and the same complexion in the Gospel and the Epistle.[39]

Analysis of the Greek Text," in *Linguistics and New Testament Interpretation: Essays on Discourse Analysis*, ed. David Alan Black, Katharine G. L. Barnwell, and Stephen H. Levinsohn (Nashville: Broadman, 1992), 271–86.

39. Eusebius, *Ecclesiastical History* 7.25.18–21.

This is a lovely summary of thematic correspondences between the two documents, as Dodd affirms: "The good bishop is quite right; most of the themes treated in the Epistle have a place also in the Gospel, and there is a general affinity of theological outlook, at least in comparison with any other part of the New Testament."[40] Dodd adds that not only are the ideas of the two writings similar but also their ways of expressing them. He then suggests that the reader go through the Epistle and underline the expressions that echo the language of the Gospel. "A glance at the result will show how few and short are those passages of the Epistles which are free from such echoes."[41]

To illustrate Dodd's point, part of Jobes's helpful chart is reproduced here.[42]

Some Similarities between John's Gospel and 1 John

Gospel of John	1 John
John 1:1 In the beginning was the Word, and the Word was with God, and the Word was God. *John 1:14* The Word became flesh and made his dwelling among us. *John 15:26* "When the Advocate comes, whom I will send to you from the Father—the Spirit of truth who goes out from the Father—he will testify about me." *John 15:27* And you also must testify, for you have been with me from the beginning."	*1 John 1:1* That which was from the beginning, which we have heard, which we have seen with our eyes, which we have looked at and our hands have touched—this we proclaim concerning the Word of life.
John 3:21 But whoever lives by the truth comes into the light . . .	*1 John 1:6* If we say, "We have fellowship with him" and walk in the darkness, we lie and do not live out the truth.
John 1:5 The light shines in the darkness, and the darkness has not overcome it.	*1 John 2:8* . . . because the darkness is passing and the true light is already shining.

---

40. C. H. Dodd, *The Johannine Epistles*, MNTC (London: Hodder & Stoughton, 1947), xlviii.
41. Dodd, *Johannine Epistles*, xlviii.
42. Karen H. Jobes, *1, 2, & 3 John*, ZECNT 19 (Grand Rapids: Zondervan, 2014), 25–27. The 1 John quotations are Jobes's translations. Her chart includes 2 and 3 John, but those sections are reproduced in this commentary's introductions to those letters. Used with permission.

John 8:12 When Jesus spoke again to the people, he said, "I am the light of the world. Whoever follows me will never walk in darkness, but will have the light of life."	*1 John 1:5* And this is the message that we have heard from him and announce to you: God is light, and there is no darkness in him at all.
	1 John 2:9 The one who says, "I am in the light," and hates their brother or sister is in the darkness.
John 1:12–13 Yet to all who did receive him, to those who believed in his name, he gave the right to become children of God—children born not of natural descent, nor of human decision or a husband's will, but born of God.	*1 John 5:1* Everyone who believes that Jesus is the Christ has been born of God.
John 15:12 "My command is this: Love each other as I have loved you."	*1 John 3:23* And this is his command: to believe in the name of his Son, Jesus Christ, and to love one another just as he gave the command to us.
John 15:7 "If you remain in me and my words remain in you, ask whatever you wish, and it will be done for you."	*1 John 3:24* And the one who keeps his commands remains in him [God], and he himself in them; and in this way we know that he remains in us: from the Spirit, whom he gave to us.
John 13:34 "A new command I give you."	*1 John 2:8* Yet I am writing you a new command.
John 14:16 "And I will ask the Father, and he will give you another advocate to help you and be with you forever"	*1 John 2:1* But if someone should sin, we have a *paraclete* with the Father— the righteous Jesus Christ.
John 17:3 "Now this is eternal life: that they know you, the only true God, and Jesus Christ, whom you have sent."	*1 John 2:25* And this is the promise that he himself promised us—eternal life.
	1 John 5:11 And this is the testimony: that God has given eternal life to us and this life is in his Son.
John 14:6 Jesus answered, "I am the way and the truth and the life. No one comes to the Father except through me."	*1 John 2:23* No one who denies the Son has the Father either. The one who acknowledges the Son has the Father also.
John 13:30 As soon as Judas had taken the bread, he went out. And it was night.	*1 John 2:19* They have gone out from us, but they were not of us.

John 20:31 But these are written that you may believe that Jesus is the Messiah, the Son of God, and that by believing you may have life in his name.	*1 John 5:13* These things I write to you who believe in the name of the Son of God so that you might know that you have eternal life.

Reflecting on these obvious similarities, Jobes asks whether we should allow the Fourth Gospel to influence our exegesis of 1 John. Her answer is appropriate: "While the overall similarities compel us in that direction, the different purposes for which the gospel and letters were written may caution against too quickly equating the sense of the two."[43]

The approach taken in this commentary is to draw on the theology of John's Gospel where appropriate, but especially when issues raised in 1 John require further illumination than the letter itself offers. This assumes that the Epistle's readers would have "filled the gaps" for themselves by reference to the Gospel. But, as Jobes cautions, we must proceed with care.

Whom John Addresses in the Letter

If 1 John is vague concerning its author, the audience is "equally shadowy."[44] One of the "letter-like" features that 1 John lacks is indication of both its author and its recipients. As a result, there is relatively little that can be discerned about the original readers of 1 John apart from a few general clues.

Clearly John's readers know Christian preaching, presumably heard from the author himself (2:7, 24).[45] They seem to belong to a single community (2:19), but this is not certain, given the generality of the letter overall. The letter offers several indications of close, personal relationship between its author and original readers, such as the affectionate terms of address, "dear children" (2:1, 12, 14, 18, 28; 3:7, 18; 4:4; 5:21) and "dear friends" (lit. "beloved"; 2:7; 3:2, 21; 4:1, 7, 11).

The author also frequently uses the first-person plural pronoun (e.g., "we are from God," 4:6) and verbs (e.g., "let us love one another," 4:7), which create an inclusive feel—the author and his readers belong together. However, the letter does not explicitly reveal whether John is physically part of the community he addresses. The "we" could be generic, equally applicable among any group of Christians whether physically proximate or not. Then again, the "we" might indicate a more immediate and proximate relationship.

---

43. Jobes, *1, 2, & 3 John*, 28.

44. Judith Lieu, *The Theology of the Johannine Epistles* (Cambridge: Cambridge University Press, 1991), 12.

45. Lieu, *The Theology of the Johannine Epistles*, 12.

Furthermore, the pastoral *tone* of the letter might indicate either a remote or proximate relationship between author and readers. In favor of a proximate relationship are the terms of affection (see above), but in favor of a remote relationship is the generality of the letter without any named individuals, references to geography, or historical events.

Putting all these factors together, it seems that the letter is written to a "Johannine community" spread in and around Ephesus in western Asia Minor (on the location, see below). John treats this community as a whole, though it may have existed physically in a variety of locations. John knows these communities personally as they have been the recipients of his preaching and teaching. They may even be churches that he originally planted.

But the scholarly tide is turning against the idea of a sectarian "Johannine community" as championed by J. Louis Martyn and Raymond Brown. Writing in 2009, Köstenberger says that the previous decade had seen a remarkable shift away from the "Johannine community" paradigm, and dramatic reassessment of the historical setting of John's Gospel is now warranted.[46] My use of the term "Johannine community," however, is not meant in a technical sense; it simply points to a community taught and influenced by the apostle John. Clearly, 1 John gives the impression of a community known and loved by John. In this sense they are designated "Johannine."

John's opponents may have split off from just one of these local communities, or they might constitute a more widespread phenomenon across the Johannine community. We can't know for sure, though the general warnings about the secessionists suggest the more widespread alternative.

The Johannine Community in Asia Minor

But where was this so-called Johannine community located? This question can be addressed with respect to John's Gospel alongside the Letters, rather than to the Letters alone, since it is accepted that they share the same author. This gives us more to work with in establishing the location of the Johannine community. There are four main options, as outlined by Jan van der Watt.

1. Ephesus in Asia Minor. The earliest traditions link John and his Gospel to Ephesus, as seen in Irenaeus (*Haer.* 3.1.1) and Eusebius (*Hist. eccl.* 3.23.1–4).[47] The supposed anti-gnostic polemic of 1 John (though, see on "opponents" above) fits with the Ephesus

---

46. Andreas J. Köstenberger, *A Theology of John's Gospel and Letters: The Word, the Christ, the Son of God*, BTNT (Grand Rapids: Zondervan, 2009), 59.

47. Jan van der Watt, *An Introduction to the Johannine Gospel and Letters* (London: T&T Clark, 2007), 124.

area, with the gnostic teacher Cerinthus living there at around AD 100. There are no serious problems with an Ephesian location, and most scholars support Ephesus as the likely location of the Johannine community.[48]

2. Alexandria in Egypt. The academic center of Alexandria was a hub for authors such as Philo and Valentinus (a gnostic) and was home to diverse ideas that resonated with John's *Logos*, his dualism, and his expression of divinity.[49] However, there are no historical accounts to place the Johannine community in Alexandria, and this location is little more than an idea that seems to fit.

3. Syria, specifically Antioch on the Orontes. John's Gospel may show some affinities with some Syrian writings, with the writings of Ignatius of Antioch, or with some local gnostic writings. But this line of argument is thin and has not convinced scholars.[50]

4. Northern Transjordan. The Jewish opponents of Jesus in John's Gospel seem to fit the synagogue Judaism found in northern Transjordan under King Agrippa II. Some argue that Johannine Christians fled there from Palestine.[51]

There is no reason to doubt the tradition that the Johannine community was located in or around Ephesus in western Asia Minor, and this enjoys current scholarly consensus. We cannot know, however, whether the community was restricted to Ephesus or was spread through the general region of which Ephesus was the main hub. Given the generality of 1 John, a wider location seems more likely.[52]

Format of This Commentary

First John is a love letter from God. As Augustine said, "It should constantly be in the mind of God's holy church."[53] It affirms the profound love of God in Christ and exhorts us to go and love likewise. This commentary examines John's teachings with an eye to the church today—the men and women who desire a deeper relationship with God, a stronger foundation for their walk, and a clearer vision for God's working in the world beyond their immediate circle—according to the commentary pattern described in the introduction to The Story of God Bible Commentary series.

---

48. Ibid., 125.
49. Ibid.
50. Ibid.
51. Ibid.
52. Köstenberger, *A Theology of John's Gospel and Letters*, 94.
53. Augustine, "Ten Homilies on the First Epistle General of St. John," 259.

1 John 1:1–4

 LISTEN to the Story

¹That which was from the beginning, which we have heard, which we have seen with our eyes, which we have looked at and our hands have touched—this we proclaim concerning the Word of life. ²The life appeared; we have seen it and testify to it, and we proclaim to you the eternal life, which was with the Father and has appeared to us. ³We proclaim to you what we have seen and heard, so that you also may have fellowship with us. And our fellowship is with the Father and with his Son, Jesus Christ. ⁴We write this to make our¹ joy complete.

Listening to the Text in the Story: Genesis 1; John 1:1–18; 19:35; 20:30; 21:24; 1 John 4:2.

This is a very unusual way to begin a letter. There is no greeting, no audience indicated, no author stated, no mention of geography or occasion—nothing that we would normally associate with the beginning of an ancient letter of any type. Hebrews is the only parallel in the New Testament. While 2 and 3 John are also odd in that their greetings are very truncated, at least it is evident that those are to be read as letters. Such is not obvious here (see the Introduction for more on the genre of 1 John). This opening creates the rhetorical effect of bold proclamation, which befits the letter as a whole. Everything John goes on to say is based on the truth and significance of the historical and spiritual realities iterated in these first four verses.

The opening verses of John's longest canonical letter raise important spiritual issues relating to Jesus Christ, the apostolic proclamation of Christ, and fellowship with God. Regarding Christ, John draws attention to his preexistence (1:1, 2), his physical existence on earth (1:1), and his status as the Word

---

1. Some manuscripts have "your" instead of "our." In 2 John 4 and 3 John 4, we see John express *his* joy at the news that his readers are walking in the truth. It makes good sense, then, that here he refers to "our" joy rather than "your" joy.

of life (1:1, 2). The apostolic proclamation of Christ consists of eyewitness testimony (1:1–3) for the purpose of bringing about fellowship with the community of believers and fellowship with the Father and the Son (1:3).

EXPLAIN the Story

Proclaiming the Word of Life (1:1–2)

First John begins in a mysterious way, much like the Gospel of John. It is not immediately obvious that John is referring to a person, since his first phrase is "*That* which was from the beginning."[2] But just as the prologue of the Gospel becomes increasingly clear that the subject is Jesus Christ, so too here.

However, not all interpreters agree that Jesus is the direct subject in these verses, but rather the message about him.[3] The main reason for this is John's use of the neuter relative pronouns ("which"; *ho*)—four times in the first verse—rather than the masculine form ("who"; *hos*) that is expected if Jesus were meant. Thus Jobes writes, "The Greek does not allow this direct reference to the person of Jesus."[4] Even if the "word of life" (1:1b) were meant, a masculine pronoun would be required since "word" is masculine in Greek (*logos*).

However, the issue is not so simple. In favor of the "which" referring to Jesus are the following points. First are the obvious parallels to John 1, in which the initially ambiguous subject is first depicted in an impersonal way (as the "Word"), but then it becomes clear that a *person* is meant (e.g., John 1:14). These parallels with John 1 (of which there are several) would all need to be understood in no-longer-parallel ways if Jesus were not the subject in 1 John 1:1–2.

Second, John says he saw and touched that which was from the beginning (1:1). It would be extremely strange to speak of a *message*, which has no tangible or physical existence, as having been *seen* and *touched*. But a person *can* be seen and touched, concerning which John's Gospel makes a special point (see below).

Third, this entity was "with the Father" (1:2; *pros ton patera*), strongly suggesting the person of Jesus rather than an abstract message, who was "with God" (*pros ton theon*) in John 1:1. A person dwells *with* another; a message does not (one might *have* a message or *know* one, but we would not say it is *with* us). We see this clearly in 1:3, where our fellowship is "with the Father and with his Son, Jesus Christ."

---

2. The neuter relative pronoun (*ho*) initially masks the fact that John is speaking about a person.
3. E.g., Dodd, Stott, Jobes. Smalley prefers to see an intentional ambivalence between the two possibilities; Stephen S. Smalley, *1, 2, 3 John*, rev. ed., WBC 51 (Nashville: Thomas Nelson, 2007), 6.
4. Jobes, *1, 2, & 3 John*, 44.

But what, then, of the neuter relative pronouns? Why say "which" when you mean "who"? Schackenburg notes that the "neuter gender often appears in Johannine usage for the masculine" (John 3:6 with 5; 4:22 with 23; 6:37a with b; 6:39 with 40; 17:2, 10 with 9; 1 John 5:4 with 5).[5] I suggest that "which" is used here in order to be purposely ambiguous, at least initially. This is how John operates in the Gospel prologue—someone reading John 1:1–18 for the first time would not know who/what is the topic until further into the prologue—so it should not surprise us if the same strategy is in effect in 1 John. The subject is progressively revealed, moving from a seemingly non-personal (hence neuter) entity to the Son of the Father, Jesus Christ.

And as the Gospel affirms, this one is "from the beginning" (1:1a; cf. 2:13). Both Johannine prologues are striking in their explicit affirmation of the preexistence of Christ.[6] While the Gospel's wording directly evokes Genesis 1:1 ("in the beginning"; *en archē*), 1 John's "from the beginning" (*ap archēs*) is less directly referential. There is nevertheless a strong echo of Genesis 1:1. As Schnackenburg comments, "The preexistent Logos, and subsequently the incarnate One, incorporates in himself the fullness of the divine life."[7]

That which was from the beginning was *heard* and *seen* and *touched* (1:1a). There is an emphasis here on the eyewitness testimony of John and those he represents (note the consistent use of "we").[8] This emphasis is also consistent with John's Gospel, in which he frequently refers to the firsthand nature of the testimony recounted (e.g., John 19:35; 20:30; 21:24). Eyewitness testimony—hearing, seeing, touching—underscores the historical and physical realities underlying the theology that John will impress upon his readers (see the Introduction to 1 John for more on eyewitness testimony).

But alongside these historical and physical realities are the eternal and spiritual truths to which they point. That which has been seen concerns "the Word of life" (1:1b; NIV supplies "this we proclaim," anticipating 1:2, 3). The "Word" (*logos*) is another unmistakable parallel to the prologue of John's Gospel (1:1, 14), which clearly refers to Jesus (John 1:14). The Word also

---

5. Schackenburg, *The Johannine Epistles*, 57. Or, as Brown suggests, the neuter functions "*comprehensively to cover the person, the words, and the works*" of Christ (Brown, *Epistles of John*, 154 [emphasis original]).

6. Contra Dodd, who thinks "that which was from the beginning" refers to "what has always ('from the beginning') been true about the word of life" (*The Johannine Epistles*, 3). That is, John's emphasis is on "the unchanged, original content of the Gospel, over against novel forms of doctrine" (*The Johannine Epistles*, 5n1).

7. Schnackenburg, *The Johannine Epistles*, 57.

8. Contra Judith M. Lieu, *I, II, & III John: A Commentary*, NTL (Louisville: Westminster John Knox, 2008), 39–40, who does not see any reference to eyewitness testimony but sees instead an allusion to Isaiah 59:9–10 and/or Psalm 115 with their focus on sensory perception. However, given John's insistence that Jesus came *in the flesh* (4:2), the multiple remarks about seeing, hearing, and touching are much more likely meant to confirm Jesus's fleshly humanity.

relates to Genesis 1 (reinforced by the "beginning" language) as God speaks his creation into existence (Gen 1:3, 6, 9, 11, 14, 20, 22, 24, 26, 28, 29). The Word is the instrument of God's creative work, as the Gospel makes explicit (John 1:3).

Here the Word is the "Word of life" (1:1b), a phrase not used in John's Gospel but consistent with the message of its prologue in any case: "In him [i.e., the Word] was life, and that life was the light of all mankind" (John 1:4). The genitive, "of life" (*zōēs*), most likely indicates source: the Word is the source of life, as in John 1:4. In spite of other suggestions,[9] the "Word of life" refers to Jesus himself, the one who gives life (1 John 5:11–12).

The "Word of life" is then called simply "the life," which becomes the focus of 1:2: "The life appeared; we have seen it and testify to it" (1:2a). The reiteration of the eyewitness claims of 1:1 is augmented now with proclamation (more prominent in 1:3). And the proclamation concerns "the eternal life" (1:2b). Thus, we see the "Word of life" referred to as "the life," and now "the eternal life."

The eternal life was "with the Father and has appeared to us" (1:2c). This points to Christ's eternal and divine nature. It also echoes the Word of John 1:1–14 who was with God from the beginning and dwelt among us.[10] And once again John reiterates the eyewitness nature of the proclamation, since this eternal Word from God *appeared* to him and his fellow witnesses.

What Exactly Was Witnessed?

What exactly does John refer to in his testimonial account? We have already argued that John is speaking of Jesus directly (and not of a message about him), but can we press further? On the one hand, he could simply refer to the incarnate Jesus Christ—his person, life, and ministry—and the fact that Christ dwelt among us in the flesh and that eyewitnesses have verified this. Alternatively, John might also refer to something more specific, such as Christ's resurrection.

Consider the eyewitness testimony recorded in John's Gospel. In John 19:35 the appeal to eyewitness testimony is found in direct response to the crucifixion of Jesus. John 20:30 refers to the disciples' witness of "many other signs" that Jesus performed—"other" (*alla*) is clearly used in distinction from the great sign just recorded—the appearance of the resurrected Jesus before Thomas (20:24–29). Note the physical nature of that incident, as Jesus invites Thomas to touch him (v. 27). This correlates with the physical aspect of the

---

9. E.g., Stott's position that the "word of life" means "the gospel of Christ" (*Letters of John*, 72–73). See also Brown, *Epistles of John*, 164–65.

10. Schnackenburg, *The Johannine Epistles*, 50.

testimony of 1 John 1:1–3. John 21:24 also relates to a resurrection account, framed explicitly by vv. 1 and 14. The explicit references to eyewitness testimony in John's Gospel refer directly to Christ's death and, more commonly, resurrection. Thus these events may constitute part of the scope of 1 John 1:1–3.

In current scholarship, it is popular to view 1 John 1:1–3 as affirming purely the incarnation of Jesus, usually because of the presupposed antignostic agenda of the letter. Jensen, however, argues against an incarnation-only reading of these verses, demonstrating several links to the resurrection accounts of John 20–21 (see above) as well as Luke 24. He makes a compelling case that "the resurrected incarnate Christ" is in view here; thus John is affirming *both* the incarnate humanity of Christ *as well as* his bodily resurrection from the dead.[11]

According to Didymus the Blind (AD 313–98), it was commonly thought in his day that John's words referred to the resurrection:

> Many think that these words apply to the postresurrection appearances of Jesus and say that John is speaking of himself and the other disciples who first of all heard that the Lord had risen and afterwards saw him with their own eyes, to the point where they touched his feet, his hands and his side and felt the imprint of the nails.[12]

We Proclaim This That You Might Have Fellowship with Us (1:3–4)

On the spiritual front, we see that Jesus's ministry, death, and resurrection are for the purpose of fellowship. What has been seen and heard is proclaimed "so that you also may have fellowship with us," and this fellowship is spiritual—it is with the Father and his Son, Jesus Christ (1:3). Through the reception of John's proclamation, believers are included in fellowship with other believers, which is to share in fellowship with the Father and the Son (1:3).

The wording "with the Father and with his Son, Jesus Christ" hints at the idea of fellowship *within the Godhead*. That is, John does not simply say that "our fellowship is with God," though that would have been perfectly appropriate. Instead, he identifies two members of the Godhead, reminding us that there is fellowship within God himself. Father, Son, and Spirit are in perfect, mutual, indwelling relationship one with another. Our fellowship with each other and our fellowship with Father and Son are derivative of the fellowship that the Father and the Son themselves enjoy. God is a God of relationship, and that is why the goal of John's proclamation is fellowship. Knowing God

---

11. Jensen, *Affirming the Resurrection*, 47–72.
12. Didymus, *Commentary on 1 John* (PG 39:1775–76).

in loving relationship is what it is all about because that is what God is all about. As Painter observes:

> Here we are dealing with the revelation of life, eternal life, bringing those who believe to *share* eternal life, not in an individualistic way but mutually sharing in eternal life with the Father and the Son.[13]

Finally, we observe that John's testimony to Christ is a source of joy: "We write this to make our joy complete" (1:4). John's joy arises both from his testimony about Christ as well as because of fellowship. As we have observed, proclamation leads to fellowship with other believers and fellowship with the Father and the Son (1:3). The prospect of others' inclusion in this fellowship is reason for joy. As Bede the Venerable wrote (AD 672/3–735),

> The joy of all teachers is complete when by their preaching they bring many into the fellowship of the holy church and also into the fellowship of God the Father and his Son Jesus Christ, through whom the church is strengthened and grows.[14]

 LIVE the Story

The prologue of 1 John challenges two opposite mistakes. The first is to deny the human, physical, fleshly reality of Christ and his resurrection. The flesh is not regarded as evil or temporary (contra Gnosticism), nor is the humanity of Jesus rejected (contra docetism). The resurrected Jesus was not some disembodied spirit (contra some forms of liberal theology).

The second mistake is the denial of the spiritual impact of Jesus's life and ministry. The historical, fleshly nature of Christ's dwelling among us serves the spiritual significance of his ministry—it is not pit against it. He has changed our spiritual situation by bringing us into fellowship with God by the Spirit. Jesus Christ is, then, a historical figure *and* a spiritual figure. He is not merely one or the other. Or, to put it another way, he is *a spiritually significant historical figure*. So we see that the historical and spiritual dimensions of Jesus's ministry are to be held together. They are not in competition but are mutually reinforcing and complementary.

The opening verses of 1 John impress upon us the need to embrace both the historical testimony to Christ and the spiritual dimensions of his life and work. Sometimes Christians are tempted to collapse their interest into one or other of these dimensions.

---

13. John Painter, *1, 2, and 3 John*, SP 18 (Collegeville, MN: Liturgical Press, 2002), 137.
14. Bede, *On 1 John* (PL 93:87).

Belief is Grounded in Historicity and Spirituality

With the rise of modernism and post-Christian skepticism, it is understand-able that believers would want to focus on the historicity of Christ's narrative and of the Gospels and other New Testament documents. Our beliefs are grounded in historical realities that were witnessed, recorded, and went on to change ancient cultures and peoples. Christianity can be afforded respect in the face of modernistic skepticism because it is grounded in neither blind faith nor naive confidence in a metaphysical construct of the universe. There are intelligent, evidence-based reasons for Christian belief. 1 John 1:1–4 certainly supports this direction for Christian apologetics.

On the other hand, this kind of interest in facts, witness, and testimony can sometimes buy into a materialistic worldview (assumed by many modern-ists and secularists), so that the spiritual and metaphysical nature of Christian-ity becomes muted or even slightly embarrassing. This trend can be seen when evangelism and apologetics appeal only to the mind with facts, apparently without acknowledgment that there is also a spiritual battle being waged for souls. Conversion is not simply a matter of being convinced by factual evi-dence but can only occur through the work of the Spirit according to the will of God. It is nothing less than spiritual rebirth and cannot be reduced to mere intellectual assent won by testimony and persuasion.

The truth of this simple fact is seen by the way that believers do not only have their minds converted; rather, they are changed through and through. The mind, body, and soul of a person are all involved together in conversion. And actions, behavior, and habits will necessarily change as a result—not only the mind.

From the opposite end of things, some Christians are apparently disin-terested in factual evidence and any historical, intellectual element inherent to Christian belief. These believers correctly recognize that Christianity is *spiritual* and is primarily concerned with fellowship with God in Christ. Such believers may therefore reject any attempt toward persuasion or appeal to reason since conversion is, after all, a spiritual matter.

Nevertheless, it is an equally serious mistake to focus solely on the spiritual elements of Christian faith to the exclusion of the historical and intellectual. Christianity is not just one of the many metaphysical constructs for under-standing the universe. It is not simply an invention of someone's imagination or a worldview built upon superstitious tradition or philosophical fancy.

Sadly, some people seem to think that Christianity is exactly those things—an invention of the imagination or a superstitious tradition. Such an attitude is humorously depicted in the film *The Invention of Lying*, starring Ricky Gervais. In the film, Mark Bellison (played by Gervais) lives in a world where falsehoods are completely unknown. An epiphany enables him to tell the world's first lie, and he begins to harness the ability to lie for his own gain.

Mark is then told that his mother is going to die, having had a heart attack, and he rushes to the hospital to see her. She is terrified of death, believing that an eternity of nothingness awaits her. At that moment, Mark invents the concept of heaven, telling her that a joyful afterlife will be hers on the other side of death. She dies happily, while the doctors and nurses are awed by this incredible new truth.

Mark's knowledge of heaven brings him worldwide attention, and he teaches people about it through "ten rules" written on two pizza boxes. He claims that these rules were revealed to him by a "Man in the Sky."

While the film is poking fun at religion, it portrays a more serious belief that Christianity is just a lie invented to make people feel better about themselves and their lives, especially in the face of death. But such skeptics do not realize that the beliefs of Christianity are grounded in a historical narrative involving real people, events, and the acts of God enfleshed in space and time. It has a historical nature. It cannot be the figment of someone's imagination.

First John 1:1–4 defies two extremes. The historical facts concerning the central figure of Christianity—Jesus Christ—and the spiritual dimensions of his ministry and mission are to be held together because they are both in fact indispensable parts of God's story in the world. John proclaims what has been seen and heard because this proclamation, and the belief it evokes, brings about fellowship with God and his people. This means that Christians must resist the materialistic trend of modern Western culture on the one hand and the anti-intellectual vagaries of self-determined spirituality on the other.

It is important for believers to self-diagnose on this point. Are we inclined to seek rationalistic credibility at the expense of spiritual engagement? This is a perilous course for the Christian and must be abandoned immediately. Christianity is not simply a more credible worldview than its alternatives; it is about fellowship with the Creator of the universe.

When John Stott was a school student in 1938, the preacher and evangelist Eric "Bash" Nash pointed him to Revelation 3:20, "Behold, I stand at the door, and knock: if any man hear my voice, and open the door, I will come in to him, and will sup with him, and he with me" (KJV). Years later, Stott reflected on the significance of this verse for his life.

> Here, then, is the crucial question which we have been leading up to. Have we ever opened our door to Christ? Have we ever invited him in? This was exactly the question which I need to have put to me. For, intellectually speaking, I had believed in Jesus all my life, on the other side of

the door. I had regularly struggled to say my prayers through the key-hole. I had even pushed pennies under the door in a vain attempt to pacify him. I had been baptized, yes and confirmed as well. I went to church, read my Bible, had high ideals, and tried to be good and do good. But all the time, often without realising it, I was holding Christ at arm's length, and keeping him outside. I knew that to open the door might have momentous consequences. I am profoundly grateful to him for enabling me to open the door. Looking back now over more than fifty years, I realise that that simple step has changed the entire direction, course and quality of my life.[15]

Stott's life from that point offers abundant evidence of the deep impact made by genuine conversion. He devoted his life to the proclamation of the gospel and teaching the Bible. He was a model of humility and loving concern for the people he met around the world. He gave freely of his time and money in service of others. For instance, the considerable royalties earned from his books were used to set up a fund for the training of majority world Christian scholars. Each area of Stott's life bore witness to the spiritual change that took hold of him.

On the other hand, are we inclined to seek spiritual experience at the expense of engagement with real-world issues of history and argument? This is also a course to be abandoned, not least because it is not authentic Christianity. God's story recorded in the Bible is grounded in God's acts in history. There is no room for the dehistoricization of Christian belief. As John Stott again comments:

> Such an emphasis on the historical revelation of the invisible and intangible is still needed today, not least by the scientist trained in the empirical method, the radical who regards much in the Gospels as "myths" . . . and the mystic who becomes preoccupied with his subjective religious experience to the neglect of God's objective self-revelation in Christ.[16]

Stott is a great example of a believer who held together these two sides of the same coin: the historical and the spiritual. He was serious about the events that occurred in time and space, involving real people in real history. And he was serious about the fact that through these events, God was revealing himself to the world in order that we might draw near to him in fellowship through Christ.

---

15. Quoted in Timothy Dudley-Smith, *John Stott: The Making of a Leader* (Leicester: Inter-Varsity Press, 1999), 95.

16. Stott, *Letters of John*, 66.

Proclamation Leads to Fellowship

John's opening verses also draw attention to the importance of proclamation. The apostles' widespread testimony to the life, death, and resurrection of Christ was no doubt a natural response. How could they not share with others what they had experienced and encountered? But more important is the connection between proclamation and relationship with God. Their encounter with the risen Lord leads to proclamation, which in turn leads to fellowship with God. As others encounter the risen Christ through the apostolic witness and respond in repentance and faith, they are drawn into the fellowship of believers which is centered on fellowship with God himself.

As the history of the church bears out, the proclamation of Christ does not remain the response of the apostles only. Their proclamation was of course extremely important since it was the original proclamation, drawing on their own eyewitness experiences and that of others, such as Mary Magdalene and the other women who first encountered the resurrected Christ. And their testimony became the source of all subsequent proclamation. All genuine proclamation of Christ draws upon their witness and broadcasts it to every people group and each new generation. This proclamation is the message that the risen Jesus is God's promised Messiah who died for the sins of the world, conquering sin and death. All who come to him in repentance and faith receive the forgiveness of sins and eternal life in loving fellowship with God.

If the church of today is interested in seeing others drawn into its fellowship and into fellowship with God, then it must also be interested in such proclamation. It is the corporate responsibility of the church to proclaim the apostolic eyewitness testimony to this generation and to all who have not heard. While John does not explicitly state it here, the implication (confirmed elsewhere) of his connection between proclamation and fellowship is that relationship with God is not possible apart from the apostolic proclamation of Christ. He alone is the Word of life, and he cannot be known truly apart from the apostolic message that testifies to him.

But the very idea of proclamation is challenged by the values of our culture today. It is often viewed as "imposing your religion" on others. Proclamation can be interpreted as intolerance of another person's worldview in our age of relativism. And with the rise of secularism, spirituality has been sidelined to one's personal life. The collective mood says, "If you want to believe that stuff (as silly as it is), that's fine, but keep it to yourself, thank you very much."

Alongside the awkwardness of proclamation in an age that prefers to confine religious belief to the private domain, the message itself offends many. It claims that all people are sinful, requiring forgiveness, while we prefer to think of ourselves as basically good. It also claims that Jesus is the only way to find forgiveness of sins, rendering other paths false, while we prefer to embrace everyone's point of view. Rather than hearing the proclamation of Christ as the glorious message about God's merciful love for us, it is often seen in a more negative light.

So it is understandable that some parts of the church have felt it necessary to adopt other approaches. If proclamation is politically incorrect, then the church will engage the world in less offensive ways. After all, the Bible affirms the importance of *promoting* the gospel through acts of love, service, generosity, prayer, and good deeds.[17] But the problem comes when we think that promoting the gospel is the *only* thing we need to do.[18] Yes, we are called to do that, but we are also called to *proclaim* the message of Jesus. Our corporate responsibility as the church is to promote *and* proclaim the gospel, with each of us working out how we may best contribute to those complementary endeavors.

As our society becomes increasingly intolerant of proclamation, it will become harder and harder to do it faithfully. It will require courageous confidence in God's goodness. It will require conviction in the face of potential negative ramifications. It will require perseverance through the trial of persecution. In the West, persecution is generally quite mild—though nonetheless real—mostly confined to verbal hostility and occasional social ostracism. But in other parts of the world, persecution is of a different order. Proclamation of Christ remains central to the persecuted church even when faced with the threat of beatings, imprisonment, and death. And throughout many such regions, the gospel flourishes in contexts of persecution. From a historical point of view, we see that persecution does not silence the proclamation of the church—it adds fuel to the flame.

The apostles gave us the testimony we must proclaim. But they also gave us an example to follow. Their world was not tolerant of their message either. In fact, they faced much harsher consequences for their preaching than most of us ever will (in the West, at least). And yet when commanded to remain silent, they chose to obey God rather than men (Acts 4:1–22). The result of their persevering proclamation, under God, was that the message of Jesus spread like wildfire throughout the Roman Empire. Let us learn from their proclamation—both its content and their commitment to speak it to all who would hear.

---

17. See John Dickson, *The Best Kept Secret of Christian Mission: Promoting the Gospel with More Than Our Lips* (Grand Rapids: Zondervan, 2010).

18. Dickson rightly affirms the importance of *both* proclaiming and promoting the gospel.

Proclamation Is a Joy

The responsibility for proclamation should not, however, be viewed as an onerous task, begrudgingly fulfilled out of duty. After the Samaritan woman encountered Jesus at Jacob's well, she couldn't help but testify about him to the people of her town—many of whom believed because of her testimony (John 4:28–29, 39). Proclaiming Jesus was a natural response after her life-changing encounter with him. It was not an onerous task.

Proclamation is the church's duty, yes, but John shows us that it is more than that too. He writes "to make our joy complete" (1:4). The apostolic proclamation of Christ is a joy for multiple reasons. First, it is the proclamation of God's truth. To speak the truth into a world of darkness is its own reward. Second, proclamation brings glory to Christ. To speak the truth about who Jesus is and what he has done for us brings him honor. Third, proclamation leads to fellowship. To introduce others to Jesus extends to them an invitation to share in fellowship with God and his people. As John Piper writes:

> The joy which is our Christian duty to pursue does not reach its climax in private communion with God. Rather, it reaches its fullest extent only when it is compounded by the joy of seeing others share in it with us. And these are not two different joys as if the good of man were somehow in competition with the glory of God. The sharing of a joy is that same joy in consummation.[19]

If we do not regard proclamation—with its truth-telling, Christ-glorifying, and fellowship-increasing fruit—to be a responsibility of joy, then we have not grasped it as the apostle John did. Perhaps we need to meditate afresh on what exactly Jesus means to us and what he could mean to others. Perhaps we need the refreshment that God's Spirit can provide so that we are not only filled with joy in our fellowship with Christ but we are also filled with joy at the prospect of making him known. Above all, let us cherish the precious fellowship we have with God in Christ and allow its benefits to overflow to the many. Pray that it may be so.

But be careful what you pray for. In God's goodness, sometimes we learn the joy of proclamation by being thrown into the deep end. Lee Strobel tells of his wonderful (and terrifying) experience of sharing Jesus with someone for the first time.

It was a hectic day at the newspaper where I worked as an editor. Several major stories erupted before deadline. Reporters were scurrying

---

19. John Piper, "How Does Christian Hedonism Relate to Evangelism?," *Desiring God.org*, January 1, 1978, http://www.desiringgod.org/articles/how-does-christian-hedonism-relate-to-evangelism.

around as they frantically tried to finish their articles. With emotions frayed, just about everyone lost their tempers.

After the last story was edited, I looked up and was surprised to see one of my bosses standing over my desk. *Uh-oh!* That wasn't a good sign. But it turned out that he wasn't there to up-braid me about some mistake or oversight. Instead, he took me off guard by asking with genuine curiosity, "Strobel, how did you get through the day without blowing your top?"

Then, apparently suspecting a link between my behavior and the fact that I went to church on Sundays, he added the words that sent a chill down my spine: "What's this Christianity thing to you?"

Whoa! For a moment I froze. Nobody had ever asked me anything like that before. In fact, I had never shared my faith with anyone. . . . And now, out of the blue, I was being put on the spot.

I didn't know what to say or how to say it. I was afraid I would utter the wrong words. I didn't want to embarrass myself or have him make fun of me. I fretted about what would happen to my career if I gushed about my faith and became known as the newsroom's "holy roller." There was a lot at stake.

My mind raced. . . . Finally, even as I was opening my mouth to reply, I made a scary split-second decision: I resolved to take a spiritual risk. I looked up at my boss. "You really want to know? Let's go into your office."

Behind closed doors, we talked for forty-five minutes. Well, to be honest, I did most of the talking. I was really nervous. Never having been trained in how to engage with others about my faith, I fumbled around and wasn't nearly as clear as I could have been. Still, in my own sincere but admittedly inept way, I tried to describe how I met Jesus and the difference he had made in my life.

An amazing thing happened. He didn't laugh. He didn't make fun of me. He didn't nervously try to change the topic or make excuses so he could leave the room. Instead, he listened intently. By the end, he was hanging on every word.

. . . I'm not sure how God used that conversation in my boss's life, but I do know this: he undeniably used it in mine. . . . There are no words to adequately describe the thrill I felt in having been used by God to communicate his message of hope to someone far from him.[20]

---

20. Lee Strobel and Mark Mittelberg, *The Unexpected Adventure: Taking Everyday Risks to Talk with People about Jesus* (Grand Rapids: Zondervan, 2009), 9–11.

CHAPTER 2

1 John 1:5-10

LISTEN to the Story

⁵This is the message we have heard from him and declare to you: God is light; in him there is no darkness at all. ⁶If we claim to have fellowship with him and yet walk in the darkness, we lie and do not live out the truth. ⁷But if we walk in the light, as he is in the light, we have fellowship with one another, and the blood of Jesus, his Son, purifies us from all sin.

⁸If we claim to be without sin, we deceive ourselves and the truth is not in us. ⁹If we confess our sins, he is faithful and just and will forgive us our sins and purify us from all unrighteousness. ¹⁰If we claim we have not sinned, we make him out to be a liar and his word is not in us.

Listen to the text in the Story: Genesis 1:3; Exodus 30:10; Leviticus 16:15–19; Psalms 36:9; 43:3; 89:15; Isaiah 60:1, 19–20; Habakkuk 3:4; John 1:9; 3:19–21; 8:12; 9:5; 12:46.

This passage contrasts walking in the light with walking in the darkness. True fellowship with God means walking in the light, since God is light. This involves truth and confession of sin, while deception and the claim to be without sin belong to the darkness. With the confession of sin comes God's forgiveness and cleansing, because God is faithful on the grounds of the blood of Jesus.

EXPLAIN the Story

After the opening verses of 1 John, with their emphasis on the proclamation of eyewitness testimony to Christ for the sake of fellowship, this passage draws on two important elements of that opening section and introduces a series of new themes to the letter. First, the notion of proclamation is continued, though the language here is slightly different.[1] Second, the theme of fellowship is at the heart of this passage, as it is in 1:1–4.

---

1. It is difficult to see any meaningful distinction between the terms translated "proclaim" (*apangellō*) in 1:2–3 and "declare" (*anangellō*) in 1:5.

The continuities between this passage and 1:1–4—proclamation and fellowship—serve to frame the new elements introduced here. First, proclamation introduces the idea of a message (*angelia*), which was "heard from him" and then declared to John's readers. Whereas proclamation in 1:1–4 is based on eyewitness testimony (1:3), here it consists of "the message we have heard from him" (1:5). Second, the message is that "God is light; in him there is no darkness at all" (1:5). Third, fellowship with God is directly tied to this message. Since God is light, and in him there is no darkness, it is a lie to claim to have fellowship with him and yet walk in the darkness (1:6). Fourth, fellowship with other believers ("one another") is dependent upon walking in the light (1:7a). Fifth, walking in the light is connected with purification from sin by the blood of Jesus (1:7b). Sixth, the introduction of the theme of sin in 1:7 leads to the discussion in 1:8–10 of the deception of claiming sinlessness. We turn now to explore these elements in turn.

God Is Light (1:5)

In 1:5 a message is introduced: "God is light; in him there is no darkness at all."[2] John declares that this message was heard "from him," likely referring to the nearest possible antecedent—"Jesus Christ" (1:3). This fits with John's testimony of having *heard* Christ (see on 1:1–4); part of what John heard from Christ is this message he now declares to his readers.

The message is simple yet profound: God is light.[3] There are Jewish and Hellenistic backgrounds for the idea of God as "light," including Zoroastrianism, Gnosticism, Plato, and the Jewish philosopher Philo. While the Greek background might have appealed to John's ex-pagan readers, Judaism is the most likely background, especially the Old Testament and the writings of Qumran.[4]

Throughout the Old Testament there is a rich series of connections between God and light. He brought light into the world (Gen 1:3). The psalmists say, "In your light we see light" (Ps 36:9); "Send forth your light and your faithful care, let them lead me" (Ps 43:3); "Blessed are those who have learned to acclaim you, who walk in the light of your presence, Lord" (Ps 89:15); "The Lord wraps himself in light as with a garment" (Ps 104:2).

---

2. It is possible that the "message" continues beyond 1:5 to include the following content in 1:6–7, but this is unlikely. It is more natural to read 1:6–7 as John's commentary on the message recorded in 1:5.

3. Yarbrough argues that this is *the* programmatic statement of 1 John: "The core of John's epistle is the conviction that there is a light, peculiar to God the Father though shared with Christ the Son, which those who know God recognize" (*1–3 John*, 50). See also Marianne Meye Thompson, *1–3 John*, IVPNTC 19 (Downers Grove, IL: IVP Academic, 1992), 40–41.

4. Smalley, *1, 2, 3 John*, 18.

Habakkuk declares, "His splendor was like the sunrise; rays flashed from his hand" (Hab 3:4). In Isaiah the Lord says, "Arise, shine, for your light has come, and the glory of the Lord rises upon you" (Isa 60:1); and in the same chapter (60:19–20):

> The sun will no more be your light by day,
>   nor will the brightness of the moon shine on you,
> for the Lord will be your everlasting light,
>   and your God will be your glory.
> Your sun will never set again,
>   and your moon will wane no more;
> the Lord will be your everlasting light,
>   and your days of sorrow will end.

John's Gospel makes strong use of the theme of light, applying it to Jesus himself. He is the "true light that gives light to everyone" (1:9). Jesus himself declared, "I am the light of the world" (8:12; 9:5). He came into the world so that people would not remain in darkness but become children of the light (12:35–36, 46).

All this raises some theological questions. The Old Testament stops short of calling God "light" (though Isaiah 60 comes close to this), preferring to see light as an attribute that proceeds from him. As such, when Jesus is *called* the light in John's Gospel, he is the personification of this attribute of God (much like "wisdom" and "word"). Then, in 1 John 1:5 John refers to *God* as light. Does this mean that Jesus (who is the light) is meant here and explicitly called "God"?

A different solution is preferable. John refers to "God" rather than Jesus, and God is light. This truth is not directly revealed in the Old Testament, but it accounts for why God is the source of light; this attribute stems forth from the one who *is* light. When therefore Jesus is revealed as the personification of this attribute, this underscores that he is sent by God for God is the source of the world's light both in a physical as well as a spiritual sense. Nevertheless, John's use of the theme of light gives voice to his implicit Trinitarianism: God is light, and Jesus is the light come into the world; he is the personification of this divine attribute as the second person of the Trinity.

We Cannot Have Fellowship with God if We Walk in Darkness (1:5c–7a)

Because God is light, there is no darkness in him (1:5c). To have fellowship with God and to "walk in the darkness" are mutually exclusive realities; to claim the first while doing the second is not to live the truth (1:6).

It is possible to understand "darkness" here as some kind of theological error or falsehood since it is contrasted to "truth" and is considered "lying" (1:6). In the next two verses, however, it becomes clear that "darkness" is a moral category: the theme of sin is introduced in 1:7 and is the main topic in 1:8–10.

"Walking" is a well-known Jewish metaphor for how one lives (e.g., Pss 1:1; 15:2; Rom 6:4; 8:4; 14:15). It is found in 1 John 1:7; 2:6, 11; 2 John 4, 6; and 3 John 3, 4.[5] Thus, walking in darkness is a metaphor for living according to sin. This idea is summarized well in John 3:19–21:

> This is the verdict: Light has come into the world, but people loved darkness instead of light because their deeds were evil. Everyone who does evil hates the light, and will not come into the light for fear that their deeds will be exposed. But whoever lives by the truth comes into the light, so that it may be seen plainly that what they have done has been done in the sight of God.

Accordingly, 1:6 states that it is impossible to be in fellowship with God while continuing to live according to sin. To claim such is simply lying. And if we lie, we "do not live out the truth." As Irenaeus wrote, "A lie has no fellowship with the truth, any more than light with darkness. The presence of one excludes the other."[6]

Immediately, this reading of 1:6 comes into tension with 1:8 in which John states that if we claim to be *without* sin, we deceive ourselves. The tension between the two verses, simply put, is that 1:6 says if you live according to sin while claiming fellowship with God, you lie; 1:8 says that if you claim to be *without* sin, you lie. How, then, are these verses to be understood together?

The most straightforward answer is that "walking in darkness" is not equivalent to "sin" but to "living according to sin." In other words, John acknowledges that all believers will commit sin—to claim otherwise is a lie— but there is a difference between committing sins and living *according to* sin. The former refers to believers' frequent failings as they seek to live according to their fellowship with God; the latter refers to not living according to fellowship with God at all.[7]

---

5. David Rensberger, *1 John, 2 John, 3 John*, ANTC (Nashville: Abingdon, 1997), 51.

6. Irenaeus, "An Exposition of the Faith," in *Early Christian Fathers*, ed. Cyril Richardson, vol. 1 of *The Library of Christian Classics*, ed. J. Baillie et al. (Philadelphia: Westminster, 1953–66), 376.

7. Baylis argues that walking in the darkness is not directly related to sin but refers to rejecting the revelation of God in Christ. Certainly we can affirm that it relates to the rejection of God's revelation, but to ignore its relationship to sin downplays the ethical significance of the "walking" metaphor and the immediate context in which sin is clearly in view. See Charles P. Baylis, "The Meaning of Walking 'in the Darkness' (1 John 1:6)," *BSac* 149 (1992): 214–22.

Believers are to "walk in the light, as he is in the light" (1:7a). We are told implicitly in 1:6 that walking in the light is essential for fellowship with God; in 1:7 John adds that if we walk in the light "we have fellowship with one another." Since walking in the light is essential for fellowship with God and leads to fellowship with one another, it is clear that these two "fellowships" are correlated (cf. 1:3). While John does not explicitly make the point, it is clear that fellowship with God leads to fellowship with his people.[8] Because God is light, those who walk in the light are united in their common walking.

The idea of walking in the light also connotes light's revelatory aspect. Light illumines the path along which we walk. As the psalmists say, "Send me your light and your faithful care, let them lead me (Ps 43:3); "Your word is a lamp for my feet, a light on my path" (Ps 119:105). Since God is light, knowing him gives sight to true reality that we may know where and how we should go. But light also gives sight to who we are. It reveals our need for purification and confession of sins, which is what John goes on to address.

The Blood of Jesus Purifies Us from All Sin (1:7b)

John then moves to another factor in the fellowship between believers: "And the blood of Jesus, his Son, purifies us from all sin" (1:7b). Sin is a prevalent theme in 1 John; this is the first of twenty-seven references to sin or sinning (*hamartia, hamartanō*).[9] John says that "sin is lawlessness" (3:4b) and that "all wrongdoing is sin" (5:17). Sin involves rebellion against God's good order and instruction. And as John says next in 1:8, no one is free from sin (cf. Rom 3:9–20).

However, sin is not only about doing the wrong thing. Sinful people are rebels against God by *position*. John writes, "The one who does what is sinful is of the devil, because the devil has been sinning from the beginning" (3:8). Sinners belong to the evil one, whose rebellion against God goes back to the beginning (cf. Gen 3). The sinner is opposed to God by allegiance to his enemy. Thus, sinful actions are but symptoms of a deeper problem, namely, the rejection of God in our hearts (cf. Mark 7:1–20).

Here John explicitly connects the death of Jesus (more specifically, his "blood") to cleansing from sin. The shedding of Jesus's blood at his crucifixion achieves the all-important removal of sin that enables believers to walk in the light.[10] The sacrificial shedding of blood in the Old Testament cleansed

---

8. Kruse, *Letters of John*, 64.
9. 1 John 1:7–2:2; 2:12; 3:4–6, 8–9; 4:10; 5:16–18.
10. Eduard Schweizer, "An Exegetical Analysis of 1 John 1:7," in *Theology in the Service of the Church: Essays in Honor of Thomas W. Gillespie*, ed. Wallace M. Alston (Grand Rapids: Eerdmans, 2000), 188–95.

Israelites from the guilt and penalty of their sin.[11] Blood was regarded as the seat of life (Lev 17:11) so that the blood of a victim was its life yielded up in death, "and the 'sprinkling' of that blood guaranteed for the worshipper the effectiveness of any sacrifice" (cf. Exod 30:10; Lev 16:15–19).[12]

It did not prevent Israelites from ever sinning again, and the repeated nature of such sacrifices attested to this obvious fact. While the shedding of Jesus's blood occurred once and thus differs from Old Testament sacrifices in this way, it likewise did not secure sinless perfectionism for its beneficiaries (at least, not in this life). As in the Old Testament, Jesus's sacrifice removed the guilt and penalty of sin, and it is in this sense that believers are purified from sin.

While contemporary notions of purity tend to relate to sexual integrity, the focus here is not limited to such matters. John points to purification from "*all* sin" and "*all* unrighteousness" (1:7, 9). Furthermore, purification is a *cleansing* (*katharizō*) from the guilt and penalty of sin. It refers to the cleansed status of people who have benefited from the shedding of blood—the objective guilt and penalty for sin has been wiped away. This will of course have implications for living a life of sexual purity, but the primary point here is that the *failure* to live in purity has been dealt with by Jesus's blood.

We Need to Confess Our Sins (1:8–10)

Reference to purification from sin in 1:7 presupposes that sin exists and is a problem requiring a solution. Since 2:2 states that Jesus's sacrifice was for the sins of the *whole world*, it would be nonsense for any (other) human being to claim to be without sin. The guilt of all has been presupposed by the sacrifice for all. So says John: "If we claim to be without sin, we deceive ourselves and the truth is not in us" (1:8). Indeed, it is more than nonsense to claim sinlessness—it is a deception and denial of the truth. In this way, John covers both poles of deception regarding sin. First, to walk in darkness or to live according to sin is to reject the truth (1:6). Second, to claim to be without sin is also to reject the truth (1:8).

Rather than claim to be without sin, John implores his readers to confess their sins (1:9). His encouragement toward confession is couched in the character of God: "He is faithful and just and will forgive us our sins and purify us from all unrighteousness." God's faithfulness and justice ensure forgiveness because he has promised to forgive those who repent and believe in Jesus. For God to withhold forgiveness from those who confess their sins would be to

---

11. While some scholars have supported the view that "blood" means "life released" rather than "death inflicted," Morris has demonstrated that "in both the Old and New Testaments the blood signifies essentially the death." Leon Morris, *The Apostolic Preaching of the Cross*, 3rd ed. (Grand Rapids: Eerdmans, 1965 [1955]), 126; see also the entire chapter concerning blood (112–28).

12. Smalley, *1, 2, 3 John*, 23.

make himself a liar. With this faithful and just God, there is nothing to fear in admitting to and confessing sin. He will forgive, and nothing is to be gained by pretending that forgiveness is not needed.

Alongside the language of forgiveness in 1:9 is the second instance of purification or cleansing language in this passage: God "will forgive us our sins and purify us from all unrighteousness." In 1:7 we are told that the blood of Jesus purifies us from all sin. In 1:9 purification from unrighteousness is procured through confession of sin and God's forgiveness. By correlating the two statements about purification in 1:7 and 1:9, we see that cleansing from sin is part of what it means to walk in the light, since walking in the light brings purification in 1:7 as does confession in 1:9. These are not two separate means of cleansing, but one is folded within the other.

John returns to the issue of claiming to be without sin in 1:10. Whereas the claim reveals self-deception in 1:8, in 1:10 it makes God out to be a liar. Whereas the claim reveals that the truth is not in us in 1:8, in 1:10 it reveals that God's word has no place in our lives. The claim to be without sin makes God out to be a liar because he has said that there are none who have not sinned (Pss 14:1–3; 53:1–3; Eccl 7:20; Rom 3:9–20).[13]

Another distinction between 1:8 and 10 is the change of tenses. In 1:8 John literally says, "If we say that we have not sin" (*ean eipōmen hoti hamartian ouk echomen*); in 1:10 he says, "If we say that we have not sinned" (*ean eipōmen hoti ouch hēmartēkamen*). While the use of the Greek perfect in 1:10 (*hēmartēkamen*) is typically translated this way, the HCSB renders the phrase as "If we say, 'We don't have any sin,'" which treats the perfect as stative rather than as referring to a past event.[14] Theologically, this translation guards against a potential error that would understand the phrase "we have not sinned" to refer only to preconversion sin. It might then be argued that John is not suggesting that all people sin—including Christians—but that once confession (= conversion) has occurred, Christians sin no longer. This is the error of sinless perfectionism and twists John's words. After all, he has already used the present "if we say we have no sin" in 1:8 that confirms that Christians still "have sin" in their lives, even postconversion.

Walking in the light involves being honest about our sin, confessing it, receiving purification from it and forgiveness of it. But the denial of sin belongs to the darkness, the home of all lies. And it is not possible to walk in darkness and have fellowship with God, because God is light.

---

13. Kruse, *Letters of John*, 71.

14. This does better in keeping with the perfect's imperfective aspect and is to be preferred. See Constantine R. Campbell, *Basics of Verbal Aspect in Biblical Greek* (Grand Rapids: Zondervan, 2008), 106–7.

 LIVE the Story

Being Honest with God

This passage contrasts two ways of living—walking in the light and walking in darkness. The first constitutes fellowship with God. That fellowship is characterized by truth, confession of sin, forgiveness, and cleansing. The second constitutes a false claim to fellowship with God, which is characterized by deceit, deception, and the rejection of truth.

Believers must remember that their relationship with God must be *honest*. God sees all and knows all—do we really think that we can keep some sins secret from him? Some believers may feel so ashamed of certain failures that they find it difficult to bring them before the Lord in confession. There is nothing to be gained, however, by pretending since God already knows the truth. But there is much to be gained by honest and repentant confession.

No one knew this better than King David. After his adultery with Bathsheba and arranging the death of her husband, Uriah the Hittite, David was confronted by Nathan the prophet concerning his grievous sins (2 Sam 11–12). It took a direct confrontation with the word of the Lord to bring David to repentance, but repent he did.

Psalm 51 records David's passionate and transparent prayer of confession. Note the honest acknowledgment of his sins (vv. 1–5, 9, 14), but also the reliance on God's character to forgive (vv. 1, 11, 14, 17) and David's requests to be cleansed from his sin (vv. 1–2, 7, 9–10, 14):

> *For the director of music. A psalm of David. When the prophet Nathan came to him after David had committed adultery with Bathsheba.*

¹Have mercy on me, O God,
　　according to your unfailing love;
according to your great compassion
　　blot out my transgressions.
²Wash away all my iniquity
　　and cleanse me from my sin.
³For I know my transgressions,
　　and my sin is always before me.
⁴Against you, you only, have I sinned
　　and done what is evil in your sight;
so you are right in your verdict
　　and justified when you judge.
⁵Surely I was sinful at birth,
　　sinful from the time my mother conceived me.

[6]Yet you desired faithfulness even in the womb;
    you taught me wisdom in that secret place.
[7]Cleanse me with hyssop, and I will be clean;
    wash me, and I will be whiter than snow.
[8]Let me hear joy and gladness;
    let the bones you have crushed rejoice.
[9]Hide your face from my sins
    and blot out all my iniquity.
[10]Create in me a pure heart, O God,
    and renew a steadfast spirit within me.
[11]Do not cast me from your presence
    or take your Holy Spirit from me.
[12]Restore to me the joy of your salvation
    and grant me a willing spirit, to sustain me.
[13]Then I will teach transgressors your ways,
    so that sinners will turn back to you.
[14]Deliver me from the guilt of bloodshed, O God,
    you who are God my Savior,
    and my tongue will sing of your righteousness.
[15]Open my lips, Lord,
    and my mouth will declare your praise.
[16]You do not delight in sacrifice, or I would bring it;
    you do not take pleasure in burnt offerings.
[17]My sacrifice, O God, is a broken spirit;
    a broken and contrite heart
    you, God, will not despise.
[18]May it please you to prosper Zion,
    to build up the walls of Jerusalem.
[19]Then you will delight in the sacrifices of the righteous,
    in burnt offerings offered whole;
    then bulls will be offered on your altar.

With true confession comes great comfort. First John 1:5–10 reminds us that God is faithful and just, which may at first strike fear in our hearts since we would justly face condemnation. Yet on account of the blood of Jesus, God's justice is expressed by fulfilling his promise of forgiveness for those who confess their sins and trust in Jesus. May all believers rejoice in the certainty of God's forgiveness!

Should we ever be tempted to think that some sins are beyond the reach of God's mercy, we would do well to remember that he is not a capricious god, sitting in heaven weighing up which sins to forgive and which to punish. No,

God is *faithful* and *just*. His promise is sure and can be trusted: the blood of Jesus purifies us from *all* sin.

Confessing Sins Today

The role of confession in the Christian life can become muted in today's world. Generally speaking, modern Western culture is moving away from the idea of personal failure and responsibility. Apart from breaking laws—in which case the state declares guilt of transgression—people ought to be free to act as we see fit, indulging our every whim and desire. We live in a culture that is dominated by a worldview in which its highest value is the freedom to fulfill our own desires. To claim that some of those desires are sinful or wrong in any way is really the only sin that can be committed today.

Consequently, the very notion of confession is becoming increasingly alien. It is something that believers must be taught to do as we reject the assumptions of secular society. Sin does exist and its power is real. We must not only accept that fact but face our own failures and embrace God's forgiveness.

Sadly, the world is not alone in shunning confession. Some corners of the church are likewise hesitant to face up to failure. The error of sinless perfectionism continues to permeate congregations around the world. To confess sin in "sinless" churches is tantamount to renouncing Christian faith. This creates an unbearable burden for many believers who would rejoice in the face of true freedom if only they were free to admit that they still struggle with sin in their lives.

Consider the Christian who struggles with pornography. I suspect this particular struggle is much more prevalent within the church than we may realize because there is a kind of shame associated with it. Many believers are too ashamed to admit that they are caught up in this pernicious sin, and as a result they do not confess it to anyone. It remains secret. It remains hidden. And therefore it remains much more difficult to overcome. This problem will only be exacerbated within "sinless" churches that pretend that real Christians do not struggle with sinful activity such as pornography. Not only will the discouraged believer keep their sin to themselves but may end up giving up on the faith because it is clearly only for people who have overcome sinful behavior.

It is much healthier to acknowledge the presence of such sins in our lives, to confess them to each other, and to help each other in overcoming them. Accountability is key in conquering sins such as pornography, but accountability only works if we are open with each other about our struggles.

Corporate Confession

Churches can undermine the role of confession in other ways too. With the widespread decline of liturgical practice in today's churches, corporate confession no longer features as it once did. Whatever the strengths and weaknesses of liturgical approaches to worship, liturgy generally does a good job of facilitating corporate confession.

For instance, the tradition of the Anglican Prayer Book, which reaches back to the sixteenth-century English Reformer Thomas Cranmer, includes corporate confession of sin followed by assurance of God's forgiveness in the face of genuine repentance. One of my favorite prayers of corporate confession is found in *An Australian Prayer Book* (said together):

> Merciful God,
> our maker and our judge,
> we have sinned against you in thought, word, and deed:
> we have not loved you with our whole heart,
> we have not loved our neighbors as ourselves:
> we repent, and are sorry for all our sins.
> Father, forgive us.
> Strengthen us to love and obey you in newness of life;
> through Jesus Christ our Lord. Amen.

An assurance of forgiveness follows, prayed by the service leader:

> Almighty God,
> who has promised forgiveness of sins to all who turn to him in faith:
> pardon you and set you free from all your sins,
> strengthen you to do his will,
> and keep you in eternal life;
> through Jesus Christ our Lord. Amen.

The advantages of corporate confession are felt beyond the gathering too. The practice *teaches* us of the importance and theology of confession, which will then more likely permeate our personal practice. It also reinforces God's promised response to confession—the assurance of forgiveness of sins.

It is not necessary to revert to liturgical practice (or to embrace it for the first time) in order to make corporate confession a regular feature of our Christian gatherings. But whichever way it is formulated, corporate confession ought to become again a standard feature of our congregations, as normal as the preaching of sermons and the singing of praises. After all, confession of sin is an essential element of the Christian life—as is hearing God's word and offering him praise. Should not that reality be reflected in our meetings together?

Being Too Comfortable with Sin

Some Christians fail to confess sin because they are uncomfortable confronting their own failings. But others fail to confess sin because they are all

too comfortable with it. Yes, they know it is sin, and they know it falls short
of God's standards, but some sins have become acceptable in their eyes. This
might happen slowly, particularly with ongoing struggles that never seem to
dissipate. The believer simply gives up. And he or she also stops confessing.

This can be understandable, since ongoing battles are wearisome, and an
apparent lack of progress can be disheartening. It's just easier to stop dealing
with it, both in resistance and confession. But the result is that the believer
allows a dark corner of his or her life to remain unexposed to the light. And
so long as the sin secretly remains, it will fester.

Dietrich Bonhoeffer perceptively addresses this issue in his classic, *Life
Together*:

> Sin demands to have a man by himself. It withdraws him from the
> community. The more isolated a person is, the more destructive will be
> the power of sin over him, and the more deeply he becomes involved in it,
> the more disastrous is his isolation. Sin wants to remain unknown. It shuns
> the light. In the darkness of the unexpressed it poisons the whole being
> of a person. This can happen even in the midst of a pious community. In
> confession the light of the gospel breaks into the darkness and seclusion of
> the heart. The sin must be brought into the light. The unexpressed must
> be openly spoken and acknowledged. All that is secret and hidden is made
> manifest. It is a struggle until the sin is openly admitted, but God breaks
> gates of brass and bars of iron (Ps. 107:16).
>
> Since the confession of sin is made in the presence of a Christian
> brother, the last stronghold of self-justification is abandoned. The sin-
> ner surrenders; he gives up all his evil. He gives his heart to God, and he
> finds the forgiveness of all his sin in the fellowship of Jesus Christ and his
> brother. The expressed, acknowledged sin has lost all its power. It has been
> revealed and judged as sin. It can no longer tear the fellowship asunder.
> Now the fellowship bears the sin of the brother. He is no longer alone
> with his evil for he has cast off his sin in confession and handed it over to
> God. It has been taken away from him. Now he stands in the fellowship of
> sinners who live by the grace of God and the cross of Jesus Christ. . . . The
> sin concealed separated him from the fellowship, made all his apparent
> fellowship a sham; the sin confessed has helped him define true fellowship
> with the brethren in Jesus Christ.[15]

While unconfessed secret sin is no doubt common, it is not acceptable
for God's people. To walk in the light is to allow the whole of one's life to

---

15. Dietrich Bonhoeffer, *Life Together* (New York: Harper & Row, 1954), 112–13.

be exposed to it. We are not to have secret sins. We are not to become comfortable with sin. We are not to pretend that some sins are immune from confession.

While we may be comforted by God's forgiveness, we should not become complacent about the need for it. After all, our forgiveness came at great cost—no less than the blood of God's Son, Jesus Christ. If we forget the seriousness of sin, we will inevitably cheapen the price he paid for us on the cross.

CHAPTER 3

1 John 2:1-6

 ## LISTEN to the Story

¹My dear children, I write this to you so that you will not sin. But if anybody does sin, we have an advocate with the Father—Jesus Christ, the Righteous One. ²He is the atoning sacrifice for our sins, and not only for ours but also for the sins of the whole world.

³We know that we have come to know him if we keep his commands. ⁴Whoever says, "I know him," but does not do what he commands is a liar, and the truth is not in that person. ⁵But if anyone obeys his word, love for God is truly made complete in them. This is how we know we are in him: ⁶Whoever claims to live in him must live as Jesus did.

Listening to the Text in the Story: Leviticus 16; Deuteronomy 6:5; John 14:15–18; 15:10–14; Romans 3:21–26.

Having discussed sin, confession, and forgiveness in 1:5–10, here John exhorts his "dear children" to avoid sin. But he also acknowledges that they *will* sin and will need the righteous advocate, Jesus Christ, who is also the precious atoning sacrifice for our sins. While this is a wonderful truth, the main thrust in this passage has to do with not sinning and keeping Jesus's commands. The person who truly knows Jesus is the one who does what he says. True believers will live out their confession of faith.

The passage fits into a wider unit that is structured around three purpose statements for John's writing (2:1–14). In the first, John states that he writes "so that you may not sin" (2:1). Second, John says that he is "not writing a new command" but an old one (2:7). The third is a group of such statements: "I write to you, dear children" (2:12, 13); "I write to you, fathers" (2:13, 14); "I write to you, young men" (2:13, 14). This passage (2:1–6) begins with the first purpose statement, "I write this to you so that you will not sin" (2:1), which sets the theme for the section.

EXPLAIN the Story

I Write This So That You Will Not Sin (2:1a)

John begins the passage by affectionately addressing his readers as "my dear children" (2:1a; *teknia mou*). This points to the loving, pastoral bond that John shares with them. He is fond of the address (1 John 2:12, 28; 3:7, 18; 4:4; 5:21), which emulates Jesus's own loving address to his disciples (John 13:33).[1]

To his dear children, John provides his first purpose statement: "I write this to you so that you will not sin" (2:1). While forgiveness and purification are available upon confession of sin (1:7–10), it is better that believers avoid sinning in the first place.

The purpose statement refers to the contents of the entire letter (lit. "I write *these things*"; *tauta*). However, the exhortation not to sin can only be *one* of the purposes of the letter since John's interests are broader than just this concern. Nevertheless, it *is* one of John's concerns and is part of walking in the light (1:7). The confession of sin is not the only expectation of those in the light; avoidance of sin is part of it too. The forgiveness of sins (1:9) is not intended to license sin; it is offered that believers might live in fellowship with God. Consequently, Christians are to live according to the purpose of their forgiveness—fellowship with God—and thereby resist sin as is fitting for such a relationship.

But If You Do Sin, We Have a Righteous Advocate (2:1b)

Though John writes so that his readers will not sin, he is obviously aware that believers *will* sin: "But if anybody does sin, we have an advocate with the Father—Jesus Christ, the Righteous One" (2:1).

But he does not just raise the *possibility* of sin—it is, rather, a certainty. John has already said that the claim to be without sin is a deception (1:8, 10). While most translations of 2:1b read, "*If* anybody does sin" (*ean tis hamartē*), English can be misleading at this point. The word "if" makes it sound possible that *no one* will sin, as though John means "*if* it happens that anyone *does* sin."[2] Given what John has already said about the inevitability of sin, however,

---

1. The expression is literally "my little children" (*teknia mou*; as CSB, ESV), but this might sound somewhat patronizing to modern ears.

2. There is a mismatch between English and Greek here, as the third class condition (*ean* + subjunctive) has a broad semantic range. As Wallace writes, "It depicts what is *likely to occur* in the *future*, what could *possibly occur*, or even what is only *hypothetical* and will not occur" (Daniel B. Wallace, *Greek Grammar Beyond the Basics: An Exegetical Syntax of the New Testament* [Grand Rapids: Zondervan, 1996], 696; emphasis original).

the phrase is better understood as "when anyone does sin." In other words, the "if" expresses an expectation rather than a mere possibility.

In the event of sin, John offers the greatest possible comfort: "We have an advocate with the Father—Jesus Christ, the Righteous One" (2:1b). Christ is described as an "advocate" (*paraklētos*)—one who appears on another's behalf as a mediator, intercessor, or helper.[3]

In John's Gospel, "advocate" is used exclusively for the Holy Spirit (John 14:16, 26; 15:26; 16:7), while here it is used of Jesus Christ. Yet it is not difficult to correlate the different uses. In John 14:16, Jesus says that God will give "*another* Counselor" (*allon paraklēton*), indicating that he considers *himself* a counselor also and that there is continuity between his work and that of the Spirit. The Spirit testifies to Jesus and reminds the disciples of his teaching (John 14:26; 15:26).[4]

Whereas the Spirit enables access to Jesus after his ascension, so Jesus enables access to the Father. He advocates on behalf of believers and thereby facilitates our fellowship with God. Thus, *advocacy* is the ministry of two persons of the Godhead (Son and Spirit) for fellowship with two persons of the Godhead (Son and Father), as the three persons together display the fullness of God who redeems us.

Jesus Christ, our advocate with the Father, is called "the Righteous One." The righteousness of Jesus is an essential qualification for dealing with human sin. In 1:7 Jesus's blood "purifies us from all sin," which in Jewish thought would only be possible if he were free from sin himself. In the Old Testament, purification required the sacrifice of a spotless animal (lit. "blameless"; e.g., Lev 1:3, 10; 3:1; 4:3, 23, 28, 32; 5:15, 18). The blood of the blameless animal was shed on behalf of the repentant sinner. With the sacrificial system in the background, John knows that purification depends on Jesus's own righteousness. Only the one without sin can bring about purification: "He appeared so that he might take away our sins. And in him is no sin" (3:5; cf. Rom 3:21–26). In this same way, Jesus's righteousness is essential to his atoning sacrifice in 2:2 (see below).

The Righteous One Is the Atoning Sacrifice for Sins (2:2a)

John writes "so that you will not sin" but acknowledges that believers *will* sin. In view of this reality, John comforts his readers with the advocacy of Jesus Christ. In 2:2 he adds further reason for comfort: Jesus is not only our advocate but is also "the atoning sacrifice for our sins."

This description of Jesus requires careful exploration as it is both important and controversial. Debate swirls around the term *hilasmos*, here translated

---

3. BDAG 766.
4. Lieu, *I, II, & III John*, 62.

"atoning sacrifice." *Hilasmos* occurs in the New Testament only here and at 4:10. However, related (cognate) words can be found in Matthew 16:22, Luke 18:13, Romans 3:25, and Hebrews 2:17, 8:12, and 9:5. Importantly, the word group occurs forty-six times in the Greek Old Testament (LXX, including the Apocrypha), which provides essential background for New Testament usage.[5] The question is, what exactly does *hilasmos* mean?

The two main alternatives involve the concepts of *propitiation* and *expiation*. *Propitiation* refers to the aversion of wrath such that God's wrath is redirected *away* from sinful humanity and *toward* a sacrificial victim. *Expiation* infers the removal of guilt so that the offense of humanity's guilt is expunged (without any necessary implication of wrath). "In short, propitiation appeases the offended person, whereas expiation is concerned with nullifying the offensive act."[6] The ideas are not mutually exclusive, since the removal of guilt and the aversion of wrath can be understood together.

First, we briefly explore the case for expiation in biblical sacrifice. Gerhard von Rad represents a number of biblical scholars who regard Old Testament sacrifice as expiatory rather than propitiatory. A key text to support the idea of the removal of guilt is Deuteronomy 21:1–9 (v. 9: "you will have purged from yourselves the guilt of shedding innocent blood"). Von Rad states, "As a rule . . . expiation is effected through the vicarious death of an animal." Furthermore, God is the one who effects expiation: "The one who receives expiation is not Jahweh, but Israel: Jahweh is rather the one who acts, in averting the calamitous curse which burdens the community."[7]

C. H. Dodd made a case for expiation on linguistic grounds, examining Greek words used in the LXX against their uses in classical Greek literature. Among other studies, he examined passages where the *hilas-* word group translates the Hebrew *k-p-r* word group and concluded that the sense is not one of "propitiating the Deity, but the sense of performing an act whereby guilt of defilement is removed."[8] Dodd became a major proponent of the expiation understanding of the *hilas-* word group in the New Testament on the basis of what he believed about LXX usage. However, Dodd's work has been criticized for limiting his study to lexical issues without looking at the wider contexts and without considering the nature of God's character and relationship with

---

5. Exod 25:17–22; 31:7; 32:14; 35:12; 38:5, 7–8; Lev 16:2, 13-15; 25:9; Num 5:8; 7:89; Deut 21:8; 2 Kgs 5:18; 24:4; 2 Chr 6:30; Esth 13:17; Pss 24:11; 64:4; 77:38; 78:9; 129:4; Lam 3:42; Ezek 43:14, 17, 20; 44:27; Amos 8:14–9:1; 2 Macc 3:33; 4 Macc 17:22.

6. Moisés Silva, ed., "ἱλάσκομαι," in *New International Dictionary of New Testament Theology and Exegesis*, 2nd ed. (Grand Rapids: Zondervan, 2014), 2:534.

7. Gerhard von Rad, *Old Testament Theology*, trans. D. M. G. Stalker, 2 vols. (London: SCM, 1975), 2:270.

8. C. H. Dodd, *The Bible and the Greeks* (London: Hodder & Stoughton, 1935), 93.

people.[9] Moreover, he has been criticized for basing his conclusions on less than 40 percent of the relevant evidence.[10]

Second, we briefly explore the case for propitiation in biblical sacrifice. Leon Morris also examined a swath of relevant passages, making the following conclusions. In secular Greek usage there are only two possible instances in which the *hilas-* word group could be understood in an expiatory sense, and these are capable of being understood in a propitiatory sense. When the *hilas-* word group is used in the Old Testament, the offense is not dealt with in an impersonal way (contra expiation). Passages that can be read in an expiatory way can also be understood in a propitiatory way, but passages that require propitiation cannot be reduced to expiation. In cultic settings, the verb took on a technical meaning, overshadowing other senses.[11] The Hebrew and Greek versions of the Old Testament do not present a picture of propitiation like crude pagan ideas of propitiating a capricious and malevolent deity. Nor do their authors evince a mechanistic understanding in which sin simply needs the right antidote. "There is a personal dimension that affects both the offending and the offended parties."[12]

Third, John's Gospel presents Jesus as the fulfilment of the Passover lamb (Exod 12),[13] as seen in John the Baptist's declaration, "Look, the Lamb of God, who takes away the sin of the world!" (John 1:29; cf. 10:11–18). Jesus is the Lamb of God who directs God's wrath away from his people, just as the blood of the lamb did that first Passover in Egypt. That is propitiation. But we *also* see expiation affirmed, since Jesus "takes away the sin of the world." He removes humanity's sin, the cause of offense against God.

Fourth, we turn to the most likely sense meant in 1 John 2:2. Given that the Old Testament sacrificial system was a means for dealing with God's wrath, that the *hilas-* word group denotes propitiation and on occasion expiation too, and that John's Gospel evidences a theology of propitiation and expiation, it seems at the outset that propitiation at least is meant in 1 John 2:2,[14] possibly along with expiation.

9. David Hill, *Greek Words and Hebrew Meanings: Studies in the Semantics of Soteriological Terms*, SNTSMS 5 (Cambridge: Cambridge University Press, 1967), 24.

10. Roger R. Nicole, "C. H. Dodd and the Doctrine of Propitiation," *WTJ* 17 (1956–57): 117–57. See also F. A. Gosling, "Where Is the God of Justice? An Examination of C. H. Dodd's Understanding of ἱλάσκεσθαι and Its Derivatives," *ZAW* 113 (2001): 404–14; K. Grayston, "Ἱλάσκεσθαι and Related Words in the Septuagint," *NTS* 27 (1980–81): 640–56.

11. Morris, *Apostolic Preaching of the Cross*, 144–78.

12. Silva, "ἱλάσκομαι," 536.

13. Andreas J. Köstenberger, *John*, BECNT (Grand Rapids: Baker Academic, 2004), 67. It is possible that John the Baptist had in mind the lamb (the suffering servant) of Isaiah 53 or the apocalyptic warrior lamb of 1 Enoch 90:9–12, but most likely the author of the Gospel uses the Baptist's statement to affirm his own theology of substitutionary atonement.

14. Contra Lieu's casual dismissal of this understanding (*I, II, & III John*, 64n16). The issues require further consideration than Lieu allows.

Propitiation remains a controversial interpretation, however. Baker and Green assert only expiation in 1 John, drawing especially on the Old Testament background of the Day of Atonement. They write:

> The importance of the connection of this text with the Day of Atonement is suggested by the relationship between impurity and sin, addressed in the rite of the Day of Atonement described in Leviticus 16. Sin results in impurity in the temple, so the ritual prescribed for the Day of Atonement calls for purification of the sanctuary/temple and the use of a scapegoat. Immediately following the purgation of the sanctuary, the high priest places his hands on the goat's head, confesses over it the sins of Israel and sends the goat into the wilderness. Thus are the sanctuary cleansed and the people's sins banished. Note that, in this rite, the scapegoat is not butchered and presented as a sacrificial offering, and there is no attempt (or necessity) to appease God. The problem is sin, which defiles us for communion with God. Jesus' death, according to the deployment of this imagery in 1 John, cleanses us and thus readies us for unfettered fellowship with God.[15]

There are problems with this analysis, however. While Baker and Green articulate well the expiatory nature of the Day of Atonement rite, they fail to show why the Day of Atonement *alone* is related to the language of 1 John. It certainly fits the purification language of 1:7, 9 (which we already agree are expiatory), and words belonging to the *hilas-* group occur in Leviticus 16. And yet elsewhere the word group is used in contexts where a sacrificial offering *is* "butchered," including the bull and ram offered for Aaron's sins in preparation for conducting the Day of Atonement rite (Lev 16:6, 11). Why are these other Old Testament sacrificial images not considered for the background of 1 John 2:2?

In his careful and detailed study, Toan Do acknowledges that the *hilas-* word group can refer both to propitiation and expiation in the LXX but that the instances in the New Testament demand an entirely different approach for proper interpretation.[16] Moreover, other New Testament instances of the word group should not be relied on for determining John's meaning. This leads to a contextual study of 1 John 2:2 and 4:10 in which he argues that *hilasmos* must refer to *expiation*, not *propitiation*.[17] Do also points to the absence of the language of wrath or anger in 1 John to argue against propitiation.[18]

---

15. Mark D. Baker and Joel B. Green, *Recovering the Scandal of the Cross: Atonement in New Testament and Contemporary Contexts*, 2nd ed. (Downers Grove, IL: InterVarsity Press, 2011), 103–4.
16. Toan Do, *Re-Thinking the Death of Jesus: An Exegetical and Theological Study of* Hilasmos *and* Agapē *in 1 John 2:1–2 and 4:7–10*, CBET 73 (Leuven: Peeters, 2014), 279–80.
17. Ibid., 206–13.
18. Ibid., 210–12, 215–75.

While Do is correct to offer caution about how John's usage of *hilasmos* relates (or does not relate) to the LXX and other New Testament uses, the effect of his approach is to ignore the overtones of propitiation that John's original readers may well have perceived. *If* the word *did* often refer to propitiation, how can we ignore such overtones in John's writing? To that point, the absence of the language of wrath or anger in 1 John does not prove that *hilasmos* must mean expiation rather than propitiation. Again, if overtones of propitiation are heard in the word, then wrath is implied; it need not be stated explicitly (though note the further comments on this, below).

Most significantly, however, it appears that Do has pit propitiation against the love of God. He associates God's *love* with *expiation* and his *wrath* with *propitiation*: "Expiation comes solely from God's love for humanity, whereas the cause for propitiation is conditioned by his wrath."[19] Since he rightly notes the strong emphasis on God's love in 1 John along with the apparent absence of his wrath, it is obvious then why Do must conclude in favor of expiation over propitiation. The former connects to love, the latter to wrath. But this is an oversimplification, as we will see below.

Even Dodd acknowledges that propitiation may be meant in 1 John 2:2: "In the immediate context it might seem possible that the sense of 'propitiation' is in place: if our guilt requires an advocate before God, we might, logically, need to placate His righteous anger."[20] To which Leon Morris simply responds, "Exactly." He adds, "If there is 'a righteous anger' of God, and the New Testament is clear that there is, then it cannot be ignored in the process of forgiveness (as Dodd does ignore it in his discussion of forgiveness)."[21] McKnight writes, "In light of the presence of wrath in the Johannine tradition, we would be remiss in omitting every sense of propitiation from the term (e.g, John 3:36; Revelation 6:15–17)."[22] Jesus is our advocate, which implies our guilt and God's wrath.[23] In this context, *hilasmos* could easily refer to the aversion of God's wrath—propitiation. As for expiation, the blood of Jesus cleanses us from all sin and unrighteousness (1:7, 9). The cleansing of sin is the removal of guilt, thus expiation.

Jobes affirms both the propitiatory and expiatory aspects of Christ's death in the Johannine material.[24] Similarly, in his book on the cross in the Johannine Writings, Morgan-Wynne allows both ideas so long as propitiation is not

---

19. Ibid., 207.

20. Dodd, *Johannine Epistles*, 26.

21. Leon Morris, *The Cross in the New Testament* (Grand Rapids: Eerdmans, 1965), 349.

22. Scot McKnight, *Jesus and His Death: Historiography, the Historical Jesus, and Atonement Theory* (Waco, TX: Baylor, 2005), 370.

23. John R. W. Stott, *The Cross of Christ* (Leicester: Inter-Varsity Press, 1986), 172.

24. Jobes, *1, 2, & 3 John*, 79.

understood to "undermine the emphasis on God's initiative."[25] One way to correlate both ideas is to see that the expiation presented in 1:7, 9 is made possible through the propitiation of 2:2. By dealing with God's righteous wrath through his death on the cross, Jesus's blood ensures that all offenses and guilt are wiped away. (This logic refers to the theological relationship between propitiation and expiation, not the order of presentation in 1 John in which, of course, expiation is mentioned first.)

The biblical presentation of propitiation differs significantly from other ancient perceptions of propitiation and divine wrath (e.g., as found in Plutarch).[26] While propitiation outside the Bible normally refers to the human appeasement of capricious gods, the New Testament portrays God as the loving initiator of propitiation. And his wrath is "his steady, unrelenting, unremitting, uncompromising antagonism to evil in all its forms and manifestations. In short God's anger is poles apart from ours."[27]

Indeed, through the death of Jesus, God deals with his righteous anger toward sin *within himself* since the Son and the Father are one (John 10:30). Moreover, God's wrath is a *righteous* response to human sin. It is not the all-too-human, irrational rage to which other gods are susceptible. Acknowledging the Trinitarian dynamic of propitiation, infused with love, we see that the biblical notion does not entail the ugly characteristics of other formulations with their capricious deities. Propitiation is an expression of God's love toward us.

As mentioned above, Jesus is only able to perform this function of propitiation by being innocent of sin himself (cf. 1 John 3:4–5). Since Jesus is this propitiation for our sins, his successful advocacy on our behalf is secured. This is no doubt John's point in referencing propitiation immediately after advocacy: Jesus is an able advocate on our behalf because he has fully dealt with God's wrath on our behalf. There is no punishment of sin left to fear.

Jesus Atones for the Sins of the Whole World (2:2b)

John is quick to add that Christ is the atoning sacrifice not for our sins alone but also "for the sins of the whole world" (2:2). This is a bold declaration of the universal scope of Christ's propitiatory act; he faced God's righteous wrath toward the sins of the whole world.

John Calvin famously understood 2:2b as referring to *the whole church scattered throughout the world* rather than the whole world per se.[28] This view

25. John Morgan-Wynne, *The Cross in the Johannine Writings* (Eugene, OR: Pickwick, 2011), 246.
26. See Jintae Kim, "The Concept of Atonement in Hellenistic Thought and 1 John," *JGRChJ* 2 (2001–5): 100–116.
27. Stott, *Cross of Christ*, 173.
28. John Calvin, *Commentaries on the Catholic Epistles*, trans. John Owen (Grand Rapids: Baker, 1999), 172–73.

did not originate with Calvin, however, and can be seen as early as Hilary of Arles (AD 401–49) who wrote, "When John says that Christ died for the sins of the 'whole world,' what he means is that he died for the whole church."[29] This has become a common interpretation of 2:2b among those who adhere to a theology of *limited atonement*, which affirms Jesus's sacrificial death paid only for the sins of the elect. This verse challenges that view since it seems, at least on the surface, to directly contradict the position.

A chief difficulty for the limited-atonement reading of 2:2b is that there is nothing in the context to support it. There is no reference to the elect only in view, nor is there any hint that the "world" (*kosmos*) should be understood in a narrow sense here. In fact, the stress on "the *whole* world" seems to rule it out *prima facie*. Furthermore, in John's writings the "world" normally refers to humanity in total opposition to God.[30] While the "world" can be understood in a more positive light in the first half of John's Gospel,[31] Salier notes that even these instances imply a negative sense since the world is the object of God's positive action.[32] Therefore, the most straightforward reading of 2:2b in keeping with Johannine language and theology is to take it at face value: Jesus died for the sins of the whole rebellious world.[33]

Nevertheless, John does not endorse any sort of universalism by which all people are saved. Throughout the letter he repeatedly distinguishes between those born of God and those who are not (e.g., 3:7–10). Clearly not all are redeemed. "Whoever has the Son has life; whoever does not have the Son of God does not have life" (5:12). This exclusivism does not undermine the sufficiency of Christ's sacrifice, which was the propitiation for all sin. Forgiveness of sins, however, is enjoyed only by those who believe in the Son. Our belief in him appropriates his propitiatory act. His achievement *for us* becomes *ours* through faith. So we may affirm that his death is sufficient for *all*, but effective for *some*.[34]

---

29. T. Zahn, *Forschungen zur Geschichte des neutestamentlichen Kanons und der altkirchlichen Literatur* (Erlangen and Leipzig: A. Reichert, 1881–1908), 3:89.

30. Lieu, *I, II, & III John*, 65.

31. N. H. Cassem, "A Grammatical and Contextual Inventory of the Use of κόσμος in the Johannine Corpus with Some Implications for a Johannine Cosmic Theology," *NTS* 19 (1972): 91.

32. W. H. Salier, "What's in a World? Κόσμος in the Prologue of John's Gospel," *RTR* 56.3 (1997): 107. Jensen notes that the only "positive" use of "world" (*kosmos*) in 1 John is in 3:17 (*Affirming the Resurrection*, 106n7).

33. Nevertheless, for a robust articulation and defense of "limited atonement," or the now preferred term, "definite atonement," see the recent tome, David Gibson and Jonathan Gibson (eds.), *From Heaven He Came and Sought Her: Definite Atonement in Historical, Biblical, Theological, and Pastoral Perspective* (Wheaton, IL: Crossway, 2013).

34. This sentiment is endorsed by Calvin—he just doesn't think it is in view in 2:2b. He writes that others "have said that Christ suffered sufficiently for the whole world, but efficiently only for the elect. . . . Though then I allow that what has been said is true, yet I deny that it is suitable to this passage" (*Commentaries on the Catholic Epistles*, 173).

Knowing Jesus Will Lead to Keeping His Commands (2:3–4)

John now returns to the concern of the (partial) purpose statement expressed in 2:1—"I write this to you so that you will not sin"—by adding, "We know that we have come to know him if we keep his commands" (2:3).

While 2:1 issues an exhortation (effectively, "do not sin"), 2:3 addresses relationship with Jesus: "We know that we have come to know him." Rather than another exhortation to avoid sin, 2:3 is about assurance—believers can know that they know Jesus. Or, perhaps more to the point, believers can know that they know the *true* Jesus rather than having been deceived by falsehoods about him. By knowing the *true* Jesus and by really *knowing* him, believers have assurance about their relationship with him.[35]

The concept of "knowing" or "knowledge" is important for John, both in this letter and in his Gospel. There are twenty-six references to the word *ginōskō* ("to know") in John's letters. While the significance of this word will be unpacked as we encounter the following twenty-five instances, we note here that John correlates "knowing" Jesus with being a genuine Christian (cf. 4:7).

This assurance of knowing Jesus is conditional in the second part of 2:3: "If we keep his commands." John is not issuing another exhortation ("keep his commands") but simply states that believers who keep his commands can have assurance of knowledge of him. There is a correlation between knowledge of Jesus and keeping his commands—the two go together. If this were misunderstood, John would effectively mean that someone could come to know Jesus *by* keeping his commands. But John does not endorse command keeping as a mechanism to ensure salvation; it is rather the necessary duty of those who *are* saved. John means that knowledge of Jesus *leads to* obedience, and in this way the two things go together. If someone truly knows Jesus, keeping his commands will be evidence of the fact.[36]

The following verse states the negative of "*truly* knowing Jesus": someone who claims to know Jesus but does not obey his commands is a liar, and "the truth is not in that person." This presents a somewhat jarring juxtaposition to 1:8: "If we claim to be without sin, we deceive ourselves and *the truth is not in us*." On the one hand, the claim to sinlessness is a lie; on the other, disobedience of Jesus's commands makes someone who claims to know him a liar. The relationship between 1:8 and 2:4 shows that keeping Jesus's commands is not equivalent to sinlessness. The keeping of his commands refers to a *disposition* of obedience rather than a disposition of rebellion (e.g., walking in darkness; cf. 1:6).

---

35. This assumes that the "him" in 2:3 refers to Jesus rather than to God the Father, but (possibly intentional?) ambiguity over pronouns is frequent in 1 John.

36. Jobes, *1, 2, & 3 John*, 82.

But What Commands Do We Keep?

The person who keeps his commands is the one who truly knows Jesus. What then are these commands of Jesus that indicate knowledge of him? While it is possible to see here a reference to the commands of God as expressed in the Decalogue (the Ten Commandments), such a reading is to be ruled out. The clearest definition John provides for these laws is found in 3:23: "And this is his command: to believe in the name of his Son, Jesus Christ, and to love one another as he commanded us." And in 2:9–10 John spells out the implications of keeping "his commands": it means showing love to one's brother and sister.[37] Consequently, a failure to love is evidence that one does not truly know Jesus, and knowing Jesus is evidenced by love.[38]

Love is clearly defined in 1 John 3:16: "This is how we know what love is: Jesus Christ laid down his life for us. And we ought to lay down our lives for our brothers and sisters." The love that is required is nothing less than the sacrificial, life-giving love demonstrated by Jesus himself. Love is rugged commitment to another. It is little wonder then that John correlates love with truly knowing God: "Whoever does not love does not know God, because God is love" (4:8). Love will be discussed further in the next section (2:7–11).

Obedience Will Make Love for God Complete (2:5a)

Keeping Jesus's commands indicates that we truly know him. Another implication of keeping Jesus's commands comes next in 2:5a: "But if anyone obeys his word, love for God is truly made complete in them." Obedience to his word appears to be synonymous with keeping Jesus's commands, given John's frequent stylistic parallelism. In this instance the result is that "love for God is truly made complete in them."

The phrase "love for God" (*hē agapē tou theou*) could be understood as an objective genitive ("love for God") or as a subjective genitive ("God's love"). There are arguments for both options. For the objective genitive reading, it can be argued that love for God is made complete by showing love to others. One cannot truly love God and yet show less than love to others. This would be parallel to 4:20: anyone who does not love his brother cannot love God. For the subjective genitive reading, since God is love (4:8, 16), believers embody his love as they show love to others. A parallel would be 4:7: believers are to love one another since love comes from God. Deciding between the two readings is difficult as both options fit well enough in the wider context. The immediate context, however, offers a slight advantage to the objective genitive

---

37. John does spell out who he has in mind by "brother and sister," but it is reasonable to conclude that he views all the children of God as brothers and sisters. That is, our brothers and sisters are fellow believers in Christ (cf. 5:1–2).

38. Yarbrough, *1–3 John*, 82–84.

reading ("love for God") since it correlates well with the phrase "if anyone obeys his word."[39] It has already been established that obedience to his word is equivalent to keeping his commands, which is to love. If the believer shows love to others, love for God is made complete in that it flows out of true love for God.[40] As 4:20 says, it is not possible to love God and not also love one's brother and sister.

Again, love is defined in 3:16: "This is how we know what love is: Jesus Christ laid down his life for us. And we ought to lay down our lives for our brothers and sisters." True love is sacrificial commitment to another, as Jesus demonstrated by laying down his life in commitment to our wellbeing. For us to love God means that we will be sacrificially committed to him. Keeping his commands and loving others will express our sacrificial commitment to God.

And This Is How We Know We Are in Him (2:5b–6)

To this point, the focus has been on truly knowing Jesus. Now we turn to knowing that "we are in him": "This is how we know we are in him: Whoever claims to live in him must live as Jesus did" (2:5b–6). There are three questions to be solved for 2:6. First, who is the "him" in the phrase "live in him"? Second, what does it mean to live in him? Third, what does it mean to live as Jesus did (lit., "walked")?

First, Jesus and the Father are the two options for understanding the "him" in the phrase "live in him." In fact, John can refer to believers being "in him" with reference to either. On the one hand, 4:16 states, "Whoever lives in love lives in God, and God in him." On the other, 5:20 reads, "And we are in him who is true by being in his Son Jesus Christ." In 2:6, however, "in him" likely refers to Jesus.

Second, what does it mean to live in Jesus?[41] In 2:27 we read, "As for you, the anointing you received from him remains in you, and you do not need anyone to teach you. But as his anointing teaches you about all things and as that anointing is real, not counterfeit—just as it has taught you, *remain*

---

39. Martin M. Culy, *1, 2, 3 John: A Handbook on the Greek Text* (Waco, TX: Baylor University Press, 2004), 28.

40. "Made complete" could also be translated "made perfect" (*teteleiōtai*). Smalley sees this as indicating a state of fulfillment: "God's love has really reached fulfillment." Thus, when a Christian obeys God (by loving brothers and sisters), "love attains completeness and maturity" (Smalley, *1, 2, 3 John*, 46).

41. The phrase "in him" (*en autō*) occurs nineteen times in 1 John (1:5; 2:5, 6, 8, 10, 15, 27, 28; 3:5, 6, 9, 15, 17, 24 [2x]; 4:13, 15, 16; 5:10) with either believers as the antecedent of "him" (nine times; 2:10, 15; 3:9, 15, 17, 24; 4:15, 16; 5:10) or with Jesus or God as antecedent (ten times; 1:5; 2:5, 6, 8, 27, 28; 3:5, 6, 24; 4:13). We are interested in the latter group, in which a number of references also refer to "remaining" (*menō*) in him (2:6, 27, 28; 3:6, 24; 4:13, 16), directly addressing the question raised about 2:6 (the NIV translates *en autō menein* as "to live in him," but it is literally "to remain in him").

in him." Here John says that the "anointing" (*chrisma*) received from Jesus teaches believers about all things, including that they *remain in him*. What is this "anointing"? Unfortunately, there are no further clues in 1 John; the word is found only in 2:20 and 2:27, and neither explains what is meant. In fact, *chrisma* is found nowhere else in the New Testament. The commentary on 2:20 and 2:27, however, argues that the anointing is that of the Spirit (see on those verses).

What, then, did the Spirit teach about *remaining in* Jesus? There are two steps required here. First, in John's Gospel the Spirit is regarded as "another advocate" (14:6) who will "teach you all things and will remind you of everything I have said to you" (14:26). So the teaching of the Spirit is *also* the teaching of Jesus.

Second, Jesus taught about *remaining in him* in John 15, using the metaphor of the vine and the branches. The metaphor speaks to the essential, organic relationship between Jesus and his believers; they must remain spiritually connected to him, else delinquent branches will be thrown into the fire and burned (v. 6).[42] In particular, v. 4 is pertinent: "Remain in me, as I also remain in you. No branch can bear fruit by itself; it must remain in the vine. Neither can you bear fruit unless you remain in me." Here is the notion of mutual indwelling as believers remain in Jesus and he remains in them. Furthermore, this mutual-indwelling relationship bears fruit as branches that remain in the vine become fruitful. Believers' works are only possible through life-giving relationship with Jesus. It is impossible to produce fruit apart from the vine.

Returning to 1 John 2:6, the metaphor of the vine and the branches informs our understanding of remaining in Jesus and why that correlates to living just as he lived. Remaining in Jesus refers to our mutual indwelling, as we are "organically" connected to him—he is in us, and we in him. 1 John's emphasis on appropriate Christian living ties to this mutual indwelling since bearing fruit is the outworking of remaining in Jesus the vine. Thus "whoever claims to live in him must live as Jesus did" means that branches connected to the vine will bear fruit. Right living results from right relationship. By remaining in Jesus, we are able to live like Jesus and for Jesus.[43]

This leads us to our third question about 1 John 2:6: What does it mean to live as Jesus lived? First, "live" is literally "walk" (*peripateō*), a common Jewish metaphor for how one conducts oneself through the course of life. "Walking" is prevalent in the Johannine Epistles, with references to walking in the

---

42. On the relationship between this metaphor and Paul's concept of union with Christ, see Constantine R. Campbell, *Paul and Union with Christ: An Exegetical and Theological Study* (Grand Rapids: Zondervan, 2012), 418–19.

43. For more on the theme in 1 John, see Robert A. Peterson, *Salvation Applied by the Spirit: Union with Christ* (Wheaton, IL: Crossway, 2015), 249–63.

darkness (1 John 1:6; 2:11), walking in the light (1:7), walking in the truth (2 John 4; 3 John 3, 4), and walking in love (2 John 6). Of these references, the most likely here is walking in love. Though found in 2 John rather than 1 John, it resonates extremely well with the latter's several exhortations to love. First John 3:16 presents Jesus's love as a model for believers to follow: "This is how we know what love is: Jesus Christ laid down his life for us. And we ought to lay down our lives for our brothers and sisters." And the following section is about love (2:7–11). Walking as Jesus walked means that believers are to walk in love, following the lead of the one who loved us enough to die for us.

LIVE the Story

Comfort, not Casual

I'm either on or off. In fifth gear or park. High energy or catatonic. The jazz tune "All or Nothing or All" could be my theme song. This means that I can easily fall into a trap that all Christians face: I'm either being too concerned about sin or too casual about sin. People who are overly concerned about sin cannot let go of their guilty feelings for past wrongs, and they struggle to accept the free and full forgiveness that Christ brings. They tend to be very strict with themselves and beat themselves up when they inevitably miss the mark. On the other hand, people who are too casual about sin can slip into licentiousness without much concern and will be tempted to use their freedom in Christ as a cloak for sin. They will remind themselves of the forgiveness they have in Christ, which will give them an excuse to continue in it.

John begins this section with an exhortation to avoid sin, even while acknowledging that sin is inevitable and that Jesus Christ is our advocate with the Father (2:1). While believers will sin (1:8, 10), John writes so that they will not. There is comfort for the sinner in that God is faithful and just and will forgive our sins when we confess them (1:9). But *comfort* should not be confused with *casual*. Forgiveness in Jesus rightly comforts sinners, but our attitude to sin should not therefore become casual. For an on/off sort of person, this nuance can be difficult to navigate because I will tend to take comfort all the way to the casual end of the spectrum. But we must not let comfort slip into a casual attitude towards sin.

I used to play in a jazz group led by the prominent Australian jazz pianist Serge Ermoll. Serge had a fearsome reputation: he was a black belt in karate, had a well-known history of alcohol and drug abuse, and was even known to have bashed up a musician or two who disrespected him. But I always knew Serge as a kind, warmhearted teddy bear. After a couple of years of playing music with him, I asked Serge why he was so gruff to outsiders when that was not the man I knew. He answered that in his experience people abuse his kindness and disrespect him. And it's true that some had treated him poorly in the past.

To me that illustrates the problem of confusing comfort with casual. Serge would have been happy for everyone to be comfortable around him as I was. But instead some people would become *too casual* with him. They would take him for granted or become rude or just disrespect him. Rather than put up with that, Serge put up a wall that most people did not have the chance to see past.

We have an advocate with the Father, Jesus Christ the Righteous One. We have good reason to know comfort in the face of our failures. But we must not let comfort slip into a casual attitude toward sin. A casual attitude will disrespect God and the sacrifice that Jesus made for our sins.

We Can Trust Our Advocate

Furthermore, Christ is a *righteous* advocate. He could only be a propitiation for our sins because he himself was righteous. And he can only be an advocate on our behalf because he himself is righteous. As a righteous advocate, we can trust him wholeheartedly.

A friend of mine, Adam, shared with me the following story about his experience of a good advocate, which I'll leave in his own words:

> I was desperate for my first paycheck having used up all my cash, and credit for that matter, relocating from college to my first job. I had no groceries, my first rent payment would be due, and I had a car payment. When I opened my check in the office (they still wrote checks back then), it was 2/3rds of what I expected. I would be able to pay rent, but not eat or buy gas. After triple checking my offer letter, I was sure a mistake was made so decided to bring it to my boss's attention.
>
> She agreed with my assessment and, while I was still in her office, she dialed HR. I could hear only one side of the conversation, but enough to know that it was moving in the direction of the difference being made up in my next check. However, being proud, I determined not to let on that I was desperate for the difference. To my relief, she authoritatively demanded, "No, you won't make it up in the next check, you'll cut him a check right away!"
>
> Having not eaten much for several days, I deposited my check and had the most enjoyable grocery shopping experience I'd ever had before or since.

Adam's boss was an example of a good advocate. She had the authority to do the right thing, and she looked out for him when it really counted. He would have been helpless without her. The illustration isn't perfect, though, because Jesus doesn't need to "fix" God's mistakes. God is right to hold us

accountable for our sins. But because Jesus has atoned for our sins, his advocacy is exactly what we need to remain in fellowship with the holy God.

Not all advocates, however, are good. I have another friend who is a medical doctor. She told me once that she had an appointment with a woman who
had recently moved from overseas. She didn't speak English, so her husband
was with her to translate. My friend examined her patient and concluded that
she was pregnant. The husband spoke with his wife for a few moments. Then
he turned to my friend and said that they had decided to have an abortion.
My friend was a bit surprised that such a decision had been made so quickly.
So she kept talking about their options and said they should go away and
think about this. She handed them some brochures to read, and then the
woman got a puzzled look on her face. It turns out that her husband did *not*
tell her that she was pregnant but requested an abortion without her knowledge. Fortunately, the abortion did not go ahead.

That is an example of a very bad mediator. There are some mediators
whom you simply cannot trust; how sad that the woman could not trust her
own husband in this way. Not so Jesus Christ. He is a righteous mediator and
advocate on our behalf. He is worthy of our trust.

Hear the joy that Ambrose of Milan (ca. AD 333–97) takes in this truth:

> I will not glory because I have been redeemed. I will not glory because
> I am free of sins but because sins have been forgiven me. I will not glory
> because I am profitable or because anyone is profitable to me but because
> Christ is an advocate on my behalf before the Father, because the blood
> of Christ has been poured out on my behalf.[44]

The Wrath of God Is Real

Jesus's righteous advocacy is grounded in his act of propitiation (2:2). We have
discussed the complex arguments regarding *propitiation* versus *expiation* (see
above). They are similar ideas, but the former involves averting the wrath of
God, whereas the latter avoids that notion.

Whatever the scholarly arguments around the issue, we can imagine why
expiation might be an attractive alternative to propitiation. For some it is dis-
tasteful to speak of God's wrath.[45] The idea is an offense to many. This may
be due to a caricatured understanding of wrath, picturing an uncontrolled,
capricious deity. But this is not the biblical presentation of propitiation nor
of God's righteous anger toward human sin. He is not a capricious god whose

---

44. Ambrose of Milan, "On Jacob and the Happy Life," in *Seven Exegetical Works*, trans. Michael
P. McHugh, vol. 65 of *The Fathers of the Church: A New Translation* (Washington, DC: Catholic
University of America Press, 1970), 133.
45. I don't mean to imply that this is the motivation of scholars who argue against propitiation.

irrational hostility requires appeasement. God's wrath is "his steady, unrelenting, unremitting, uncompromising antagonism to evil in all its forms and manifestations."[46] Nevertheless, expiation enables us to sidestep the issue by focusing on the removal of guilt rather than God's wrath.

While we want to affirm the goodness of guilt being removed through the death of Jesus and the biblical concept of expiation, we cannot reject the notion of God's wrath. The Bible is clear about its reality whether we like it or not. In the end if we abandon the notion altogether, we will necessarily distort the Scriptures.

Some will find propitiation unpalatable because of some unpalatable examples of it outside the Bible. These are usually set in the context of capricious gods with irascible anger. In times past, thousands of innocent children were sacrificed to appease the Hindu goddess Ganga by throwing them into the Ganges River in India. But this is not the nature of propitiation in the Bible. Rather than an irascible and capricious god, the true God is holy and just. Moreover, he chooses to propitiate *himself*. Within the intra-Trinitarian relationships of the Godhead, the Father's anger toward sin is averted through the sacrifice of the Son. This is God dealing with the problem of sin for us rather than we trying to placate an unreasonable god.

It is right that our rebellion engenders the wrath of a holy God. And yet we know that God is deeply loving and committed to our forgiveness. That is the point of 2:2—Jesus is the propitiation for our sins. He averted God's just wrath away from us, its deserved objects, and took it upon himself. That is a truth about which we ought to rejoice! Though our sin be so awful that we deserve God's wrath, his mercy and love causes it to be removed from us by the gift of his Son.

Knowing Jesus

How do you know if you know Jesus? I've always thought that Matthew 7:22–23 are among the scariest verses in the Bible. Jesus says:

> Not everyone who says to me, "Lord, Lord," will enter the kingdom of heaven, but only the one who does the will of my Father who is in heaven. Many will say to me on that day, "Lord, Lord, did we not prophesy in your name and in your name drive out demons and in your name perform many miracles?" Then I will tell them plainly, "I never knew you. Away from me, you evildoers!"

Some who think they know Jesus will be told, "I never knew you." So how do you know if you *really* know Jesus? First John 2:3–6 provides a diagnostic to check if we are the real deal or not. The short answer is that the one who

---

46. Stott, *Cross of Christ*, 173.

keeps Jesus's commands (2:3), keeps his word (2:5), and walks in love (2:6) is the one who truly knows Jesus.

But the point is that this is a *diagnostic*. John does not issue imperatives here, commanding believers to do these things. No, it's the other way around: if you truly know Jesus, that relationship will bear real fruit. We need a diagnostic because relationships are intangible. You can't look at a relationship. You can't touch it. But the qualities of our relationships are revealed by what we do and say. It becomes clear who and what you love by what you do.

So, how do "knowing" and "doing" relate? Relationships have what I would call *volitional power*. In short, if you know someone, you are more likely to do what they ask. It's a cliché in mafia movies that someone will say, "I know a guy." This means they can get a favor done because of a friendship. The relationship has volitional power.

That's why the old adage is true: *It's not what you know, but who you know.* I've experienced this in the jazz-music scene. When it comes to booking musicians to play a gig, the natural tendency is to choose people you know. And you are more likely to choose your friends. I used to think this was unfair. Shouldn't a musician's success be based on ability rather than friendships? But now I see that there is something lovely about that. Musicians want to make music with their friends. While we should not form cliques that exclude others, there is something inherently good about wanting to share in pursuits with our friends.

We are relational beings. This is because God is a relational God. He is three persons in one. Father, Son, and Spirit exist together in mutually indwelling relationship. And the relational nature of the Trinity is reflected in his creation, especially within the experience of his image bearers, human beings. The universal and fundamental nature of our relational existence means that it's *meant* to be *who* you know rather than *what* you know.

This is about theology. Is the goal of theology the *what* you know, or is it the *who* you know? I can learn many facts about God and the Bible, learn its original languages, read theology books, quote the church fathers from memory. But what is the point of all of that if I don't also have the *who you know*? Of course theology should be about the *who*. It's about knowing God. And this knowing is relational. Yes, facts and information are important, but we mustn't let other things get in the way of our relational knowing of God. Don't put the *what* ahead of the *who*. Because relationships have volitional power, when we truly know Jesus we will keep his commands.

Love of God

John moves from knowing to loving in 2:5. Love is sacrificial commitment modeled on Jesus's sacrificial love for us. Whoever obeys his word, in them love for God is made complete. This is another diagnostic. John is not saying, "Obey his word, then your love for God will be complete." No. He is saying that someone with real love for God will naturally obey because of sacrificial commitment to him. Love for God includes love of his holy character. Love for God means that we will want to please him. Love for God means we will be committed to his glory. Again, the intangible nature of the relationship is revealed by what we do.

The reason that love for God will result in obedience is that love motivates. Love is a very powerful motivator! Discipline is helpful, but love is more powerful than discipline. That other old adage is also true: *If you love your job, you'll never work a day of your life.* The meaning of this saying is that a job you love will not feel like work because, well, you love it!

I love teaching the Bible. Whether in class or preaching, I love to do it. I also love writing books and playing music. These activities do not require great discipline from me. My love for them is enough to get them done. Grading papers, on the other hand, requires all the discipline in the world!

In our battle against sin, the winning solution is not greater discipline. Discipline is helpful, but love is more powerful than discipline. In the end, we are engaged in a competition of "loves"—our love for sin versus our love for God. That's what it comes down to. As Augustine once said, "Love, and do what you will."[47] Love shapes our will. Love is the most powerful motivator there is. If we truly love God we will live his way.

A few years ago a friend shared his testimony at church. Mike revealed to the congregation that through most of his adult life he had struggled with same-sex attraction and gay pornography. As a Christian, he hated this sin in his life yet didn't seem to be able to escape it. He first attacked the problem with discipline. He got rid of his computer at home and disconnected the internet; for ten years he had no online access in his house! He removed himself from any and all situations that might cause him to stumble. And Mike found that these disciplines were helpful but that they didn't really resolve his struggle.

Increasingly, Mike decided to put more time and effort into reading the Bible, listening to sermons, and drawing near to God in prayer. He read his Bible every morning and night, listened to podcast sermons during the day at work, and went to Bible-study groups at night. The effect of all this study was that his love for Jesus grew and grew. The more he studied God's word, the more his desire for God developed. Eventually, he was pleased to report,

---

47. This famous quote comes from Augustine's Homily on 1 John 4:4–12 for Easter Saturday, AD 407 (*Nicene and Post-Nicene Fathers*, first series, vol. 7, ed. P. Schaff, trans. H. Browne [Buffalo: Christian Literature Publishing Co., 1888], 504).

God enabled him to overcome his struggle with sin. Mike said that the key was to love God more and more. As his love grew, his struggle diminished.

None of us will vanquish sin this side of eternity, but Mike's testimony demonstrates the power of love for God. We would do well to increase our devotion by being immersed in God's word, by reflecting on his character and mercy, by deeply trusting his promises, and by sincere worship in all of life. We will not achieve perfection, but the one who truly loves God will keep his word.

CHAPTER 4

1 John 2:7–11

 LISTEN to the Story

> ⁷Dear friends, I am not writing you a new command but an old one, which you have had since the beginning. This old command is the message you have heard. ⁸Yet I am writing you a new command; its truth is seen in him and in you, because the darkness is passing and the true light is already shining.
>
> ⁹Anyone who claims to be in the light but hates a brother or sister is still in the darkness. ¹⁰Anyone who loves their brother and sister lives in the light, and there is nothing in them to make them stumble. ¹¹But anyone who hates a brother or sister is in the darkness and walks around in the darkness. They do not know where they are going, because the darkness has blinded them.

Listening to the Text in the Story: Leviticus 19:18; Matthew 22:37–40; John 13:34–35; 2 John 5–6.

Love is the topic of this passage. Even though the word is only used once (2:10a), it will become clear that love is indeed the theme of the whole section. "Love for God" is mentioned in the previous passage (2:5b), and now the focus is on love toward others. Love of God and one another is a major theme of the letter (2:15; 3:11, 15–17, 23; 4:7–12, 19–21; 5:1–3).

The passage has two parts. First, John focuses on an "old command" that he also calls a "new command" (2:7–8). We will see that this old/new command is love. Second, he draws a strong distinction between hate and love—hate lives in darkness, while love is in the light (2:9–11).

EXPLAIN the Story

John Writes an Old/New Command (2:7–8)

John says he is not writing a new command but an old one. This old command is one his readers "have had since the beginning" and is "the message you have had since the beginning" (2:7). We're not explicitly told what this old command is, and before that becomes clear we see that John deliberately "contradicts" himself in the very next verse—"Yet I am writing you a new command." What is this command that John calls "old" and "new" at the same time?

The command is love. Not only is that what John goes on to address in the second half of the passage, but love can be understood as both old and new. It is *old* because it goes all the way back to Moses: "Love your neighbor as yourself" (Lev 19:18).[1] It is *new* because love is also the commandment of Jesus (John 13:34; cf. Matt 22:37–40).[2] Indeed, John later specifies love as a command (3:23; 4:21). All of this, together with the fact that love is a major theme of the letter, strongly suggests that the "old command" of 2:7 and the "new command" of 2:8 are both "love one another."

This understanding is confirmed in comparison with 2 John 5–6, which displays striking parallels with this passage and explicitly makes the point that the command is love:

> And now, dear lady, I am not writing you a new command but one we have had from the beginning. I ask that we love one another. And this is love: that we walk in obedience to his commands. As you have heard from the beginning, his command is that you walk in love.

John Writes to His "Beloved" (2:7a)

Given the theme of the passage, it is likely no accident that John literally calls his readers "beloved" (*agapētoi*)—appropriately translated "dear friends."[3] While "dear friends" nicely captures the intimacy of the address, "be*loved*" shows the connection to the theme of love that pervades the passage. John loves his readers, just as he will encourage them to love one another. He addresses his readers this way another nine times across his three letters (1 John 3:2, 21; 4:1, 7, 11; 3 John 1, 2, 3, 11).

John Writes an "Old Command" (2:7)

And so, the "old command" is what they "have had since the beginning" (2:7b). "The beginning" could refer back to Moses ("Love your neighbor as

---

1. Brown writes that John "is implicitly equating the commandment of Jesus with the Decalogue, the covenant demand of the OT" (*Epistles of John*, 265). See also Yarbrough, *1–3 John*, 97.

2. Kruse attempts to explain the old/new juxtaposition by appealing to Jesus's "new command" of John 13:34 while also acknowledging that by the time John composes his letter, Jesus's words were long past (*Letters of John*, 83). While an interesting suggestion, the juxtaposition is better explained by recognizing that Jesus's "new command" stands in direct continuity with the law of Moses, which he summarizes as love for God and love for neighbor (Matt 22:37–40).

3. "Dear friends" is an appropriate translation since few people use the word "beloved" anymore.

yourself"), or John might mean the beginning of their Christian lives. The latter is probably right, since 2:7c says, "This old command is the message you have heard." The "message you have heard" would then be the message of Jesus that they heard at the very beginning of their walk with him.[4] Jesus proclaimed both the love of God and love for one another.

John Writes a "New Command" (2:8)

About the "new command," John says in 2:8, "Its truth is seen in him and in you." In the context of John's letter, this means that love is enacted and observed, first in Jesus, second in his people. In 3:16 John says, "This is how we know what love is: Jesus Christ laid down his life for us." Love is enacted by Jesus and observed by all who look to him.

But love is also seen in the lives of those who follow Jesus. As John writes in 2:8, "Its truth is seen in him *and in you*." Indeed, the second half of 3:16 states, "And we ought to lay down our lives for our brothers and sisters." Throughout the letter, the love of God and of Jesus is connected to the love of believers. John no doubt derives this theme from Jesus's own words, recorded in John 13:34–35:

> A new command I give you: Love one another. As I have loved you, so you must love one another. By this everyone will know that you are my disciples, if you love one another.

The reason John can say that the *truth* of love (the new command) is "seen in him and in you" (2:8b) is "because the darkness is passing and the true light is already shining" (2:8c). Here love is connected to light; the truth of love can be seen in the true light. But what does John mean by "darkness" and "light"?

In 2:8c we are told that the darkness is passing (*paragetai*). The best clue for understanding this is to note 2:17: "The world and its desires pass away" in which the same verb is used (*paragetai*). The darkness is a metaphor for the world in opposition to God.

The true light, then, refers to life in Christ, through which one is taken out of allegiance to the world for fellowship with the Father and the Son (1:3). The true light "is already shining" because even now, while this dark world continues in its darkness, those who enter into fellowship with God enter into the light.

The new command, love, is seen in Jesus and in his people. Jesus's love, and the love of his disciples, is the light shining in the darkness of the world in rebellion against God. This has direct implications for John's readers, as 2:9–11 will make clear.

---

4. So Kruse, *Letters of John*, 82.

Hate Belongs to the Darkness; Love Belongs to the Light (2:9–11)

The old/new command of love means that hate is to be entirely shunned. The "light" of 2:8c is incompatible with hate so that anyone who "hates a brother or sister is still in the darkness" (2:9). The same is said in 2:11a. Hate belongs to the darkness—the world in rebellion against God. A hater does not belong to Jesus but to the world. By the same token "anyone who loves their brother and sister lives in the light" (2:10a). Light and love go together.

What does John mean by "hate" and "love"? The Greek word for hate, *miseō*, can be meant in a very strong way (e.g., *to hate, detest*),[5] but it can also mean something milder, such as *to show disfavor, disregard*.[6] Yarbrough argues that it is unlikely that John means "hate" in the strong sense, since a Christian community would not have struggled with such intensely hostile, even homicidal, animosity toward each other.[7] However, this should be balanced by the fact that John excludes the "hater" from fellowship in the light. In other words, their hatred must be serious enough to exclude them from true relationship with Christ. This would suggest that the *milder* meaning of "hate" is less likely, contra Yarbrough. After all, would John mean to say that showing disregard to someone else—perhaps unintentionally or accidentally—is serious enough to exclude him or her from the light (cf. James 4:1–2)?

Love is a rich theme throughout the letter and is given clear definition in 3:16: "This is how we know what love (*agapēn*) is: Jesus Christ laid down his life for us. And we ought to lay down our lives for our brothers and sisters." Furthermore, love is not "with words or speech but with actions and in truth" (3:18). Love is, then, as much about action as anything else. It involves rugged, self-sacrificial commitment to others, modeled on Jesus's own self-sacrifice for us.[8] Indeed, loving is more than simple imitation of Jesus (though it is not less than that) since God himself *is* love. To love is to live in God, and he in us (4:16).

McKnight provides some further categories to think through the nature of biblical love as we learn of it from God's own love. Defining love broadly as "rugged commitment," he adds that it is a commitment to be "with" and "for" another person "unto" Christlikeness. Love is "rugged commitment" because it is often hard work. It is "with" because love is about sharing presence together.

---

5. BDAG 652 §1.
6. BDAG 653 §2.
7. Yarbrough, *1–3 John*, 104.
8. While John uses the *agap-* word group throughout the letter, this should not be taken as evidence to support the common view that *agapaō* alone is the Greek word for "Christian love." As Smalley points out, *phileō* appears alongside *agapaō* in John's Gospel where "it can refer to the love of God, of Jesus, or of the Christian. As a result we should not attempt . . . to draw sharp distinctions in meaning between the two verbs" (*1, 2, 3 John*, 61).

It is "for" because love means you will be their advocate, on their side. It is "unto" because love is directional; it moves toward the one to whom we surrender our love.[9] These "love prepositions" give shape to our understanding of what love is as revealed by God's love in Christ.

John does not address love and hate in general terms. They are both seen in respect to one's "brother and sister."[10] While John occasionally refers to love in more general terms (e.g., 2:15; 4:18), his dominant concern is love for God and love for brothers and sisters. No doubt "brothers and sisters" refers to fellow believers. This would be in keeping with John's inspiration—Jesus's own exhortation—"As I have loved you, so you must love *one another*" (John 13:34). This does not mean that believers will not extend love to others who do not belong to Jesus, but that is not John's concern here. The light that shines in a dark world is the love that believers exhibit toward one another.

The dichotomies of love/hate and light/darkness present life through stark contrasts. While our experience tends to be more complicated and nuanced, John's point is to remind his readers that there are ultimately only two allegiances. Ultimately either one is of the world and in darkness, or one belongs to Jesus and the light. Hate and love therefore become outwards signs of someone's true spiritual reality.

Living in the Light vs. Walking in the Darkness (2:10b, 11b)

While some may claim to be in the light, their hate for a "brother or sister"[11] reveals that they are in fact in darkness (2:9). They seemed to be genuine believers, but their hatefulness reveals otherwise. Only those who love their brothers and sisters can be regarded as being in the light (2:10).

Those living in the light have "nothing in them to make them stumble" (2:10b). Literally, "there is no stumbling block *in it*" (*skandalon en autō ouk estin*),[12] meaning that *in the light* (not "in them") there is nothing to cause stumbling. That is, John does not say that there is nothing *in them* (the believers) that will cause stumbling but that *in the light* stumbling will be avoided. The light reveals all, allowing the believer to direct his or her steps with care.

However, the hater is "in the darkness" and so "walks around in the darkness" (2:11a). Walking is a familiar Jewish idiom for one's life conduct (cf. 1:7; 2:6). Thus darkness defines one's being *and* one's doing. John says, "They do not know where they are going, because the darkness has blinded them"

9. Scot McKnight, *A Fellowship of Differents* (Grand Rapids: Zondervan, 2014), 53–59.

10. While some translations simply have "brother," the Greek word *adelphos* refers to fellow believers, whether male or female (Jobes, *1, 2, & 3 John*, 96).

11. Quotation marks are used here because the "brother and sister" are not, in fact, spiritual siblings of the hater, since it turns out that the hater is not a genuine believer.

12. Smalley, *1, 2, 3 John*, 58.

(2:11b). Spiritual darkness is disabling; those in it are hopelessly blinded to the way they should go. The implications of this are huge for every aspect of life in the world.

 LIVE the Story

Loving Brothers and Sisters

Jesus's radical instruction to love our enemies is powerful (Matt 5:44; Luke 6:27). But a failure to love our brothers and sisters—our fellow believers—is also powerful, in a negative way. While Jesus instructs us to love our enemies, he also instructs us to love *one another*, and this is how the world will know that we belong to him (John 13:34–35). We ought to demonstrate sacrificial commitment to one another.

Loving one another is harder than it sounds. In fact, love for each other can be one of the greatest challenges believers will face. But why is it sometimes so hard? I wonder if the "brother and sister" imagery can help us to work this through. While we may love our *literal* brothers and sisters, quarrels among siblings are stereotypically prevalent in many households. Sibling rivalry can cause deep and lasting relational damage among family members. We can treat our siblings with a harshness that most of us would never extend to nonfamily members. Why is that?

When we are really close to someone, like a sibling, we can sometimes lose respect for him or her, perhaps because we see him or her as an extension of ourselves. When this happens, we tend to view his or her faults and failings in a more acute way than we would if it were someone else. We might take more offense at things they do or say than we would if we were not so close. This means that as we rightly develop close bonds with our *spiritual* brothers and sisters in Christ, our intimacy can inadvertently cause us to treat each other with disrespect. In such cases, being "with" others does not translate to being "for" them. Closeness has bred antagonism rather than advocacy. And if that's the case, it's impossible to be heading "unto" Christlikeness together.

And of course there are plenty of other reasons that cause Christians to fall out with each other, such as theological disagreements, differences of opinion over how church should be run, politics, parenting, and many other things. Part of the pain of such disagreements is that we are supposed to be united; we are supposed to be of one mind (Phil 2:2). So when we disagree, it hurts. And when we add hurt to our differences, that's when divisions can set in. But our divisions can be overcome by love. Sacrificial commitment puts our own desires on hold in order to uphold another. It enables us to put aside our own hurts and exercise patience and forbearance. As Bede says, "The person who loves his brother puts up with everything for the sake of unity. Such an attitude keeps us from hurting anyone unduly."[13]

Charles Spurgeon and Joseph Parker both led prominent churches in London in the 19th century. One Sunday, Parker spoke of the impoverished condition of the children welcomed by Spurgeon's orphanage. However, Spurgeon heard that Parker had criticized the state of the orphanage itself. He attacked Parker the next Sunday from his pulpit. The incident was printed in the newspapers and was widely discussed throughout the city. Sadly, crowds gathered to Parker's church the following Sunday to witness his rebuttal. "I understand Dr. Spurgeon is not in his pulpit today, and this is the Sunday they use to take an offering for the orphanage. I suggest we take a love offering here instead." The crowd was delighted. The ushers had to empty the collection plates three times.[14]

This is an example of a division between two Christian pastors, caused by a misunderstanding and a hasty overreaction. But Parker responded to Spurgeon's harsh response with grace and love, which immediately healed the rift. It is so easy to respond poorly in the face of an unjust offense from a brother or sister in Christ, but Parker modeled the way we should go. We should respond in love, forgoing the injustice to ourselves and seeking the best for another.

Failure to love is also one of the worst indictments of the church in the eyes of the outside world, and rightly so. If there is rabid conflict and infighting within the church, how can we possibly claim to be people of love to a world that desperately needs it? Notice how the newspapers in Spurgeon's day reported his conflict with Parker. Thankfully the rift was mended quickly, but imagine how an ongoing feud between Spurgeon and Parker would have damaged the work of the gospel. Imagine how such a feud would have dishonored Christ.

When a brother or sister wrongs us, we would do well to remember the extent of Jesus's love. He endured ridicule and mockery for the sake of love. He was the recipient of injustice, yet he did not retaliate (1 Pet 2:23). Sacrificial love bears the cost of any offense against oneself and chooses to respond with kindness. If more believers were able to overcome their anger, distrust, and resentment with love, we would see much more unified and loving churches.

Loving our brothers and sisters involves more than just overcoming conflict. Even in the absence of difficulty, love can be hard because love requires proactivity. We are so often absorbed in the busyness of life and its attendant tasks that we miss opportunities to extend sacrificial love toward others.

---

13. Bede, *On 1 John* (PL 93:91).
14. "Spurgeon's Orphanage," Bible.org, February 2, 2009, www.bible.org/illustration/ spurgeon's-orphanage.

There are few things that communicate love more than unprompted acts of costly service. Not only does a costly act indicate love, but an *unprompted* act demonstrates that you have been mindful of another. You've considered their need without them having asked, and you've proactively sought out their good. By God's grace our churches are filled with examples of this kind of love, and it surely does shine a light into a dark, self-centered world. Indeed, it reflects the love of the Father who took the first step in reaching out to us by sending his Son.

About five months after my family and I moved from warm, sunny Sydney to the Chicago area, I returned to Australia for a couple of weeks to preach at a student conference. While I was gone, my family experienced snow for the first time. My kids had never even *seen* snow before, so we were not used to dealing with snowy winters. My wife had a bit of a hard time negotiating our first snowfall in my absence. On the day of that first snowfall, the pastor of our new church and his wife—David and Helen Jones—quietly came to our house that night and shoveled out our driveway. Once they were done, they gave us the shovels!

Now, this was a *Sunday* night, after a busy weekend of pastoral ministry at a church of eight hundred members. When I heard about their act of kindness in Australia, I was deeply encouraged. Knowing that I was gone, David and Helen had taken action to help my family out. I'm sure they thought it just a small gesture, but it meant a lot to us, and we learned that this ministry couple doesn't just preach love. They *live* it.

According to John, God is love—it flows from him, and it is demonstrated in Jesus Christ dying for us. As people who know God and know his love in Jesus Christ, we are to express the same love toward each other. This is not merely the imitation of Christ—following his example of love—but reflects something much deeper. Love is God's own nature. By loving each other we demonstrate that we truly understand who God is and that we truly know him.

Hating Brothers and Sisters

Every family has conflicts, and all brothers and sisters battle each other from time to time. But that is different from a prolonged stance of hatred. If siblings come to that point—to a settled position of hate—they will effectively cease to be siblings. It is this kind of unrepentant, active hate that tears families apart.

Instead of loving, sacrificial commitment, hate is self-serving antipathy toward another. If hate is committed to anything, it is the destruction of its object. Hate enjoys seeing the enemy suffer. Hate longs for its enemy to suffer misfortune. Hate justifies selfishness and pride.

Individuals within our churches who adopt a prolonged stance of hate threaten to tear our churches apart. More than that, according to John they reveal themselves not to be a true brother or sister. Their hatred reveals that they belong to the darkness, not the light.

As with any sin, the Scriptures instruct us to rebuke a person stuck in sin. If they are unrepentant after multiple attempts to win them over, Jesus said to "treat them as you would a pagan or a tax collector" (Matt 18:15–17). That sounds a little harsh, but what Jesus means is that by their stubborn refusal to repent, such a person has excluded themselves from the fellowship of God's people. We are then simply to acknowledge the truth of that reality.

Nevertheless, there is always hope for such a one. John says that the hater "is still in the darkness" (2:9); literally, the hater "is in the darkness *until now*" (*heōs arti*). The phrase "until now" implies that this current situation may not last forever. The hater is *still* in the darkness, but he or she may eventually come into the light.

We have no control over other people's hearts. We might encourage, rebuke, and instruct, but we can't bring the hater to repentance. We can lead a horse to water, but we can't make it drink. All that is left to do is pray. We can pray that God's love will shine light into their heart so that they will come into a true knowledge of who God is. We can pray that God will remove the hatred from their heart.

Living in the Light vs. Walking in Darkness

John equates loving our brothers and sisters with living in the light (2:10). Indeed, light and love are connected in 1 John. John declares that "God is light" (1:5) and that "God is love" (4:16b). God is both light and love. Therefore, it is not surprising that anyone who loves their brother and sister lives in the light. Light and love go together in the very person of God.

To live in the light, then, involves living according to love. Believers are to shape their lives by this guiding principle—love. When decisions must be made, the loving choice is always the right one. When we need to choose between our own interests and the interests of another, love directs us to choose the other.

When John says that there is nothing in the light to make believers stumble, it means that love will never cause us to trip up. Since love is always the right choice, it will not lead us astray. It may be difficult. It may hurt at times. But living by the light of God's love is the safe, right, and true way we should go.

On the contrary, living in the darkness is to live by the rule of hate and lovelessness. The trouble with these things—apart from being wholly opposed to God!—is that they are not reliable guides. Living by hate and lovelessness does not lead to good places. Hate tends to turn inward and devours the hater, leaving him or her as an empty shell or as a rotten fruit. It spirals from one negative place to the next without recourse for correction. Hate does most damage to the hater.

John says that those walking by darkness do not know where they are going; the darkness has blinded them (2:11). People in the dark do not know what lies before them, nor do they know that everything is going to work out in the end. Their destination is uncertain and unknown. They may *think* they know where they're going, but the reality is that they are deceived.

One way that the church can reach out to people ruled by darkness is to demonstrate what it looks like to live by love. Rugged commitment to one another, being "with" and "for" each other "unto" Christlikeness, stands out in a culture marked by individualism and self-interest. By offering sacrificial acts of love, forgiveness, and mercy, the world can see another way. Rather than being characterized by the rhetoric of judgment and division, Christians should be known for their love. That is the most attractive characteristic we can offer the world. And it points people straight to the God who is love.

Bill Bright, founder of Campus Crusade for Christ (these days called Cru), tells the following story.[15]

> Two gifted attorneys had great professional animosity, even hatred one for the other. Even though they were distinguished members of the same firm, they were constantly criticizing and making life miserable for each other. One of the men received Christ through our ministry and some months later came for counsel.
>
> "I have hated and criticized my partner for years," he said, "and he has been equally antagonistic toward me. But now that I am a Christian, I don't feel right about continuing our warfare. What shall I do?"
>
> "Why not ask your partner to forgive you and tell him that you love him?" I suggested.
>
> "I could never do that!" he exclaimed. "That would be hypocritical. I don't love him. How could I tell him I love him when I don't?"
>
> I explained that God commands His children to love even their enemies and that His agape, supernatural, unconditional love is an expression of our will which we exercise by faith. . . .
>
> Together we knelt to pray and my friend asked God's forgiveness for his critical attitude toward his law partner and claimed God's love for him by faith.

15. Bill Bright, "5 Truths about Love: You Can Love with God's Love by Faith," Cru, http://www.cru.org/train-and-grow/classics/transferable-concepts/love-by-faith.4.html.

Early the next morning, my friend walked into his partner's office and announced, "Something wonderful has happened to me. I have become a Christian. And I have come to ask you to forgive me for all that I have done to hurt you in the past and to tell you that I love you."

His partner was so surprised and convicted of his own sin that he responded to this amazing confession by asking my friend to forgive him. Then to my friend's surprise, his partner said, "I would like to become a Christian, too. Would you show me what I need to do?"

Choosing to love may hurt and it may humble us. It may require us to ask for forgiveness and let go of injustices. But God's love will overcome our stubborn hearts if we let it. And it will lead others to the God who is love.

CHAPTER 5

1 John 2:12–17

 LISTEN to the Story

¹²I am writing to you, dear children,
    because your sins have been forgiven on account of his name.
¹³I am writing to you, fathers,
    because you know him who is from the beginning.
I am writing to you, young men,
    because you have overcome the evil one.
¹⁴I write to you, dear children,
    because you know the Father.
I write to you, fathers,
    because you know him who is from the beginning.
I write to you, young men,
    because you are strong,
    and the word of God lives in you,
    and you have overcome the evil one.

¹⁵Do not love the world or anything in the world. If anyone loves the world, love for the Father is not in them. ¹⁶For everything in the world—the lust of the flesh, the lust of the eyes, and the pride of life—comes not from the Father but from the world. ¹⁷The world and its desires pass away, but whoever does the will of God lives forever.

Listening to the Text in the Story: Matthew 5:27–30; 6:12–13; Mark 7:20–23; John 12:25; 16:8–11; 1 John 4:4; 5:4.

If love for brother and sister marks out true believers in the previous passage (2:7–11), love for the Father marks them in this passage. While love for brother and sister is contrasted with hate, love for the Father is contrasted with love for the world.

The passage has two parts. The first lists John's various reasons for writing, but the focus is on *to whom* John is writing. He is writing to people who have been transformed by God. The second part of the passage focuses on the dichotomy between loving the world versus loving the Father—these "loves" are incompatible.

The two parts of the passage work together to remind John's readers of who they are on account of the work of God in their lives and to warn them that their love for him is incompatible with love for the world. As Jensen affirms, this passage is "the topic paragraph for the body of 1 John."[1] (See the introduction to 1 John for more on this concept.)

EXPLAIN the Story

John's Readers Have Been Shaped by God (2:12–14)

These verses are normally understood as articulating John's reasons for writing. This is understandable, since they are structured by the repeated formula, "I am writing to you . . . because . . ." and "I write to you . . . because . . ." But on closer inspection, it seems that John's focus is on *who* his recipients are and why he is writing *to them*. In other words he is saying, "I am writing *to you* . . . because . . ."

Each "because" clause focuses on the *spiritual state* of John's readers. John writes to *them* because of what God has done in their lives. He wants to encourage them to live out their true identity as people who are loved by God.

John writes in semipoetic form. There are two stanzas (2:12–13, 14) with three couplets each. The first three couplets begin with "I am writing to you" (*graphō hymin*), while the second three couplets begin with "I write to you" (*egrapsa hymin*).[2] The two stanzas stand in parallel, with the addressees of each couplet repeated in order:

Stanza 1
  Children
  Fathers
  Young men
Stanza 2
  Children
  Fathers
  Young men

---

1. Jensen, *Affirming the Resurrection*, 104.

2. It is not clear what the switch from the present (*graphō*) to aorist indicative (*egrapsa*) is meant to communicate. The NIV correctly treats the aorists as "epistolary aorists," indicating present time. The study of verbal aspect sheds some light on the issue: the aorist conveys a holistic view of the action rather than just a past action. See my *Basics of Verbal Aspect in Biblical Greek* (Grand Rapids: Zondervan, 2008), 34–39, 83–102. In addition, Kruse points out that for this expression, the present-tense form (*graphō*) is consistently used in 1:1–2:13, but in 2:14–5:21, the aorist (*egrapsa*) is consistently used (*Letters of John*, 87n59).

Variation occurs in the "because" clauses, with each indicating something of the addressees' spiritual state:

Stanza 1

> I am writing to you, dear children,
>> *because your sins have been forgiven on account*
>> *of his name.*
> I am writing to you, fathers,
>> *because you know him who is from the beginning.*
> I am writing to you, young men,
>> *because you have overcome the evil one.*

Stanza 2

> I write to you, dear children,
>> *because you know the Father.*
> I write to you, fathers,
>> *because you know him who is from the beginning.*
> I write to you, young men,
>> *because you are strong,*
>> *and the word of God lives in you,*
>> *and you have overcome the evil one.*

There are two parallels among the "because" clauses. First, the middle couplet of both stanzas addressed to "fathers" says "because you know him who is from the beginning" in both instances. Second, the third couplet of both stanzas addressed to "young men" says "you have overcome the evil one," though in the second stanza this follows two additional lines in the "because" clause.

We ought not to make too much of the parallels within the "because" clauses. It is the overall impression made throughout that is most important. These are people whose sins have been forgiven, who know the Father, and who have overcome the evil one.

Who Are John's Addressees? (2:12–14)

John writes to "dear children," "fathers," and "young men."[3] Since he calls his readers "dear children" throughout the letter, it is likely that this address includes everyone.

---

3. John uses two different Greek words for "children" in vv. 12a and 14a (*teknia, paidia*), while using the same words for the other two groups. It's hard to say why he uses two different words for children but the same words for fathers and young men, but perhaps it is because "children" refers to the whole group. All of John's readers fit under the address of "dear children." By using two overlapping terms, John emphasizes the whole scope of this group.

Why, then, does John go on to specify two subgroups within the "dear children"? It may be that fathers and young men are the leaders and future leaders of the group. Or, perhaps these are two groups inclined to come into conflict with each other. Then again, it is possible that the "threefold pattern echoes the standard categories of age and participation in civic life in the ancient world."[4]

Moreover, is there something special about fathers and their knowledge of "him who is from the beginning?" Is there a special way in which young men "overcome the evil one"? Why focus on these characteristics?

And why are the subgroups both male? Women are included in the first address, "dear children," but it is not clear why the focus shifts to (older and younger) men in particular.[5]

While some questions remain, the main rhetorical point is clear: all of John's addressees have been shaped by God through the forgiveness of sins, knowledge of the Father, and overcoming the evil one.

Do Not Love the World (2:15–17)

John's affirmation of his readers' spiritual status provides the backdrop for the exhortation to follow: "Do not love the world or anything in the world" (2:15).[6] If 2:15–17 had not been preceded by 2:12–14, it would sound as though John were chiding his readers for something they were doing wrong. But as it is, the exhortation reads as a *warning* so that they do not fall into love of the world. They are people who know the Father, who have had their sins forgiven, and who have overcome the evil one. They are to make sure that their good standing is not compromised by the allure of the world.

Love of the world is incompatible with love for the Father.[7] This strong antithesis helps us to understand what John means by the "world." "World" (*kosmos*) is capable of a variety of meanings, including a neutral

---

4. Lieu, *I, II, & III John*, 87. If so, this would naturally exclude women from the addressees altogether, since "Greek divisions of the 'ages of man' were not interested in women since they would not grow up to play their part in the life of the city" (ibid.).

5. Kruse says that "fathers" and "young men" do not exclude female readers (as a first-century way of speaking), but this is extremely unlikely (*Letters of John*, 88n60). See Jobes, *1, 2, & 3 John*, 104, for the fact that "young men" (*neaniskoi*) is never used in an inclusive sense.

6. Some commentators interpret the negated present imperative (*mē agapate*) as indicating an ongoing action (e.g., Kruse, *Letters of John*, 94), but this represents a mistaken understanding of imperative verbs. The imperfective aspect of the present imperative normally conveys a *general instruction* rather than an ongoing action. Its nuance is not so much temporal as characteristic. See my *Verbal Aspect and Non-Indicative Verbs*, SBG 15 (New York: Peter Lang, 2008), 91–95. See also Douglas S. Huffman, *Verbal Aspect and the Prohibitions in the Greek New Testament*, SBG 16 (New York: Peter Lang, 2014).

7. The phrase could mean "the Father's love," depending on how the genitive is understood (*hē agapē tou patros*). But "love for the Father" is more likely since a comparison is made with love for the world.

sense.[8] However, John's use is typically negative, depicting a rebellious humanity in opposition to God. Consider, for example, Jesus's frequent discussion of the world's antipathy toward himself, his Father, the Spirit, and his followers in the farewell discourse of John's Gospel (14:17, 19, 27; 15:18, 19; 16:20; 17:25). While the "world" can be understood in a more positive light in the first half of John's Gospel,[9] Salier notes that even these instances imply a negative sense since the world is the object of God's positive action.[10] Furthermore, Jensen notes that the only "positive" use of "world" in 1 John is found in 3:17.[11] For John, the "world" is the whole of humanity in rebellion against God. Clearly John's meaning here in 2:15–17 is likewise negative because his examples of "everything in the world" are "the lust of the flesh, the lust of the eyes, and the pride of life" (2:16). Lust and pride are roundly condemned by Jesus (Matt 5:27–30; Mark 7:20–23). Such things do not come from the Father but from the world.

John adds that "the world and its desires pass away, but whoever does the will of God lives forever" (2:17). He anticipates a time when rebellious humanity with its sinful appetites will no longer remain. However, those who belong to God—identified as those who do his will—remain forever. Clearly, then, John does not regard believers as part of the "world." Otherwise he would have directly contradicted himself, since we are meant to love our brothers and sisters who are part of the world!

Since the "world" is rebellious humanity, John's instruction not to love the world or anything in the world does not pertain to "neutral" or "good" things in the world. Food, for example, is not part of rebellious humanity, so love of food is appropriate, especially if we thank God for his provision of it. The point is that we are not to love anything that is opposed to God. The source of such things is not the Father. However, we can easily acknowledge that good things in the world (meant in a neutral sense) are from him.

In this passage John addresses people who have been transformed by God through the forgiveness of sins, knowledge of the Father, and overcoming of the evil one. And as such people they ought not to love the world. Their love is for their heavenly Father, which is incompatible with love for the things of the world.

---

8. E.g., John 21:25: "Jesus did many other things as well. If every one of them were written down, I suppose that even the whole world (*kosmon*) would not have room for the books that would be written."

9. N. H. Cassem, "A Grammatical and Contextual Inventory of the Use of κόσμος in the Johannine Corpus with Some Implications for a Johannine Cosmic Theology," *NTS* 19 (1972): 91.

10. W. H. Salier, "What's in a World? Κόσμος in the Prologue of John's Gospel," *RTR* 56.3 (1997): 107.

11. Jensen, *Affirming the Resurrection*, 106n7.

We Have Been Shaped by God

As John writes to the children, fathers, and young men, it is clear that their identities have been shaped by the work of God. *God* has forgiven their sins; *he* has enabled them to know him; and *he* has caused them to overcome the evil one. This set of qualifying features is not self-determined, even though they require the believers' cooperation. And so, John's very reasons for writing to *them* are due to the fact that they are the recipients of God's transformative work.

As we live the Christian life, this point is important to remember. It means that there is never a place for pride among believers. Even the most mature, godly, and gifted followers of Jesus cannot claim credit for their achievements and status.

The mature believer can take no more credit for their transformation than a beautiful butterfly having gone through metamorphosis. We may marvel at its beauty. And we may be amazed when we consider the butterfly's previous appearance as a caterpillar. But we cannot say, "Wow, butterfly, you have done a great job at becoming so beautiful!" The process of metamorphosis is not under the caterpillar's control, and the final product is beyond its imagination. Truly their final appearance is a work of art, but the caterpillar is not the artist. The caterpillar/butterfly is the canvas that displays the work of the artist.

So we are not the artists of our own beauty. We are the canvas. God is the artist. He has transformed us from belonging to a world in rebellion against God with its lusts and pride and brought us into relationship with himself. He has forgiven us our ugly sins. He has given us true knowledge of our beautiful God. He has enabled us to overcome the monstrous evil one.

John writes to such transformed people, and the transformation has been remarkable. Believers are identified by these beautiful, life-changing characteristics. Compared to their former selves, they are as different as the butterfly is from the caterpillar. But we can no more boast in our transformed state than can a butterfly. Marvel? Yes. Rejoice? Yes. Admire the beauty of others' transformation? Absolutely. But we must remember who the true artist is and give him the glory.

Our Sins Have Been Forgiven

One of the characteristics of this radical transformation is the forgiveness of sins. There are several important implications that flow from forgiveness. First is the restoration of relationship with God. Since we once belonged to the rebellious world and like the world were set in our opposition to God, such restoration with the God who made us is nothing short of radical. It changes everything. Now that we are reconciled to God through the forgiveness of our sins, we are free to live in harmony with and in familial relationship with him as those who now belong to him. Knowing God as Father alters the way we see him.

Second, reconciliation with God through the forgiveness of sins changes the way we see ourselves. We may now identify ourselves as children of the Father—as precious members of his family. We need not take our cues for identity and worth from the values of this world—always seeking to measure up to others through achievement, respect, or fame. Instead we may stand secure in the Father's loving arms, knowing we are loved, valued, and respected—whatever our successes or failures in life.

Third, reconciliation with God through the forgiveness of sins alters the way we see the world. We can see it for what it truly is: God's incredible creation, deeply disfigured by human rebellion. It is a fleeting world characterized by a mixture of good as well as deep-seated evil. The good reminds us that it is still God's creation, and he has not abandoned it. The evil reminds us of humanity's desperate need for salvation and of the ultimate day of judgment that God has appointed. On that day he will rectify all that is wrong with the world by bringing it to account. And so the way we now see the world is shaped by thankfulness for God's goodness and his common grace seen in myriad ways, yet it is also shaped by a longing for the renewal of his creation, the rectification of all that stands against him, and God's final work of bringing evil to account.

The transforming power of forgiveness is beautifully illustrated in Victor Hugo's *Les Misérables*. When the former convict, Jean Valjean, finds accommodation with the trusting and generous Bishop Myriel in the town of Digne, he repays the bishop's kindness by stealing his silverware and silver plates. He is arrested and brought back to the bishop. However, rather than allow Valjean to receive the just penalty for his crime, the bishop gave him his silver candlesticks too, "reminding" him in front of the police of his promise to use the silver to become an honest man. This act of forgiveness and mercy from the bishop transforms Valjean. He becomes a repentant, honorable, and dignified man.

In much the same way, God's amazing generosity and forgiveness offer transformative power. Not only are our debts canceled and our crimes not held against us, but God showers gifts upon us like the bishop with his silver candlesticks. If we have truly taken hold of God's forgiveness and reflected on its deep significance, we cannot help but to be transformed by it.

We Know God

Flowing out of reconciliation with God is the awesome privilege of truly knowing God. Rather than rebels who only "know" God as enemy, we have been brought into a loving relationship with him as his children. As true children of his family, we have a relational knowledge of him.

It does not mean that we know everything there is to know about God—of course not—but neither does that fact mean that God is unknowable. Rather, relational knowledge means that we know him *truly* even if aspects of God remain unknown to us. To know him truly means that we know *who* he is— we understand his character, his purposes, and his wisdom. Just as we might truly know a fellow human without knowing everything about that person, so also we may truly know God.

Knowledge of God is also transformative. J. I. Packer begins his classic book *Knowing God* with an apt quote from the nineteenth-century preacher, C. H. Spurgeon, which is equally apt here:

> It has been said by someone that "the proper study of mankind is man." I will not oppose the idea, but I believe it is equally true that the proper study of God's elect is God; the proper study of a Christian is the Godhead . . . .
>
> There is something exceedingly *improving to the mind* in a contemplation of the Divinity. It is a subject so vast, that all our thoughts are lost in its immensity; so deep, that our pride is drowned in its infinity. . . . No subject of contemplation will tend more to humble the mind, than thoughts of God. . . .
>
> But while the subject *humbles* the mind, it also *expands* it. He who often thinks of God, will have a larger mind than the man who simply plods around this narrow globe. . . . The most excellent study for expanding the soul, is the science of Christ, and Him crucified, and the knowledge of the Godhead in the glorious Trinity.
>
> And, whilst humbling and expanding, this subject is eminently *consolatory*. Oh, there is, in contemplating Christ, a balm for every wound; in musing on the Father, there is a quietus for every grief; and in the influence of the Holy Ghost, there is a balsam for every sore. Would you lose your sorry? Would you drown your cares? Then go, plunge yourself in the Godhead's deepest sea; be lost in his immensity. . . . I know nothing which can so comfort the soul; so speak peace to the winds of trial, as a devout musing upon the subject of the Godhead.[12]

---

12. As cited in J. I. Packer, *Knowing God* (London: Hodder and Stoughton, 1973), 13–14. The message was delivered at New Park Street Chapel in Southwark, England on January 7, 1855.

As Spurgeon so clearly articulates, growing in our knowledge of God changes us. Revealing himself to us is part of his transforming enterprise.

We Have Overcome the Evil One

Having a new relationship with God as Father means that our relationship to "the evil one," the devil, has changed too. He is the spirit at work in those who continue in their sinful rejection of God (3:8), and we also were once under his influence. All people are either the children of God or the children of the devil, as John so starkly puts it (3:10). But now our relationship to the evil one has been fundamentally changed. Having become children of God, we no longer belong to the devil. Our overcoming the evil one is therefore a result of God's work in making us his children.

This change of relationship to the evil one has strong transformative power. His values are no longer ours. We do not share his priorities. His opposition to God no longer enjoys our cooperation. Instead, we have been turned against him. We have been inverted in our values, priorities, and opposition. We have defected. Or, perhaps better, we have *been* defected. We have been taken across to the other side, and our allegiance is now with our heavenly Father. Some of the implications of this change of allegiance will be explored below.

Loving the Father, Not the World

As John writes to people who have been forgiven their sins, who know God, and who have overcome the evil one, he implicitly draws on the reality that our identity shapes how we live. Since our identities have been transformed by God, our lives ought therefore to be transformed. This is how 2:12–14 and 2:15–17 are related: the first segment reminds John's readers who they have become; the second exhorts them to live accordingly. Or, more precisely, it exhorts them to *love* accordingly.

It is one thing to modify behavior. It is another thing to change who and what we love. But if we have truly been transformed by God, having been made his children and having come to know him, then our "loves" will ultimately shift. Love for the Father (2:15) is incompatible with love for the world and its worldly values. We will ultimately choose one or the other.

While we have addressed the "power of love" for Christian living already (see on 2:1–6), in this instance the notion of "love allegiance" is especially in view. It is the love of God *over and against* love for the world that John wants to see in his readers.

I'm an Abraham Lincoln fan. While reading Doris Kearns Goodwin's biographical work, *Team of Rivals: The Political Genius of Abraham Lincoln*, I was struck at how often people who had been opposed to Lincoln eventually turned toward him and sometimes even grew to *love* Lincoln. The most obvious reason for this change of attitude toward him was that they got to know him. A strong example of this change in attitude is Lincoln's secretary of state, William Seward. Before Lincoln's presidential nomination by the Republican Party, Seward was far more famous than Lincoln. He was certain to win his party's nomination and was understandably shocked and upset that this relatively unknown hick from Illinois had somehow stolen the nomination that Seward thought was rightfully his.

In spite of Seward's animosity toward him, President Lincoln appointed Seward as secretary of state. For the first year or so of Lincoln's presidency, Seward remained opposed to Lincoln, believing the common misconception that he was a dull, ape-like fool. In fact, Seward contented himself to believe that he could effectively run the country by manipulating Lincoln as his puppet.

Nothing was further from the truth. The turning point came when, to Seward's shock, he realized that he had been outsmarted and outmaneuvered by Lincoln, who knew all along what Seward thought of him and what he was trying to do. The first thing that changed was Seward's respect for Lincoln. He realized he was dealing with no dull-witted hick. Lincoln was *very* sharp.

Lincoln held no grudge but forgave Seward for his arrogance and duplicitousness. Over the months and years to follow, Lincoln and Seward developed a close friendship. Lincoln would spend countless evenings at Seward's home, talking by the fireplace and enjoying each other's company. Seward's allegiances eventually changed to the extent that he would frequently and publicly say that Lincoln was the greatest, wisest man he ever knew.

On the night of Lincoln's assassination, the conspirators also attacked Seward in his home. He survived but was rendered unconscious for several days. When he woke, lying in his bed, he realized by himself that Lincoln must have been assassinated. Two factors led to this conclusion. First, the flag at the White House was raised to half-mast (he could see it from his bedroom window). Second, if Lincoln lived, Seward knew that he would have been by Seward's bed, waiting for his friend to regain consciousness. After receiving confirmation of Lincoln's death, Seward wept for two days.

Here was an example of a man's allegiance turned around. Seward had been Lincoln's adversary. He did not respect him, like him, or care for him. But after getting to know Lincoln and after experiencing his forgiveness, wisdom, and affection, Seward developed a great love for his friend, President Lincoln.

To know God is to love him. As we grow in our knowledge of him, so too will our love grow. Our allegiance shifts from the loves of this world to love for our heavenly Father. And since they are in opposition, it is not possible to love both the rebellious world and God. Thus if we do love the world, John sees this as evidence that we do not yet have love for the Father. Anyone who struggles to let go of his or her love of the world should focus more on the Father. Let us mediate on his forgiveness. Focus on his mercy. Reflect on his love. Get to know him better. As we know God more fully, our affections will follow. To know him is to love him.

CHAPTER 6

1 John 2:18-27

 LISTEN to the Story

¹⁸Dear children, this is the last hour; and as you have heard that the antichrist is coming, even now many antichrists have come. This is how we know it is the last hour. ¹⁹They went out from us, but they did not really belong to us. For if they had belonged to us, they would have remained with us; but their going showed that none of them belonged to us.

²⁰But you have an anointing from the Holy One, and all of you know the truth. ²¹I do not write to you because you do not know the truth, but because you do know it and because no lie comes from the truth. ²²Who is the liar? It is whoever denies that Jesus is the Christ. Such a person is the antichrist—denying the Father and the Son. ²³No one who denies the Son has the Father; whoever acknowledges the Son has the Father also.

²⁴As for you, see that what you have heard from the beginning remains in you. If it does, you also will remain in the Son and in the Father. ²⁵And this is what he promised us—eternal life.

²⁶I am writing these things to you about those who are trying to lead you astray. ²⁷As for you, the anointing you received from him remains in you, and you do not need anyone to teach you. But as his anointing teaches you about all things and as that anointing is real, not counterfeit—just as it has taught you, remain in him.

Listening to the Text in the Story: Daniel 8–12; Hosea 3:5; John 14:15–31; 17:22–23; Hebrews 1:2; Revelation 13.

The message of this new section is summarized by 2:26: "I am writing these things to you about those who are trying to lead you astray." Those who "went out from us" (2:19) deny the Father and the Son (2:22). But believers are to remain in the Son and the Father (2:24), having been forewarned about those trying to lead them away.

In the first half of the passage, John sets up a strong contrast between the two groups (2:18–23). The first are "antichrists" (2:18–19); the second are those who have an "anointing from the Holy One" (2:20).

The second half of the passage (2:24–27) is an exhortation based on the first half. Having established his readers' anointing of the Spirit and acceptance of the truth, John encourages them to remain in Christ.

EXPLAIN the Story

Antichrists Have Come in the Last Hour (2:18–19, 22–23)

After again addressing his readers affectionately as "dear children" (*paidia*), John states that "this is the last hour" (2:18a). We know it is the "last hour" because "many antichrists have come" (2:18b–c). This raises two questions: What is the "last hour," and what or who are these "antichrists"?

There is little information given in John's letters to answer the former question,[1] but we may understand the "last hour" from related language elsewhere in the New Testament. First, John's Gospel employs the terminology of "hour" (but not "*last* hour") with differing senses. Yarbrough identifies three decisive "hours" in the Gospel:

> The first was when Jesus laid down his life for the salvation of God's people (John 2:4; 7:30; 8:20; 12:23, 27; 13:1; 16:32; 17:1). . . . The second was when Jesus through the Spirit would confirm to the apostles the meaning of Jesus' life and ministry for their gospel mandate (John 16:2, 4, 25). The third is yet to come, the time when Christ appears and final judgment takes place (John 4:21, 23; 5:25, 28).[2]

While we might expect 1 John's "last hour" to match the Gospel's *third* hour (since it is the "last" of the three outlined by Yarbrough), the third hour of the Gospel refers to yet future events, while 1 John's "last hour" clearly refers to a current temporal reality.[3]

Second, the biblical phrase "last days" can be seen as parallel to John's "last hour."[4] The "last days" language from Acts, 2 Timothy, Hebrews, James, and

---

1. The "last hour" is only mentioned here in the entire Bible. It is also the only place in which either word, "hour" (*hōra*) or "last" (*eschatos*), occur in the Johannine Epistles.

2. Yarbrough, *1–3 John*, 142.

3. The terminology of "hour" refers to a temporal period or to a stage in an unfolding eschatological schema. In this way, 1 John can use "last hour" to speak of a last period or epoch in salvation history. It need not line up with the Gospel's three "hours" more precisely than that.

4. The singular "last day" is only used in John's Gospel (6:39–40, 44, 54; 11:24; 12:48), while the plural "last days" is found in Acts 2:17, 2 Tim 3:1, Heb 1:2, Jas 5:3, and 2 Pet 3:3. While we might have expected the Gospel's use of "last day" (singular) to most closely approximate 1 John's "last hour" language, it does not refer to the same thing. Throughout John's Gospel, the "last day" refers to the day of final judgment and resurrection (apparently in parallel with the Gospel's third "hour"). Again, this cannot be what is meant by 1 John's "last hour," since it refers to a current temporal reality.

2 Peter refers to a current reality.[5] This is especially clear in Hebrews 1:2: "But in these last days [God] has spoken to us by his Son." The "last days" refers to the current era of salvation history, between Jesus's ascension and his return (see Isa 2:2, Hos 3:5, and Mic 4:1 for the Old Testament background of the term).

Third, the "last hour" has a *possible* Old Testament background in Daniel 8:17, 19; 11:35, 40; 12:1. These are the only places where the eschatological use of "hour" (*hōra*) is found in the Greek Old Testament. The "hour" refers to "the eschatological time when the opponent of God's people will attempt to deceive them."[6] Beale suggests that John sees Daniel's prophecy as beginning to be fulfilled in the deceptive work of the antichrists.[7]

So the "last hour" refers to our current stage of salvation history, between Jesus's ascension and return, parallel to the "last days" language of the Old and New Testaments.[8] It is the period when deceivers will come.

We know it is the last hour because "many antichrists have come" (2:18). John's readers "have heard that the antichrist is coming," but his point is that *many* antichrists have already come. Despite popular notions—often associated with the book of Revelation—that "*the* antichrist" is some singular evil person, it is not a solo figure that John is concerned about here.[9] Moreover, the term "antichrist" is *only* found in 1 and 2 John,[10] and it is used the same way in each reference.[11]

John provides information about these antichrists in the immediate context. "They went out from us," he says (2:19a), which showed "that none of them belonged to us" (2:19b). These antichrists have broken away from the group of true believers (or the apostolic community).[12] They have formed an alternate group that stands opposed to John's readers.

---

5. While some interpreters prefer to see 2 Tim 3:1 and 2 Pet 3:3 as referring to a yet-future reality rather than a currently existing period (cf. Lieu, *I, II, & III John*, 98), this is unnecessary. The use of a future-tense form in both verses simply means that certain events are to be expected within the current period. They do not necessarily point to a future era *per se*, and in fact the broader context of both verses favors a present-era reading.

6. G. K. Beale, "The Old Testament Background of the 'Last Hour' in 1 John 2,18," *Bib* 92 (2009): 254.

7. Beale, "The Old Testament Background of the 'Last Hour,'" 231–54.

8. The "last day" (singular) of John's Gospel may well refer to a literal day that marks the end of this "last hour" with the return of Christ. If such is the case, while it may seem counterintuitive, John's "hour" is the larger category within which the "day" will be found.

9. For a similar reading, see Jobes, *1, 2, & 3 John*, 123–24. She comments: "This suggests the shocking announcement that while Jesus' original readers (as many readers today) may have been expecting a larger-than-life evil person to arise, the kind of heretical teaching going around was actually an evil of similar proportion that could effectively destroy the church" (123).

10. 1 John 2:18, 22; 4:3; 2 John 7.

11. While the *term* is only found in 1–2 John, the *concept* of an antichrist is arguably found in Revelation 13 (cf. 2 Thess 2:3–12). For the possible Jewish background to the concept of "antichrist," see Brown, *Epistles of John*, 332–36.

12. Edward M. Curtis, "The First Person Plural in 1 John 2:18–27," *Evangelical Journal* 10 (1992): 27–36.

The antichrists deny that Jesus is the Christ, which is probably why John coined the term (2:22a). This may be a reference to their docetic beliefs that deny the humanity of Jesus, since the Christ (= Messiah) is a human descendant of David. To count Jesus as the Christ would be to acknowledge his human birth and ancestry. In any case, docetism seems to be in view with the fourth use of the term "antichrist" in 2 John 7: "Many deceivers, who do not acknowledge Jesus Christ as coming in the flesh, have gone out into the world; any such person is the deceiver and the antichrist."

In addition to possible docetic beliefs, Jensen suggests that part of the error of the antichrists is their denial of Jesus's bodily resurrection.[13] If he is correct to detect references to Jesus's resurrection in 1:1–3 (as endorsed in this commentary), it follows that denial of the resurrection is at least in part in view here. The resurrection is key to understanding Jesus as the Christ since "the event that demonstrates that Jesus, as opposed to any other Jewish man, is the Christ, is his physical resurrection (cf. John 20:31; Acts 2:25–36; 13:32–7; Romans 1:4)."[14] According to apostolic testimony, the resurrection declares Jesus to be the Christ, and thus it follows that the antichrists deny that Jesus is the *resurrected* incarnate Christ.

John says that an antichrist denies the Father and the Son (2:22b). He adds in the next verse that "no one who denies the Son has the Father" (2:23a), which means that if one gets it wrong about Jesus they will also get it wrong about God the Father. You can't have one without the other. Thus, there is no possibility of being right with God for an antichrist. Rejection of the truth about Christ puts a person completely outside the family of God.

But You Have an Anointing from the Holy One and Know the Truth (2:20–21)

In contrast to the rebel group of antichrists, John's readers "have an anointing from the Holy One," and they all "know the truth" (2:20).[15] The main thrust here is on knowing the truth, as John emphasizes in the next verse: "I do not write[16] to you because you do not know the truth, but because you do know it and because no lie comes from the truth" (2:21).

Since the antichrists deny that Jesus is the Christ, the "truth" that John's readers already know is likely the fact that Jesus *is*, in fact, the Christ. Jesus

---

13. Jensen, *Affirming the Resurrection*, 116–17.

14. Jensen, *Affirming the Resurrection*, 116.

15. Some manuscripts read "and you know all things" rather than "all of you know the truth." The context favors the NIV reading as it contrasts John's readers with those who have deserted the community of faith; see Culy, *I, II, III John*, 52. However, Black argues the other way for stylistic reasons (David Alan Black, "An Overlooked Stylistic Argument in Favor of πάντα in 1 John 2:20," *Filologia Neotestamentaria* 5 [1992]: 205–8).

16. On the tense-form *egrapsa*, see the note at 2:14.

as the Christ is an absolutely key conviction of orthodox believers and marks them as such. In keeping with the tone of the letter so far, John writes to confirm and encourage believers in what they already know, rather than needing to correct them toward the truth.

Knowing the truth seems to derive from their "anointing from the Holy One." We are not given many clues as to what this anointing refers to, since the word (*chrisma*) only occurs here and in 2:27 in the entire New Testament. It is, however, found eight times in the Greek Old Testament—seven times in Exodus referring to anointing with oil and once in Daniel referring to the Anointed One (Exod 29:7; 30:25; 35:17, 19; 40:9, 15; Dan 9:26). In Exodus, anointing by oil is used to *set people apart* for a special purpose.

The clues in 1 John 2:27 are that this anointing is "from him"—which could refer to the Father or the Son—"remains in you" (2:27a), "teaches you about all things," and is "real" (2:27b). These clues all point to the anointing as the reception of the Holy Spirit. In John 14:15–31 Jesus promises that he will ask the Father to give "another advocate" to the disciples who will "be with you forever—the Spirit of truth" (14:16–17a). The Holy Spirit "will teach you all things and will remind you of everything I have said to you" (14:26). Smalley also points to certain Old Testament references to anointing in the Spirit (1 Sam 16:13; Isa 61:1),[17] and Kruse looks to the related verb, *chriō*, used mostly to refer to Jesus being anointed with the Holy Spirit (Luke 4:18; Acts 4:27; 10:38).[18] The major alternative to the anointing referring to the Spirit is to view it as referring to the word of God.[19] Dodd and de la Potterie are the main exponents of this view, as summarized in Brown, who concludes that "overall the evidence favoring the thesis that the anointing is by the word is weaker than that for an anointing by the Spirit."[20]

That the Spirit will come from the Father and the Son, remain with the disciples, and teach them all things corresponds well with the anointing from the Holy One that remains in John's readers and enables them to know the truth. Their anointing is the reception of the Holy Spirit.

Thus there are three key elements that differentiate John's readers from the antichrists. First, they have not separated themselves into a rebel group.

---

17. Smalley, *1, 2, 3 John*, 100.

18. Kruse, *Letters of John*, 103.

19. Another possibility is to see the anointing in a literal, sacramental way, as argued by Connell. But this is less plausible than the major options adopted by most commentators. See Martin F. Connell, "On 'Chrism' and 'Anti-Christs' in 1 John 2:18–27: A Hypothesis," *Worship* 83 (2009): 212–34.

20. Brown, *Epistles of John*, 346–47. Marshall combines the two views, concluding that "the anointing is the Word taught to converts before their baptism and apprehended by them through the work of the Spirit in their hearts (cf. 1 Thess. 1:5f.)" (I. Howard Marshall, *The Epistles of John*, NICNT [Grand Rapids: Eerdmans, 1978], 155).

Second, they accept the truth that Jesus is the Christ. And third, they share in the Holy Spirit.

Remaining in the Son and in the Father (2:24–27)

The second half of the passage is an exhortation built on the contrast established in 2:18–23. "As for you," John says, "see that what you have heard from the beginning remains in you" (2:24a). The truth about Jesus as the Christ is the entry point of their Christian lives, which is why John calls it "the beginning." And it is to be pursued passionately. As Bede writes, "Follow with all your heart that faith and that teaching which you received from the apostles at the beginning of the church, for only this will make you partakers of divine grace."[21] Adherence to the fundamental truth enables John's readers to "remain in the Son and in the Father" (2:24b). The heart of their Christian lives is relationship with God.

Being "in" the Son and the Father is John's profound concept of mutual indwelling (see on 2:5b–6). It is a spiritual union that reflects the mutual indwelling of the Son in the Father and the Father in the Son (cf. John 17:22–23). There is no more profound way to envisage believers' relationship to God; we are *in* the Son and Father.

As a consequence of remaining in the Son and the Father, believers receive "what he promised us—eternal life" (2:25). The relationship of mutual indwelling will be an eternal one, which is the primary benefit of eternal life—being able to enjoy relationship with God without end. Eternal life is not an abstract prolongation of life for its own sake; its purpose is eternal relationship with God. What is eternal life? It is that we should know the only true God and Jesus Christ, the one he sent (John 17:3).

There is a clear correlation here between truth and relationship. True relationship with God is predicated on knowing and believing the truth about Jesus Christ. Thus truth plays a vital role in authentic spirituality. For John it is simply not possible to relate truly to God while denying the central truths that bring us to him.

Verses 26–27 reiterate the overall concern and exhortation of the passage. John says he is writing[22] about "those who are trying to lead you astray" (2:26). It is not enough that the antichrists have left the fold of true believers; they seek to add to their number by drawing others out from the faithful.

But John is not overly concerned. His readers have received their anointing of the Holy Spirit and therefore "do not need anyone to teach" them (2:27a). Carson points out that there is likely an allusion here to the new-covenant

---

21. Bede, *On 1 John* (PL 93:96).
22. On the tense-form *egrapsa*, see the note on 2:14.

promises of Jeremiah 31:33–34.[23] God will put his law within his people and write it on their hearts. "No longer with they teach their neighbor . . . because they will all know me" (Jer 31:34). According to Carson, John's purpose for this allusion is to say, "You do not need anyone to teach you in a mediating sort of way."[24] This is seen against those trying to lead John's readers astray:

> Thus if any group claims, as some Gnostics were wont to do, a special insight that only they and those who joined them enjoyed, part of John's response is in terms of Johannine theology that itself claims to fulfil Old Testament promises regarding the dawning and nature of the new covenant, a new covenant that would guarantee the gift of the Spirit and consequent illumination to all within its embrace, forever relegating to the sidelines those who claim the authority of specially endowed mediating teachers.[25]

Having asserted that they do not need anyone to teach them, John nevertheless exhorts his readers to heed the teaching of their anointing: "Just as it has taught you, remain in him" (2:27b).

John does not correct his readers in this passage. Instead he makes it clear that they know the truth because of their anointing—because they have the Holy Spirit. As such, he is able simply to affirm what their anointing has already taught them—that they must remain in Christ. The fact that they have the Spirit means they know the truth, which means they will remain in the Son and the Father. None of that is true of the antichrists, whose departure from the group of the faithful signals the absence of the Spirit, denial of the truth, and lack of communion with God.

 LIVE the Story

Who is the Antichrist?

I've never really understood some people's fascination with antichrist identification. I suppose it is seen as an indicator that "the end is near," and therefore the speculation serves a hopeful end. After all John says that "this is how we know it is the last hour" (2:18). There have no doubt been hundreds of candidates for the title "antichrist" suggested over two millennia, ranging from Nero to Adolf Hitler or to Mikhail Gorbachev. But such speculation is misguided.

---

23. D. A. Carson, "'You Have No Need That Anyone Should Teach You' (1 John 2:27): An Old Testament Allusion That Determines the Interpretation," in *The New Testament in Its First Century Setting: Essays on Context and Background in Honour of B. W. Winter on His 65th Birthday*, ed. P. J. Williams et al. (Grand Rapids: Eerdmans, 2004), 269–80. See also Jobes, *1, 2, & 3 John*, 132.

24. Carson, "'You Have No Need That Anyone Should Teach You,'" 279.

25. Ibid.

John says that "even now many antichrists have come" (2:18). There is not *one* Antichrist (capital *A*) whose presence signals an imminent judgment-day scenario. There are *many* antichrists (small *a*). And these antichrists are not necessarily prominent political figures who will attempt to doom the world. No, these antichrists in fact began in the community of God's people but later defected (2:19). They deny that Jesus is the Christ and so in that sense are simply *anti*-Christ.

There may be another motivation driving the "search for the antichrist." Among some there is a desire to know of God's intervening action in the world *ahead of time*. Such knowledge would allow people time to prepare or to warn others. While the Scriptures certainly do instruct us to be prepared and to warn others, they do not encourage us to speculate about times and places. Jesus explicitly warns against such speculation and warns of listening to people who engage in it (Matthew 24).

Rather than worrying about the specifics of *when* and *how*, we ought to be concerned to remain faithful as we expectantly wait and to proclaim Jesus to others while there is time left to do so. The specifics of *when* and *how* is God's business; in fact, Jesus even says it is for the Father alone to know (Matt 24:36). If we trust the Father to act according to his wisdom and plan, we need not worry about his business. Especially since he has told us not to. Rather, excessive attention given to *when* and *how* God will bring an end to the world as we know it expresses a lack of trust in his sovereign goodness and perfect timing. All we need to know is that it *will* happen. Let God take care of the rest.

"To Betray, You Must First Belong"

The "little *a*" antichrists are nevertheless a real concern for the church.

Harold Adrian Russell Philby, known as Kim Philby, was one of the most treacherous double agents in British history. After years of secretly betraying his country by working as a British intelligence officer and Soviet spy, he finally defected to the USSR in 1963 where he remained until his death in 1988.

On the fiftieth anniversary of his defection to the USSR, the *Telegraph*'s Neil Tweedie reflected on Philby's betrayal in a piece called "Kim Philby: Father, Husband, Traitor, Spy."[26] While Philby pretended to serve his country, he was secretly a committed communist. This duplicity led him to betray fellow British agents, oftentimes resulting in their deaths.

The *Telegraph* piece references Michael Smith, a historian of MI6, who thinks that scores, maybe even hundreds of MI6 and CIA agents were doomed by Philby's activities. "The number of MI6 operations destroyed and agents killed as a result of Philby's betrayal is impossible to calculate," he says. "But

---

26. Neil Tweedie, "Kim Philby: Father, Husband, Traitor, Spy," *The Telegraph*, January 23, 2013, http://www.telegraph.co.uk/history/9818727/Kim-Philby-Father-husband-traitor-spy.html.

operations mounted into the Baltic states, Poland, Albania, and the southern Soviet Union were all compromised by Philby's involvement."[27]

Before his true allegiance was revealed, Philby climbed high within the British intelligence world, being promoted (ironically) to head the anti-Soviet section of MI6. He became the principal liaison between British and U.S. intelligence agencies. Leading up to his defection, however, MI6's suspicions about Philby grew but could not be confirmed. He managed to flee just as they began to close in on him.

Kim Philby's treacherous and destructive acts of betrayal all stemmed from his inner convictions. He believed in communism, and this internal commitment caused him to breach trust, give others over to death, and abandon his family and country.

There is something especially pernicious about double agents. It is not so much that they are committed elsewhere—there are always people who hold different commitments whether to another country, political philosophy, or religion. The element that makes double agents so reprehensible is their duplicity and betrayal. They claim to be one thing when they are in fact another. They infiltrate our ranks, creating relationships of trust and intimacy, all the while with the intention of working against us. The spy's chilling words, "To betray, you must belong" stand as a warning to us in the church. There have always been double agents within our ranks. And because they seemed to belong to us, their betrayal is both dangerous and painful.

Within the church now there will be people who claim to follow Christ, but in fact their allegiances lie elsewhere. They appear to be Christians and share in the partnership, friendship, and community of God's people. But all the while they are secretly serving another lord.

Eventually, their defection reveals the truth. Just as Kim Philby's defection to the USSR finally confirmed his true loyalties, so the person who eventually leaves the church once and for all reveals his or her true spiritual situation. Though sad and painful, the defection brings their duplicity to an end— "Their going showed that none of them belonged to us" (2:19).

Though the church has been "infiltrated" by double agents, it is not our place to conduct spiritual witch hunts or McCarthy-style accusations. God knows the heart, and we must be content to allow him to be the judge. After all, Jesus said that the wheat and weeds would be allowed to grow intermingled until harvest time (Matt 13:24–30, 36–43). What then can we do about it?

The church ought to continue to teach and proclaim Christ. As the focal point of our allegiance to God, the message of Christ will simultaneously

---

27. Ibid.

encourage his true followers while also prompting double agents to reveal their true colors. Jesus divided people in his own day, and he continues to do so now. By the strong and faithful proclamation of Christ, people will eventually pick sides. Over time this will lead to double agents making the step toward final defection. Only then will we have confirmation of their ultimate loyalties.

Remaining in Him

The rather depressing topic of double agents in the church has a more positive counterpart—the exhortation for believers to "remain in him" (v. 27). We have an anointing of the Holy Spirit, who teaches us about all things including the need to remain in the Son and in the Father. But what does it mean to "remain in him"?

Remaining in him is John's way of speaking about continuing in a relationship of mutual indwelling. The Son is in us by the indwelling of his Spirit, and we are in him. The bond of mutual indwelling is difficult to illustrate since there are few natural parallels in the world we know. But probably the clearest parallel is that of marriage. A husband and wife become one flesh, and their souls are intermingled. The status of this relationship is established at a particular point in time and is intended to be permanent. But as all married couples know, marriage requires continual nurturing. The one-flesh status has been established, but the relationship needs to be renewed with each day. Without intentional effort to confirm, affirm, and nourish this one-flesh relationship, a marriage can easily fall into disrepair.

In fact, all relationships require nurturing. Even formal relationships, like marriage and family, must be nurtured to enhance their quality and to ward off atrophy. There is a parallel here with our relationship with Christ. It is a "formal" relationship in the sense that our status changes at a certain point—the point of conversion. At this moment, we enter into a relationship of mutual indwelling with Jesus that is intended to be permanent. Yet, like marriage, this permanent formal relationship must be nourished and enhanced. We must grow in our relationship with Christ. We ought to go deeper with him. Our relationship with him ought to head in a positive direction rather than wither through neglect. Clearly John is concerned that some believers may experience just that, and a withering relationship with Jesus is an extremely precarious spiritual situation. Just as we might encourage a married couple to invest in their relationship, so believers ought to invest in their relationship with Christ. As the Spirit teaches us, let us remain in him.

CHAPTER 7

1 John 2:28–3:10

 ## LISTEN to the Story

²⁸And now, dear children, continue in him, so that when he appears we may be confident and unashamed before him at his coming.

²⁹If you know that he is righteous, you know that everyone who does what is right has been born of him.

¹See what great love the Father has lavished on us, that we should be called children of God! And that is what we are! The reason the world does not know us is that it did not know him. ²Dear friends, now we are children of God, and what we will be has not yet been made known. But we know that when Christ appears, we shall be like him, for we shall see him as he is.

³All who have this hope in him purify themselves, just as he is pure.[1] ⁴Everyone who sins breaks the law; in fact, sin is lawlessness. ⁵But you know that he appeared so that he might take away our sins. And in him is no sin. ⁶No one who lives in him keeps on sinning. No one who continues to sin has either seen him or known him.

⁷Dear children, do not let anyone lead you astray. The one who does what is right is righteous, just as he is righteous. ⁸The one who does what is sinful is of the devil, because the devil has been sinning from the beginning. The reason the Son of God appeared was to destroy the devil's work. ⁹No one who is born of God will continue to sin, because God's seed remains in them; they cannot go on sinning, because they have been born of God.

¹⁰This is how we know who the children of God are and who the children of the devil are: Anyone who does not do what is right is not God's child, nor is anyone who does not love their brother and sister.[2]

Listening to the Text in the Story: Numbers 8:21; John 3:5–8; 2 Corinthians 3:18; Hebrews 2:14.

---

1. Verse 3 is here taken with vv. 4–6 rather than with vv. 1–2 (contra NIV), for reasons laid out in the commentary on the verse.

2. Verse 10 is taken as its own paragraph rather than with vv. 7–9 (contra NIV).

Two interlocking themes are threaded through this passage. The first is about being the *children* of God; the second is about acting *rightly* as God's children. Both themes are seen in the opening two verses (2:28–29) and in the concluding statement of 3:10. Everyone who does what is *right* has been *born* of God (2:29), and this is how we distinguish between the *children* of God and the *children* of the devil: anyone not doing *right* is not God's *child* (3:10).

John advances his argument through the inner three paragraphs (3:1–2, 3–6, 7–9). The first paragraph affirms that believers really are God's children. The second establishes the importance of right living and avoiding sin. The third paragraph draws on the two themes of childhood and right living in order to contrast those born of God with those born of the devil. Those who do right show themselves to be children of God, while those who sin show themselves to be children of the devil.

EXPLAIN the Story

Everyone Who Does Right Has Been Born of God (2:28–29)

The opening two verses frame the rest of the passage.[3] Continuing in Jesus will give believers confidence before him when he returns. The evidence for such confidence is what John goes on to address.

John establishes a key theological point that will undergird the rest of the passage: "If you know that he is righteous, you (also) know that everyone who does what is right has been born of him" (2:29). But who is John talking about? God the Father or the Son? Given that the "him" of the previous verse refers to Jesus ("continue in him," "unashamed before him at his coming"), the natural conclusion is that *Jesus* is the "he" of v. 29. But then again, at the end of the verse John speaks of being "born of him." If this also refers to Jesus, then it is the only place in the New Testament that speaks of being born of Jesus. Elsewhere, believers are born of God the Father (or the Spirit; cf. 3:9; 4:7; 5:1, 4, 18; John 3:3–8; 1 Pet 1:3). Most likely the referent of "he/him" has changed

---

3. The exhortation to "continue in him" (2:28a) is the same as the "remain in him" of 2:27c (*menete en autō*). It is for this reason that some commentators take v. 28 with the preceding passage rather than with what follows (e.g., Jobes, *1, 2, & 3 John*, 132–33). However, there are three reasons for taking v. 28 with what follows rather than what precedes. First it begins, "And now, dear children." The phrase "and now" (*kai nyn*) is a natural marker of a segment break (F. F. Bruce, *The Epistles of John: Introduction, Exposition and Notes* [Grand Rapids: Eerdmans, 1970], 78), and the term "children" (*teknia*) is found at the beginning of several new sections in the letter and anticipates one of the key themes of 2:28–3:10. Second, v. 28 refers to "his coming," referring to the return of Christ, which is also referred to in 3:2b ("when Christ appears"). Third, v. 28 mentions being confident and unashamed when Jesus returns. The remainder of 2:29–3:10 is concerned with being identified as children of God by right living, which connects strongly to believers' confidence before Christ when he returns.

from Jesus in v. 28 to the Father in v. 29. This is a common phenomenon in 1 John. It is possibly a deliberate technique used to affirm the close association between Father and Son. If God is righteous, those who do right must have been born of God.

Being "born of God" is a distinctly Johannine theme. First mentioned here in 1 John, it occurs twice more in this passage (3:9), and five more times in the letter (4:7; 5:1, 4, 18 [twice]). The strongest connection outside of 1 John is found in John 3:1–8 when Jesus tells Nicodemus that he must be born again (or born from above).[4] It refers to spiritual rebirth instigated by God through the Spirit, bringing about a dramatic new life. This new life is oriented toward God in Christ, leaving behind the old life with its allegiance to the world, the flesh, and the devil. According to 1 John, being born of God depends on believing that Jesus is the Christ (5:1). It produces love for fellow believers (4:7), and it enables them to overcome the world (5:4) and the life of sin (5:18).

There is a "family ethic" at work here: people will live in a way that is consistent with their parents or household: the Jones family does it *this* way, while the Smith family does it *that* way. John is not saying, "Since you are a child of God, you should act like him." Instead, this is how to *identify* someone who is born of God. Everyone who does what is right has been born of him.

The emphasis throughout 2:28–3:10 is on *identifying* who is born of God and who is born of the devil. Since John is writing to believers who are under threat from a splinter group, the purpose of this passage is to assure the faithful that *they* are the ones who come from God; the other group has revealed that they come from someone else.

The Father's Love Makes Us His Children (3:1–2)

The first step of John's argument is that believers really are the children of God. Verse 1 begins with a note of wonderment and exclamation: "See[5] what great love the Father has lavished on us, that we should be called the children of God!"[6] John revels in our status as God's children and delights in the love

---

4. While the phrase "born of God" is not used in John 3, the concept is clearly there ("born of the Spirit" occurs in v. 8). See Schnackenburg (*Johannine Epistles*, 162–69) for the helpful excursus, "Being Children of God and Being Born of God."

5. Runge analyzes "see" (*idete*) as a "meta-comment." A meta-comment occurs when the author stops what they are saying in order to comment on what is *going* to be said; e.g., "I want you to know that . . ."; "Don't you know that . . ." This interrupts the flow of the text, causing the comment to stand out and attracting the reader's attention to the proposition to follow. In this case, John is calling his readers to reflect on God's love: "*See* what great love the Father has lavished on us." See Steven E. Runge, *Discourse Grammar of the Greek New Testament: A Practical Introduction for Teaching and Exegesis* (Bellingham: Lexham, 2010), 101.

6. Literally, "See what kind (*potapēn*) of love the Father has given (*dedōken*) to us." The word *potapos* normally means "what sort of, what kind of" but in some contexts calls for the sense "how

of God. None of this is taken for granted. It is truly remarkable that human beings might be called the children of the holy, eternal God.

We are not only *called* children of God; "that is what we *are*!"[7] (3:1b). God's love does not simply effect a name change. Believers really *are* his children. Our status has changed. We have been given new life. We have a new orientation and a new family. The childhood is real, just as his fatherhood is real.

Three immediate implications follow from being children of God. First, "the world does not know us" for the reason that "it did not know him" (3:1c). The disassociation of the world toward God will be paralleled toward his children. Such disassociation constitutes further evidence that believers really are God's children.

Second, while we are now children of God, "what we *will be* has not yet been made known" (3:2a). This cryptic phrase points forward to the return of Christ (as the next phrase indicates), suggesting that the children of God will at that time become something even more. Since this "has not yet been made known," not even John knows what they will become.

Third, whatever the children of God will become, "we know[8] that when Christ appears,[9] we shall be like him" (3:2b). Christ's "appearing" refers to his return.[10] When Christ returns, the children of God "shall be like him." Again, the children of God will undergo some kind of change or transformation on the last day.[11] Whatever that transformation looks like, the important point is that it will bring believers into the likeness of Jesus.

John indicates the cause of this transformation when Jesus returns: "For we shall see him as he is" (3:2c). The notion of seeing God is part of the eschatological hope both in Judaism and Christianity.[12] Keener points out that

---

great, how wonderful" (BDAG 856). Moreover, *dedōken* literally means "he has given" but together with this use of *potapos*, "he has lavished" (NIV) is an appropriate interpretation.

7. There are no exclamation marks in Greek, but their inclusion in this translation is appropriate.

8. "We know" (*oidamen*) is another meta-comment, drawing attention to the proposition to follow: "*We know* that when Christ appears, we shall be like him" (Runge, *Discourse Grammar*, 101 [see the fuller description of this term in the note at 3:1]).

9. Literally, "we know that when he/it is revealed . . ." (*oidamen hoti ean phanerōthē*). The subject of the verb "revealed" could be *he* (Jesus) or *it*, referring back to "what we will be" in the previous clause. In favor of the latter, the same verb is used in each clause (*phaneroō*). This would mean something like "what we will be has not yet been revealed. But we know that when it *is* revealed, we shall be like him . . ." In favor of the former, Jesus is twice described as having been "revealed" (*ephanerōthē*) in this passage (vv. 5a, 8b). Both instances clearly refer to his first coming; that is, his earthly ministry. On balance, it is more likely therefore that v. 2b means "we know that when *he* is revealed," referring to Christ's second coming (so NIV).

10. Smalley, *1, 2, 3 John*, 138.

11. John does not specify the way(s) in which we will be "like him," and this is probably because the nature of that transformation is precisely what has not yet been made known (see the paragraph above).

12. Schnackenburg, *Johannine Epistles*, 160.

in the Fourth Gospel, John alludes to Mount Sinai, declaring that "we have seen his glory" just as Moses once did. "God revealed His goodness to Moses (Exod. 33:19), but the full revelation of His character is unveiled in the Word become flesh."[13] This version of the "divine vision" is much more likely the background to John's thought than the Hellenistic concept of the "vision of the divine," which is "a distant, theoretical, passionless intellectual construct."[14]

It is not clear how seeing Jesus "as he is" will effect such a transformation among believers. John probably means that we will encounter Jesus Christ in his full glory as the risen and ascended Lord of all (cf. 2 Cor 3:18). As Schnackenburg comments, "Becoming like God seems to be the consequence of glory, the radiant light of divine glory."[15] The sheer power of his glorious presence will be enough to effect the transformation of God's children.

So we see three implications flowing from being children of God. For the present time, the world will treat believers in line with their treatment of God. In the future, we will undergo some kind of transformation. And this will occur when Christ returns, whose glorious presence will make us like him.

No One Who Lives in Him Keeps on Sinning (3:3–6)

The second step of the argument is next: the one who remains in Jesus is not able to remain in a life of sin. The way people live indicates their true identity.[16]

The first identity marker is that "all who have this hope in him purify themselves, just as he is pure" (3:3).[17] Acts of purification are found frequently in the Old Testament, performed for a variety of reasons, often in connection to temple worship (e.g., Num 8:21). In the New Testament, the verb "to purify" is used the same way in some instances (John 11:55; Acts 21:24, 26; 24:18), and metaphorically or spiritually in others (Jas 4:8; 1 Pet 1:22). It has to do with preparation to encounter God's presence. Here, one of the marks

---

13. Craig S. Keener, "Transformation through Divine Vision in 1 John 3:2–6," *Faith and Mission* 23.1 (2005): 17.

14. Keener, "Transformation through Divine Vision," 17–18.

15. Schnackenburg, *Johannine Epistles*, 160.

16. The paragraph is structured through the repetition of the phrase "everyone x–ing . . . ," translated variously as "all who have this hope" (v. 3; *pas ho echōn tēn elpida tautēn*), "everyone who sins" (v. 4; *pas ho poiōn tēn hamartian*), "no one who lives in him keeps on sinning" (v. 6a; *pas ho en autō menōn ouch hamartanei*), and "no one who continues to sin has either seen him or known him" (v. 6b; *pas ho hamartanōn ouch heōraken auton oude egnōken auton*). Along with the shared theme of vv. 3–6, this structuring device lends cohesion to the unit. This is why verse 3 is here taken with vv. 4–6, not with vv. 1–2 (contra NIV). The coherence is clearer when the same translation is used each time: "Everyone who has this hope" (v. 3), "everyone who sins" (v. 4), "everyone who remains in him does not continue to sin" (v. 6a), "everyone who continues to sin has not seen him nor known him" (v. 6b). The "everyone who . . ." motif contributes to the interest of *identification* in this passage. John is sorting out identity markers that indicate who the children of God are and who they are not.

17. The phrase "this hope" forms a pivot from the previous paragraph, which pointed forward to the transformation of God's children at the return of Christ.

of the true children of God is that they purify themselves. There is a reverence and respect for God; believers are not casual in his presence. This is the appropriate stance for those who would stand in God's presence, since "he is pure."

The second identity marker is that "everyone who sins breaks the law" (3:4a). This is not really about breaking the law (whether the law of Moses or some other law).[18] Literally John says that everyone who sins "does lawlessness" (*tēn anomian poiei*). So what is "lawlessness"?

Sin and lawlessness are mutually defining: "Sin is lawlessness" (3:4b). This parallels 5:17: "All wrongdoing (*adikia*) is sin." So, sin = wrongdoing = lawlessness. Lawlessness is a disposition toward wrongdoing.[19] Lieu points out that in 2 Thessalonians 2:3–8 lawlessness refers to the manifestation of opposition to God. "As *anomia* (lawlessness), sin puts its perpetrator firmly in the camp of the archopponent of God. . . . Sin has a systemic and not a mere occasional character."[20]

Sin and lawlessness are incompatible with the true children of God. John says, "You know[21] that he appeared so that he might take away our sins" (3:5a). Our sin has been dealt with through Jesus's death for us. In him is no sin (3:5b), and he has removed our sin. This means that sin and Jesus are incompatible.

The third identity marker confirms the point: "No one who lives in him keeps on sinning" (3:6a).[22] Sin is understood as a *disposition* of lawlessness and wrongdoing.[23] Living in such a way is incompatible with living in Jesus. John is not claiming that believers will be without sin (see 1:8, 10). But someone living in Jesus has been cleansed of sin. They have left the old disposition behind. This means that anyone who *does* live in sin cannot be identified as a child of God. They have not "seen him or known him" (3:6b).

Conduct Reveals the Children of God and the Children of the Devil (3:7–9)

The third step in John's argument contrasts those born of God with those of the devil. One's true "father" is revealed by their conduct.

---

18. Lieu, *I, II, & III John*, 128.

19. See Colin G. Kruse, "Sin and Perfection in 1 John," *Faith and Mission* 23.1 (2005): 23–33.

20. Lieu, *I, II, & III John*, 128–29.

21. "You know" (*oidate*) is a meta-comment, drawing attention to the proposition to follow: "*You know* that he appeared so that he might take away our sins" (Runge, *Discourse Grammar*, 101 [see the fuller description of this term in the note at 3:1]).

22. "*Keeps on* sinning" is an interpretative translation. Literally, everyone remaining in him "does not sin" (*ouch hamartanei*).

23. See the excursus on sinless perfectionism in Kruse, *Letters of John*, 126–32, for a helpful overview of the issues and arguments put forward by various scholars. Kruse's own tentative conclusion is that "sin" here refers to a settled position of rebellion against God, which is impossible for believers to hold.

John warns, "Do not let anyone lead you astray" (3:7a).[24] Identifying people is a protective measure. Believers are not to be led astray by those identified as children of the devil. Such identification involves contrast: "The one who does what is right is righteous" (3:7b), but "the one who does what is sinful is of the devil" (3:8a).[25]

But the righteous person and the sinful person have one thing in common: they both bear their respective family resemblances. The one who does right is righteous "just as [God] is righteous" (3:7b); the one who does what is sinful is of the devil "because the devil has been sinning from the beginning" (3:8a). And the diametric opposition of these two "families" is obvious: "The reason the Son of God appeared was to destroy the devil's work" (3:8b; cf. Heb 2:14).

The appearing of the Son of God (3:8b) no doubt refers to Jesus's earthly ministry, including his incarnation, death, and resurrection. The destruction of the devil's work through the appearing of the Son of God is seen in two ways in 1 John. As Yarbrough points out, death itself has been destroyed (1:2; 2:25; 3:14–15; 5:11, 13, 20). Also, activities that are hostile to God have been destroyed in the life of the believer, as seen throughout the letter.[26]

The emphatic conclusion to the argument focuses on being born of God, which is mentioned at the beginning and end of 3:9. Not only will the one born of God not continue to sin (3:9a), but "they *cannot* go on sinning" (3:9b). They *will* not and they *can*not.

There are two reasons given: "Because God's seed remains in them" (3:9a) and "because they have been born of God" (3:9b). These parallel statements draw on the organic relationship between "seed" (*sperma*) and birth. The literal sense of 3:9a is "because his seed remains in him"; the second pronoun, "him," could refer to the believer or to God. This phrase could then mean that believers themselves are God's seed (i.e., his offspring; cf. John 8:33, 37) and *they* remain in *him* (= God).[27] Brown considers this possibility but concludes that the reading is not as likely as the understanding that it is God's seed that remains in believers.[28] Given the connection between the Spirit and new birth (John 3:5–8) and their anointing of the Spirit (2:20), which remains

---

24. This is a meta-comment, drawing attention to the proposition to follow: "*Do not let anyone lead you astray*: the one who does what is right is righteous, just as he is righteous" (Runge, *Discourse Grammar*, 101 [see the fuller description of this term in the note at 3:1]).

25. "Of the devil" (*ek tou diabolou*) is the same construction as (born) "of God" (3:9; *ek tou theou*), which parallels their respective "fatherhoods."

26. Yarbrough, *1–3 John*, 188–89.

27. See J. de Waal Dryden, "The Sense of ΣΠΕΡΜΑ in 1 John 3:9: In Light of Lexical Evidence," *Filologia Neotestamentria* 11 (1998): 85–100.

28. Brown, *Epistles of John*, 410–11.

in them (2:27), this "seed" is another way of referring to the Holy Spirit.[29] Believers are born of God, and his Spirit remains in them as confirmation of his fatherhood.

Because the Spirit remains in believers, they are not able to continue in sin. Again, this is not about sinless perfectionism. It is about an orientation toward God and a disposition to live his way. We have been born into God's family and therefore are now shaped into the family likeness by the power of the Spirit. As such, believers are not to be led astray by those whose father is the devil.

The Concluding Statement (3:10)

John concludes by reiterating the main point of this section: we can know who the children of God are and who the children of the devil are. "Anyone who does not do what is right is not God's child, nor is anyone who does not love their brother and sister." The reference to not loving brother and sister connects this passage to one of the prevalent themes of the letter: love goes hand in hand with truly knowing God. Failure to love is evidence of not belonging to God. And we see that lack of love is synonymous with failing to do right; as Augustine said, "How can we avoid sin? By keeping the commandment of Christ. And what is that commandment? It is that we should love. Love, and sin is undone."[30]

By clearly identifying who the children of God *are* and who they are *not*, John's readers are able to avoid being led astray (3:7) and may have confidence before Jesus when he comes (2:28).

 LIVE the Story

Doing Family with God

One of the main themes of this passage is the fact that God has made us his children. For many believers, the idea is perhaps so familiar (excuse the pun) that we don't notice how utterly extraordinary it is to be called the children of God. But extraordinary it is.

John draws a strong dichotomy between the children of God and the children of the devil. All people are either one or the other. This means that before

---

29. Brown, *Epistles of John*, 410–11. The other major possibility is that the seed is God's word. However, "nothing in Johannine literature associates the word with the begetting of the Christian, even though that is found elsewhere in the NT" (ibid., 410).

30. Augustine, "Ten Homilies on 1 John 5.2," in *Tractates on the Gospel of John 112–24, Tractates on the First Epistle of John*, trans. John W. Rettig, vol. 92 of *The Fathers of the Church: A New Translation* (Washington, DC: Catholic University of America Press, 1995), 187.

we ourselves became children of God, we were naturally children of the devil. And this is why it is extraordinary to be called the children of God—we used to belong to the evil one, but now God has claimed us as his own.

Adoption changes everything for a child. Rather than growing up in poverty, she grows up with every need provided. Rather than living in a home destroyed by drug abuse, he thrives in a family girded by love. Rather than surviving on the streets, she is given every chance at a healthy future. A child's environment, relationships, wealth, opportunities, and prospects are permanently altered. And so our neighborhoods, towns, and cities are riddled with stories of lives radically and positively transformed by adoption.

While the New Testament sometimes uses the image of adoption for our relationship to God (e.g., Gal 4:5; Eph 1:5), John's image is even stronger than that. The believer is *born of God* (2:29; 3:9). Former children of the devil become the children of God through a process of *rebirth*. This emphasis is seen in 3:9 in which John refers to "God's seed," which "remains in" the children of God. By referring to this "seed" (*sperma*) John claims that the children of God bear a "genetic" relationship to God. It is not merely a case of adoption without genetic relationship, as great as adoption is. The children of God are "genetically" related to God, since we are born *through his seed*.

To know God as Father is the greatest possible privilege for a human being. He is the Creator and Sustainer of the entire universe. He has no need of us, and we deserve his condemnation. But he has lavished us with fatherly love so that this awesome, almighty, and ever living God now calls us his children. More than that, he has *made us* his children through rebirth. What could be more life changing than that?

Becoming a child of God has profound implications for our "earthly" relationships too. John indicates that "the world does not know us" because it does not know our Father (3:1). To belong to him will result in alienation from the world, sometimes including our natural families.

In his book *When the Church Was a Family*, Joseph Hellerman tells the story of the young mother, Perpetua, whose loyalty to Christ caused unrest within her natural family.[31] In North Africa in AD 202, Perpetua kept an intimate personal diary as she sat in prison during the weeks leading up to her martyrdom. Her diary records the increasing estrangement between Perpetua and her earthly father. Charged with the capital offense of faith in Christ, Perpetua's father tried to have her recant so that she could return to her family. Perpetua stood her ground in this contest of loyalties, even while her father appealed to her loyalty to her family of origin:

31. Joseph H. Hellerman, *When the Church Was a Family: Recapturing Jesus' Vision for Authentic Christian Community* (Nashville: Broadman & Holman, 2009), 113–15.

Have pity on my grey head—have pity on me your father, if I deserve to be called your father, if I have favored you above all your brothers, if I have raised you to reach this prime of your life. Do not abandon me to be the reproach of men. Think of your brothers, think of your mother and your aunt, think of your child, who will not be able to live once you are gone. Give up your pride! You will destroy all of us! None of us will ever be able to speak freely again if anything happens to you (*Passion of Perpetua* 5.2–4).[32]

Hellerman observes the realization that followed the father's appeal to family loyalty.

Perpetua remained unmoved and claimed that soon her father "no longer addressed me as his daughter but as a woman" (5.5). Perpetua's father finally realized that his daughter was no longer a member of her natural family. She had instead made an irrevocable commitment to the family of God; she was no longer his "daughter."[33]

Becoming a member of the family of God does not mean that we ought to disown our natural families (indeed, we bear godly responsibilities to them). But they may choose to disown us. And when there is a contest of loyalties between our natural family and the family of God, it is clear which must take precedence. By giving us new birth, God has forever changed our ultimate allegiances. We belong to him now.

Children Bear the Family Resemblance

Sometimes it is obvious that two people are related. Perhaps they look similar, share similar mannerisms, or share a way of looking at the world. These similarities are sometimes due to genetics, such as similar looks, but often they arise from living together. Mannerisms, attitudes, and worldviews are shared through spending a lot of time together rather than through genetics.

My children are, I'm told, obviously related to my wife and me. My son looks a lot like me, one daughter looks like my wife, and our other daughter is a blend of us both. But just as obvious as looks are their temperaments. While I think that temperament is related to genetics, it is also influenced by environment. Our kids are not all the same, that's for sure, but they have each picked up mannerisms, attitudes, and ways of speaking from my wife and me. Some of this is good, and some of it is not so good, but that's not the point here. The point is that they each bear a family resemblance that goes beyond genetics. It comes through sharing our lives together.

---

32. Cited in Hellerman, *When the Church Was a Family*, 114.
33. Ibid., 114.

As God's children, we share his "genetics" though his Spirit who lives in us. We have been reborn into God's family and permanently belong to it. As such, we are to bear the family resemblance. We will no longer live according to the ways of sin, as we did as the devil's children, but will "look like" our heavenly Father. While John draws on the "genetic" connection to our Father (3:9), he also points to our relational connection: "No one who continues to sin has either seen him or known him" (3:6). Living according to the family likeness involves *seeing* God and *knowing* him. That is, it is about *being like* our Father. We see what he is like, we know who he is, and we are to live in the likeness of his character and person.

In this way, the believer shares the family likeness both through "genetics" and through shared life together with God. Just as my children share genetic traits with my wife and me, they have also learned behaviors and attitudes from living with us. The combination of genetics and shared living is a powerful one indeed.

And so, the children of God *are* and *ought to be*. We *are* already genetically related to God our Father as his children—his seed lives in us. But we *ought to be* his children in the way we live and behave. Through both factors, the family likeness will be powerfully robust. It will be obvious that we are his children.

Perfect Children?

While the children of God are expected to share in the family likeness, John does not expect believers to be entirely without sin. John's clarity about this (see 1:8, 10) helps us to understand what he means by the statement of 3:6a: "No one who lives in him keeps on sinning." Since he has already warned of the deceitful claim of sinlessness, 3:6a cannot be understood to endorse sinless perfectionism.

As argued above, sin is understood as a *disposition* of lawlessness and wrongdoing. It is a settled state of rebellion against God. That is why sin (so understood) is incompatible with membership in the family of God; we can't be *with* him if we are *against* him. But believers are not free from *sins*—understood not as a disposition of rebellion against God but as moments of failure.

In any family, children will do the wrong thing from time to time—that's simply human nature. Indeed, children may well struggle to overcome inappropriate behavior as they mature. But none of this disqualifies children from family membership. Loving parents ought not to excuse inappropriate behavior—it should be addressed appropriately—but neither do they cast out their kids for being kids. Instruction and expectation are met with understanding and forgiveness.

A proper understanding of sin in the life of believers is absolutely crucial. Sadly, whole movements of the church have been shaped around misunderstandings in this area. Wesleyan perfectionism and the Keswick movement are prominent examples. Promoting the ideal of sinlessness after conversion, the teachings of these movements hold believers to a standard that no one can meet—not if we are honest about ourselves and honest about sin.[34]

While the desire for holy living is of course commendable, perfectionism makes two key errors.[35] First, it misunderstands the New Testament teaching about sin after conversion. While the New Testament affirms maturity, holiness, and godly living, it also acknowledges that we will not achieve perfection in these things until we receive our incorruptible resurrection bodies (cf. 1 Cor 15:35–58).

Second, it dilutes sin. In order to be "sinless," sin tends to be understood as outward and obvious failures like lying, stealing, adultery, and so on. If sin is restricted to such things, then I can imagine how someone might claim to have become sinless in their postconversion life. Mind you, if sin is understood this way, we can also observe "sinlessness" in *pre*conversion life too—indeed, some nonbelievers could claim sinlessness.

However, sin is far more pervasive than this, infecting our deepest thoughts, desires, and attitudes of the heart; it does not merely consist in obvious, outward manifestations of disobedience. Even a fleeting moment of desiring our own glory above God's, for example, is sinful. And who is entirely free of such moments? With this more pervasive understanding of sin, no human being other than Jesus can possibly claim sinlessness—before *or* after conversion. Even with the indwelling of the Holy Spirit, believers still struggle against the flesh (Gal 5:16–17). We do not need to give in to the desires of the flesh, but the struggle is still there, and we will often fail in it.

Furthermore, the very fact that the New Testament is full of exhortations to walk according to the Spirit, to resist sin, and to strive toward maturity and holiness assumes that the postconversion experience will involve an ongoing struggle against sin and the failure to live perfectly. If sinless perfectionism were the expectation of the apostles, much of the New Testament would not have been written.

Confident Children

This passage begins with an exhortation to "dear children" to "continue in him" so that we may be confident and unashamed when Jesus appears (2:28). The ensuing discussion about who are and who are not the children of God

---

34. For the history, theology, and critique of the Keswick movement and its relationship to Wesleyan perfectionism, see Andrew David Naselli, "Keswick Theology: A Survey and Analysis of the Doctrine of Sanctification in the Early Keswick Movement," *Detroit Baptist Seminary Journal* (2008): 17–76.

35. There are other errors too; Naselli offers fifteen points of critique (ibid.).

is designed to offer such confidence. In short, those who are identified as the real children of God have no reason to fear but every reason for confidence before God.

It is a great tragedy when a child grows up unsure of his or her parents' love. Sometimes this is because the parents are not good at expressing their love, or they are better at expressing criticism or disappointment. And sometimes— even worse—the parents may not actually love the child. Whatever the reason, it is a tragic impediment for a child to grow up feeling unloved. There is nothing more formative than parental love and nothing more destructive than the lack of it.

The unloved child will not remain a child forever, of course, and he or she will no doubt go into adulthood bearing the consequences of feeling unloved. Countless studies could be cited about the long-term effects of such a childhood, but there is one effect that I want to focus on here: insecurity.

A lack of parental love or a lack of *feeling* parental love will predictably lead to deep-seated insecurity. Instead of feeling grounded, affirmed, and valued as a loved child, an insecure child may not feel worthwhile, will lack confidence, and will struggle to form deep relationships. And childhood insecurity will usually blossom into full-fledged adult insecurity that will seem irreversible.

Many people spend their lives with a similar experience of insecurity when it comes to God. Perhaps they doubt they're good enough for him. Maybe they imagine God as aloof and unloving. Perhaps they liken him to the austere father figure they knew growing up. Whatever the case, they do not know God as the loving Father revealed by Jesus.

But the God who is there is a Father who has lavished love on us (3:1). He has made us his beloved children through sending his Son to die for our sins and giving us his Spirit. He is merciful, loving, and full of grace. Yes, it is true that we do not want to end up on the wrong side of God. But as his children, we know that we are on his right side. And this knowledge gives us confidence. As we continue in Jesus, we may be confident children of our loving Father.

In Alan Stanley Tretick's famous photos of John F. Kennedy sitting at the Resolute Desk in the Oval Office, it is not JFK who is the center of attention but his son, John Jr., who is playfully located underneath the desk. The young John Jr. sits at his dad's feet while JFK does his work. The picture says so much about the bond of loving family relationships. The president of the United States is not accessible to just anybody. And not just anyone can walk into the Oval Office, let alone sit themselves under the Resolute Desk. But John Jr. had free access to President Kennedy. He had access to the Oval Office. He could sit under the Resolute Desk whenever he wanted. Because the president of the United States was his *father*.

When we know God as Father, we have confidence in his presence. We have access to him. We know that he accepts us and cherishes us. We know that we have nothing to fear from him. He hears our prayers as we address him as "our Father in heaven."

LISTEN to the Story

¹¹For this is the message you heard from the beginning: We should love one another. ¹²Do not be like Cain, who belonged to the evil one and murdered his brother. And why did he murder him? Because his own actions were evil and his brother's were righteous. ¹³Do not be surprised, my brothers and sisters, if the world hates you. ¹⁴We know that we have passed from death to life, because we love each other. Anyone who does not love remains in death. ¹⁵Anyone who hates a brother or sister is a murderer, and you know that no murderer has eternal life residing in him.

¹⁶This is how we know what love is: Jesus Christ laid down his life for us. And we ought to lay down our lives for our brothers and sisters. ¹⁷If anyone has material possessions and sees a brother or sister in need but has no pity on them, how can the love of God be in that person? ¹⁸Dear children, let us not love with words or speech but with actions and in truth.

Listening to the Text in the Story: Genesis 4:1–16; Matthew 5:21–22; John 10:11; 15:12–13, 18–25.

While the previous passage was primarily concerned with identification, this passage offers direct application: believers are to love one another.

There is a strong correlation between love and life, as well as hate and death. Love is evidence that we have eternal life. Those who hate remain in death. With their confidence of eternal life, believers are able to lay down their lives for others, just as Jesus did. While love makes us willing to give up our lives for others, hate makes others willing to take life. Love is expressed in practical terms. Believers are to provide for those in need, showing love in action.

EXPLAIN the Story

Love One Another (3:11)

The theme of the passage is stated up front: "We should love one another" (3:11b). This is the message John's readers "heard from the beginning" (3:11a), which likely refers to the beginning of their Christian lives.[1] Love is a fundamental teaching of Christianity. It would no doubt have been impressed upon John's readers from the moment of their conversion to Christ. Indeed, it would have been part of the proclamation that led to their conversion, since the gospel of Jesus Christ declares the eternal love of God.

As is the case throughout the letter, love is directed toward "one another." This is not to say that Christians should not show love to those outside the church, but John's concern here is in-house. Love among brothers and sisters is especially important in the context of division. The splinter group threatened to undermine Christian unity and was ultimately an unloving development.

Not like Cain, the Murderer of His Righteous Brother (3:12)

John draws on the dramatic example of Cain, who murdered his brother Abel (Gen 4:1–16). Cain "belonged to the evil one" (3:12a) and is therefore an exemplar of the children of the devil (discussed in the previous passage; 3:10).[2] According to John, Cain murdered his brother "because his own actions were evil and his brother's were righteous" (3:12b).

John's interpretation of Genesis 4:1–16 is more explicit than the text itself regarding Cain's motivation for murder. If anything, Cain seemed to struggle with jealousy (v. 5), but the Lord warned him, "If you do what is right, will you not be accepted? But if you do not do what is right, sin is crouching at your door" (v. 7). The contrast here between doing right and wrong suits John's focus, since he has already established the same contrast in the previous passage. The one who does right is a child of God; the one who does wrong is a child of the devil (1 John 3:7–10). Cain's actions were evil (*ponēra*) because he belonged to the evil one (*tou ponērou*).

It is a curious fact that Cain of all people is the only Old Testament figure explicitly mentioned in 1 John (see the introduction to 1 John). Menken suggests that John's intention was to associate Cain with his opponents, which "made the opponents appear as evil, and it served the purpose of blackening

---

1. Yarbrough, *1–3 John*, 197.
2. Painter, *1, 2, and 3 John*, 233.

them and of warning the community about them."[3] This is the reason why Cain is the only exception to the pattern: "In this case the Old Testament parallel was too obvious to let it go."[4] And so Cain is not mere (negative) example; he is also a "type" to be avoided.

Abel is not mentioned by name but is twice referred to as Cain's brother (3:12). This is not accidental but suits John's purposes since he is interested in love for our brothers and sisters. Fratricide is especially heinous. It is also no accident that Abel's actions are described as righteous. He is an exemplar of the righteous children of God, having been murdered by his hateful brother. John draws on this motif of hatred toward the righteous in the next part of the passage (3:13–15).

Hatred Produces Fratricide (3:13–15)

The themes raised by the Cain-and-Abel story carry through to John's following point. Having established the fundamental differences of identity between the righteous children of God and the evil children of the devil (3:7–10), John now addresses the inevitable conflict between the two groups.

John's "brothers and sisters" ought not to be surprised[5] "if the world hates you" (3:13).[6] The "world" (*kosmos*) in John's writings normally refers to rebellious humanity; it is the world opposed to God.[7] In the immediately preceding context, John had written about the "world" that "the reason the *world* does not know us is that it did not know him" (3:1). This statement is part of the unfolding contrast that John develops through 3:1–10. As such, it is clear that John equates the "world" with the children of the devil. The children of the devil will hate the children of God.

Being hated by the world is anticipated by Jesus in John 15:18–25. The world will hate Jesus's disciples because "it hated me first" (v. 18) and because of their association with him (vv. 19–21). Hating Jesus also spells hatred for his Father (vv. 23–24). As far as John is concerned, the world hates the whole family of God: Father, Son, and all God's children.

John draws yet another contrast between the two groups, but this time love is the basis of comparison rather than doing right or wrong (cf. 1 John 3:7–10):

---

3. Maarten J. J. Menken, "The Image of Cain in 1 John 3,12," in *Miracles and Imagery in Luke and John: Festschrift Ulrich Busse*, ed. Jozef Verheyden, Gilbert van Belle, and J. G. Van der Watt, BETL 218 (Leuven: Leuven University Press, 2008), 211.

4. Ibid.

5. "Do not be surprised" (*mē thaumazete*) is a meta-comment, drawing attention to the proposition to follow: "*Do not be surprised* if the world hates you" (Runge, *Discourse Grammar*, 101 [see the fuller description of this term in the note at 3:1]).

6. This is the only time John addresses his readers as brothers and sisters (*adelphoi*), no doubt "prompted by the reference to 'brotherly' love (or the lack of it)" in 3:12 (Smalley, *1, 2, 3 John*, 177).

7. Kruse, *Letters of John*, 134–35. See also the commentary on 2:2.

"We know that we have passed from death to life, because we love each other. Anyone who does not love remains in death" (1 John 3:14). The presence or absence of love indicates spiritual status. Love indicates spiritual life, while the absence of love indicates spiritual death.

Life and death are key themes throughout the passage. "We have passed from death to life" (3:14) is another way to speak of new birth or having been "born of him" (2:29). Such birth to new life is the essential criterion for being called the children of God (2:29–3:1), and it is effected by God's "seed," the Holy Spirit (3:9; cf. John 3:5–8).

Remaining in death, however, is the natural spiritual state of all left in the world. Since passing from death to life is necessary to receive eternal life, those who have not yet made that transition remain spiritually dead. Life in the world is death, and dead people are not able to love those who no longer belong to the "world."

Spiritually dead people not only lack love; they also hate: "Anyone who hates a brother or sister is a murderer" (1 John 3:15a). This statement draws on the Cain-and-Abel story to show that the antipathy of the evildoer for the righteous person gives birth to murderous intent. In this way, evildoers follow their father the devil, who "was a murderer from the beginning" (John 8:44).

The hater *is* a murderer, which is presumably true according to John whether or not *actual* murder ensues. This is similar to Jesus's alignment of murder to anger in the Sermon on the Mount (Matt 5:21–22).[8] While Jesus stops short of saying that the angry person *is* a murderer, the point is clear: the attitude of the heart will be judged too, alongside actualized evil.

If love is the sign that one has passed from death to life, then it follows that "no murderer has eternal life residing in him" (1 John 3:15b). This should not be understood to mean that there is no possibility of forgiveness for someone who has committed murder. If a murderer were to turn to Christ and receive new birth in the Spirit, then he or she would no longer be included in the group that John describes here. In this context a murderer is someone who holds hate toward others and stands in opposition to the righteous children of God.

Love Offers Life (3:16–18)

Since love is the defining characteristic of those who have passed from death to life (3:14), it is important to understand what kind of love John has in mind. Here we find one of the best-known (and loved) verses in the letter: "This is how we know what love is: Jesus Christ laid down his life for us" (3:16a).

---

8. Painter, *1, 2, and 3 John*, 241.

Jesus's self-sacrifice for others is anticipated in John's Gospel.[9] He gives his flesh for the life of the world (John 6:51); he is the good shepherd who "lays down his life for the sheep" (10:11). Jesus's giving of himself in death was *for us*—the propitiation for "our sins" and "for the sins of the whole world" (1 John 2:2).

But Jesus's death is not only theologically significant; it is exemplary.[10] While Cain was an exemplar of hate in action, Jesus is *the* example of love in action. His love puts others ahead of his own life, and so believers are to do the same: "And we ought to lay down our lives for our brothers and sisters" (3:16b). This is no doubt an echo of Jesus's teaching in John 15: "Love each other as I have loved you. Greater love has no one than this: to lay down one's life for one's friends" (vv. 12–13). Just as hate takes away life, so love offers life.

John immediately applies the principle of sacrificial love in practical and domestic terms. Someone with material possessions should have pity on a brother or sister in need (3:17a). If not, then "how can the love of God be in that person?" (3:17b). Clearly John sees the instruction to "lay down our lives" (3:16b) metaphorically. That is, it does not only point to the literal offering of one's life (in death)[11] but to a "laying down" of self-interest in service of others.

The "love of God" (*hē agapē tou theou*) could refer to God's love toward us or our love toward him. The phrase is used both ways in 1 John (2:5; 4:9; 5:3), but here it more likely means "God's love" for us.[12] God's love cannot be in the person who does not show love to others.

John speaks of God's love being "in" a person (or *not* in them in this case; 3:17b). God's love within us is the driving force required to love others. It is the fuel of love. This means our love does not only involve following Jesus's example but is a relational power that indwells our hearts and prompts the expression of love toward our brothers and sisters.

Finally, John concludes with a summary exhortation: "Dear children, let us not love with words or speech but with actions and in truth" (3:18). Love

---

9. Lieu is correct to observe that John does not specify the way in which Jesus's laying down his life was "for us" and that the context is devoid of any kind of explicit atonement theory. Her own solution, however, is extremely unlikely. She argues that John refers to "Jesus' readiness to give himself up at his arrest so that his disciples can go free" (*I, II, & III John*, 149–50). This ignores statements such as John 1:29 and 6:51 which connect Jesus's death to the removal of sin and to the giving of life to the world (not only his disciples).

10. Gary M. Burge, *The Letters of John*, NIVAC (Grand Rapids: Zondervan, 1996), 162.

11. It is safe to assume that a literal offering of life (in death) would be included by John's instruction, following the model of Jesus's own physical death.

12. Our "love of God" makes some sense in that if we do not show love to people in need, how can we claim to have love for God? (See Culy, *I, II, III John*, 89.) But given that John has just said, "This is how we know what love is: Jesus Christ laid down his life for us" (3:16a), it is more likely God's love for us that is in view here (so Brown, *Epistles of John*, 450).

that is powered by God's love and follows the example of Jesus is love that *acts*. It is expressed by deeds in the ways that we care for each other. Love is proved in this, while words alone can ring hollow. While John writes, "Let us not love with words or speech," it would be silly to infer that love *should not* be expressed by words or speech (alongside action). His point is not that love can't be expressed verbally but that words alone are not enough. We may speak of love, but without deeds to prove our words they mean little.

Love "in truth" means that love in action does not operate alone. There is a cognitive element to love that aligns it with the truth of Christ.[13] In John's writings, "truth" refers to the spiritual truths God has revealed in Christ.[14] Much like Paul's "speaking the truth in love" (Eph 4:15), love and truth must go together. Without truth we cannot genuinely love, since love comes from God.

This passage draws a connection between love and life as well as hate and death. Love shows that we have eternal life, while those who hate remain in death. Genuine love takes action in caring and providing for those in need and is powered by God's love in us, as modeled by Jesus.

LIVE the Story

Murder is Hate in Action

The writer, professor, and political activist Elie Wiesel once said, "The opposite of love is not hate, it's indifference."[15] This sentiment has been repeated by preachers ever since, as Wiesel touches on something true about love. He understands that love is about concern for others expressed in mindful and proactive gestures. In this sense, indifference certainly is the *absence* of love. Love does not ignore; love does not neglect; love is not apathetic.

But I don't know if John would agree that the opposite of love is indifference. In his customary binary fashion, it seems clear that John regards *love* and *hate* as opposites. While love seeks the welfare of another, hate seeks destruction. Indifference is the absence of love, but hate is its opposite. While hate does not necessarily lead to murder, John claims that anyone who hates is a murderer nonetheless (3:16). This is because hate gives birth to murder, as was the case for Cain, who murdered Abel, and as Jesus intimated (Matt 5:21–22). Murder is hate in action.

---

13. It is possible that "in truth" means that love is proved true in action. But this is a less likely understanding of the Greek expression.

14. Jobes, *1, 2, & 3 John*, 159.

15. Elie Wiesel, Interview with Alvin P. Sanoff, "One Must Not Forget," *U.S. News & World Report*, October 27, 1986, 68.

Hate stands opposed to life and is destructive to the one who does the hating as well as the one who is hated. As the Baptist minister Harry Emerson Fosdick wrote, "Hating people is like burning down your own home to get rid of a rat."[16] And Augustine stated, "Whoever hates is a murderer. You may not have prepared any poison or committed a crime. You have only hated, and in doing so, you have killed yourself first of all."[17]

And yet many people struggle with feelings of hatred, even though they may know it is wrong. Surely the cure to hate is the love of Christ. Hate and love cannot coexist, so the way to defeat hate is to be consumed by love through the grace of God. To this end, let us make good use of the prayer found in the 1662 *Book of Common Prayer*:

> From envy, hatred, and malice, and from all uncharitableness,
> Good Lord, deliver us.

The Lord is able to deliver us from hatred. Rather than give in to resentment and hostility which give birth to hatred, we may draw near to God and seek his deliverance from such things.

Don't Be Surprised if the World Hates You

John briefly evokes Jesus's words in John 15:18–25 by saying that we ought not to be surprised if the world hates believers in Christ (1 John 3:13). The disciple of Jesus has decided to undo allegiance to the world and instead belongs to Christ. This new allegiance will inspire hatred from the world since the world does not love the Son or the Father (for more on the "world" in John's writings, see comments on 2:15–17).

Such hostility from the world can be difficult to take for some believers. They do not see themselves as opposed to the world and find it unreasonable that the world should be opposed to them. From a theological point of view, it *is* unreasonable that the world should be opposed to followers of Jesus because it is unreasonable for the world to oppose Jesus himself. He is God the Son, come to give us life. Why would we oppose him? The answer is that our hearts are rebellious and in their natural state reject God and the one he has sent. Indeed, only by a miraculous work of the Spirit can anyone turn from such a situation and believe.

Opposition may be unreasonable, but it is not surprising. Believers should expect hatred from the world. But we should not give the world extra cause for

---

16. *As I See Religion* (New York: Harper & Brothers, 1932).
17. Augustine, "Sermon 49," in *Sermons, Volume 2: 20–50 on the Old Testament*, ed. J. E. Rotelle, vol. 3/2 of *The Works of St. Augustine: A Translation for the 21st Century* (Hyde Park: New City Press, 1990), 338.

hatred. If the world chooses to hate the followers of Jesus, then so be it. But sometimes Christians can make things worse for themselves in unnecessary and sometimes ungodly ways. Christians can provoke hatred by being unnecessarily judgmental, harsh, and mean-spirited. This is not what Jesus had in mind when he said the world would hate his followers. Such behavior brings disrepute to Jesus rather than honor. And yet Christians who engage in it will often think of themselves as serving God. They will gladly bear the world's hatred because it confirms their standing with the Lord. But this is off course.

The world will hate believers because our allegiance is to Jesus. But we ought to engage the unbelieving world with love, respect, and charity. Our words should be gracious, and our hearts forgiving. After all, it is only by God's grace that we are right with him. There is no room for pride. There is no room for hostility. There is no room for self-righteous indignation.

That said, our allegiance to Jesus means that we will hold beliefs and attitudes that the world may find offensive. There could hardly be a more potent example of this in recent times than the offense taken at many Christians' attitude toward gay marriage. While some Christians *are* no doubt homophobic and bigoted, the world now assumes that this is true of *all* Christians who want to defend traditional marriage.

To hold a different view on marriage now equates to bigotry. This is partly due to clever rhetoric on the part of the movement for marriage equality, who have framed the conversation in terms of equality rather than asking the question, "Should we change what marriage is?" Once the conversation became about equality, anyone who opposes gay marriage is seen to be a bigot.

There's more to say about the ins and outs of that particular conversation, but they are not the point here. The point is that Christians are currently facing quite hostile opposition regarding "marriage equality." Moves are afoot to change legalities for Christian institutions that do not recognize the new definition of marriage. Federal funding may be at risk. And personal animosity is rampant.

It is vital that in the face of such vitriolic opposition, believers do not respond in kind. We must always show grace, forgiveness, and charity. If the world hates us, we will not be surprised. Rather, we will be prepared to respond in a way that brings honor to Jesus.

Rosaria Butterfield was a leftist professor of literature at Syracuse University. As a feminist and lesbian, she was speechless when in 1997 the Christian group Promise Keepers held a two-day event at the university. She criticized the university's decision to allow the group to use the campus for a weekend, and she wrote an article in the local newspaper attacking Promise Keepers.

She received quite a lot of hate mail in response to her newspaper article, but one letter stood out. It was from the pastor of the Syracuse Reformed Presbyterian Church, Ken Smith. The letter was respectful and kind but probing, as Smith asked Butterfield to defend her presuppositions.

The letter bothered Butterfield and caused her to consider the validity of her historical materialist worldview. The letter also initiated a friendship with Ken and his wife Floy. Her previous experience of Christians included those "who mocked me on Gay Pride Day," but that was not what Ken did: "He did not mock. He engaged."[18] Ken and Floy "entered my world. They met my friends. We did book exchanges. We talked openly about sexuality and politics."[19]

Rosaria began to read the Bible, reading it several times over the course of a year. She fought against it with all her might, but it overflowed into her world. One day on her own accord she "rose from the bed of my lesbian lover, and an hour later sat in a pew at the Syracuse Reformed Presbyterian Church."[20]

"Then, one ordinary day, I came to Jesus, openhanded and naked. In this war of worldviews, Ken was there. Floy was there. The church that had been praying for me for years was there. Jesus triumphed."[21]

The beautiful story of Rosaria's unlikely conversion demonstrates how important it is to show grace and charity in the face of opposition. It all began with Ken's gracious letter in response to Rosaria's hostile newspaper article. The tone of that letter, along with the warm friendship that followed, were the factors that God used to bring Rosaria to faith in Christ. And now as a wife and mother with a ministry to college students, she too faces hostility from an unbelieving world.

Sadly, too many believers respond to hostility with hostility in turn. But hate mail does not lead people to repentance. And it does not honor Christ. Rather, gracious forgiveness, love, and mercy are what our world needs in the face of its opposition to Jesus.

Sacrifice is Love in Action

In direct contrast to hate which takes life, love offers life. It does so by laying down one's own life and by giving life to others (1 John 3:16–17). Jesus Christ is of course the preeminent example of such love. But John does not regard

---

18. Rosaria Champagne Butterfield, "My Train Wreck Conversion," *Christianity Today* 57.1 (2013), 112.
19. Ibid.
20. Ibid.
21. Ibid.

Jesus's death simply as an *example* of love. It is for him the *definition* of love: "*This is how we know what love is*: Jesus Christ laid down his life for us" (3:16; emphasis added).

There is an apocryphal story about a medieval monk who announced he would be preaching the following Sunday evening on the love of God. Come Sunday, as the shadows fell and the light ceased to come in through the cathedral windows, the congregation gathered. In the darkness of the altar, the monk lit a candle and carried it to the crucifix. First, he illumined the crown of thorns; next, the two wounded hands; then, the marks of the spear wound. In the hush that fell, he blew out the candle and left the chancel. There was nothing else to say.

Love is defined by sacrificial giving of oneself for another. John immediately applies this point with respect to material possessions and those in need (3:17). Love is to be expressed in actions and truth (3:18). This application gives us the second of two broad ways in which we may lay down our lives for others. The first is literal: like Jesus, a person might give his or her physical life for the sake of another. The second is figurative: laying down one's life means giving something up for another. If you have material possessions but your brother or sister is in need, love will share those possessions. Love means the giver goes without something for the sake of the recipient.

Being willing to die for the sake of another is the supreme act of sacrificial love. Many Christians, I suspect, have at one time or another imagined scenarios in which they could be called upon to offer the supreme sacrifice. Perhaps in a war-conflict scenario. Perhaps pushing someone out of the way of an oncoming truck while taking its blow. Maybe drowning after saving someone else from a strong tidal current.

There may be an element of heroism in such imagined scenarios—a sense of glory as the life-saving hero. It would certainly be a good way to "go out." But the reality is not glamorous; it is frightening and tragic. Nevertheless, we ought to be properly prepared to offer our lives if and when the time comes.

The other type of laying down one's life is also demanding. Giving things up for others is not a onetime action; it is a lifelong discipline. Showing concern for the needs of others is a daily struggle against selfishness. Sustaining an interest in the welfare of others is an ongoing expression of love. While we may experience loving *moments*—when we are good at putting the needs of others ahead of our own—it is another thing to live a loving *life*. A life lived in regular and consistent service to others is only possible through the indwelling of God's love (3:17).

Sharing material possessions is offered as just one example of laying down one's life for brothers and sisters, but it is the example John chose and probably lay close to his heart. If anyone sees a brother or sister in need but has no pity on them, how can the love of God be in that person? It may be that John has the parable of the Good Samaritan in mind here (Luke 10:30–37). A man attacked by robbers and left half dead is passed over by a priest and then a Levite. But a Samaritan *took pity on him* (v. 33). The word Jesus uses here for "took pity" (*splanchnizomai*) is the same one John uses when he talks about not having pity for someone in need (*splanchnon*—Jesus uses the verb; John uses the equivalent noun). Jesus's point is that the Samaritan man is the true neighbor of the robbed and beaten man in that scenario. John's point is that a *lack* of such pity on someone in need reveals a lack of God's love in the heart.

Bob Lotich shares the following story:

> Years ago [a preacher] noticed the family standing in front of him at a New Orleans convenience store did not have enough money to pay for their few items. He tapped the man on the shoulder and said, "You don't need to turn around, but please accept this money." The man took the money without ever seeing the preacher.
>
> Nine years later, the pastor was invited to speak at a church in New Orleans. After the service, a man walked up to the preacher and shared this story about how he had come to faith in Christ: "Several years ago, my wife and our child were destitute. We had lost everything, had no jobs, no money and were living in our car. We also lost all hope, and agreed to a suicide pact, including our child. However, we decided to first give our son some food, so we drove to a convenience store to buy him some food and milk.
>
> While we were standing in line at the store, we realized that we did not have enough money to pay for these items, but a man behind us asked us to please take the money from his hand and not look at him. This man told us that 'Jesus loves you.'
>
> We left the store, drove to our designated suicide site, and wept for hours. We couldn't go through with it, so we drove away. As we drove, we noticed a church with a sign out front which said, 'Jesus loves you.' We went to that church the very next Sunday, and both my wife and I were saved that day."
>
> He then told the pastor, "When you began speaking this morning, I knew immediately that you were the man who gave us that money." How did he know? The pastor was from South Africa and had a very distinct

accent. He continued, "Your act of kindness was much more than a simple good deed. Three people are alive today because of it."[22]

Compassion, generosity, and giving are traits shared by those who truly know the love of God. His compassion and generosity toward us teach us how to love others. We consider their needs, give unselfishly, and love with actions. Who knows how God will use such expressions of love?

1 John 3:19-24

LISTEN to the Story

¹⁹This is how we know that we belong to the truth and how we set our hearts at rest in his presence: ²⁰If our hearts condemn us, we know that God is greater than our hearts, and he knows everything. ²¹Dear friends, if our hearts do not condemn us, we have confidence before God ²²and receive from him anything we ask, because we keep his commands and do what pleases him. ²³And this is his command: to believe in the name of his Son, Jesus Christ, and to love one another as he commanded us. ²⁴The one who keeps God's commands lives in him, and he in them. And this is how we know that he lives in us: We know it by the Spirit he gave us.

Listening to the Text in the Story: Matthew 25:36–40; John 14:14–16; 16:23–26.

This passage is about reassurance. John speaks of hearts at rest and of confidence before God. Believers may receive whatever they ask from God because they keep his commands. And those keeping his commands live in him, while we know he lives in us by the Spirit.

EXPLAIN the Story

We Have Reassurance before God (3:19–21)

Since the splinter group adheres to falsehoods, John seeks to reassure his readers that they are on the right side of the truth: "This is how we know that we belong to the truth . . ." (3:19). Belonging to the truth is the objective side of it, while setting "our hearts at rest in his presence" is the subjective side.[1]

---

1. Literally, "before him we persuade our heart" (*emprosthen autou peisomen tēn kardian hēmōn*), which means that our hearts are "persuaded" of the reassurance that believers have of belonging to the truth; see BDAG 792.

Objective reality and subjective comfort go hand in hand: being on the right side of truth enables believers to take comfort in the presence of God.

The reassurance comes in two parts. First, "if our hearts condemn us, we know that God is greater than our hearts, and he knows everything" (3:20a). Our hearts may "condemn us" because we struggle with sin (1:8, 10), but God is "greater than our hearts." The essence of this reassurance is that our right standing with God is not determined by our subjective feelings. God is bigger than that.[2] From love, the Father has made us his children (3:1). This means that believers can have assurance in his presence even if we experience subjective guilt.

The fact that God "knows everything" (3:20b) is a counterintuitive reassurance too. God knows about our sin, and there is nothing hidden from his view. But this is ultimately reassuring because he has brought us into his family even while knowing the full extent of our sin. There is no reason to doubt his love now that believers may have become aware of their sin; God has been aware of it from the beginning and yet still reached out to make them his children.

In the second part of his reassurance John states, "If our hearts do not condemn us, we have confidence before God" (3:21). Not everyone will struggle with the subjective feelings of guilt before God.[3] Without their hearts condemning them, their subjective experience is one of confidence. Such believers feel safe in their standing before God; they know that he has accepted them in Christ.

We Have Confidence in Petition (3:22)

Believers' confidence extends beyond status and standing before God; believers receive from God whatever they ask (3:22a; see also 5:14–15; John 14:14–16; 15:7, 16; 16:23–26). Such a statement may sound like a blank check that God will grant whatever wish believers may ask him. But the following clauses shed further light. The reason we "receive from him anything we ask" is "because we keep his commands and do what pleases him" (3:22b). While it

---

2. Other interpreters suggest that "God is greater than our hearts" means that "he ministers comfort to the individual" (Yarbrough, *1–3 John*, 211); that "the love and mercy of the Father are present to heal" (Smalley, *1, 2, 3 John*, 193); and that "it is God who will exercise judgment and apportion condemnation or praise" (Marshall, *Epistles of John*, 198). Closest to the understanding presented here is that of Jobes who writes, "Reassurance cannot come from within us, but must come from the objective truth about God and his gracious mercy that sent Jesus to the cross" (*1, 2, & 3 John*, 168).

3. Painter understands a sequential situation such that once "the accusing heart is persuaded and reassured in 3:20," the same group of people have confidence before God (3:21; Painter, *1, 2, and 3 John*, 248). While this is possible, it seems more likely that two groups are in view: those with an accusing heart on the one hand and those who already have confidence before God on the other.

may seem so at first glance, Schnackenburg rightly asserts that this "can hardly be meant to suggest the condition on which their being heard depends."[4] So what, then, does it mean?

Keeping his commands is discussed further in 3:22–23. If believers "do what pleases him," it is evidence that their wills are aligned with God's.[5] This alignment of wills is an important factor in understanding the so-called blank check that we may receive anything we ask. Confidence in petition is grounded in a believer's alignment with God's will and in the context of loving relationship. Alignment with his will can be seen in one's lifestyle, which is why confidence in petition is associated with doing what is pleasing in God's sight. Such alignment gives the believer confidence that their requests will be received favorably.

God's Command Is to Believe and Love (3:23)

While keeping God's commands (plural) is mentioned in 3:22, this is narrowed to "his command" (singular) in 3:23. This switch from plural to singular indicates that all God's commands are essentially summed up in the single command "to believe in the name of his Son, Jesus Christ, and to love one another as he commanded us" (3:23).

The *name* of Jesus Christ "represents the full significance of the person and their authority," and believing is but one aspect of believers' activities conducted *in his name* (2:12; cf. John 14:13; Acts 2:38; 4:30; 5:41; 9:27; 16:18; Eph 5:20; 2 Thess 3:6).[6] Moreover, Jesus is identified as God's Son (1 John 1:3, 7; 5:20). The sonship of Jesus emphasizes his special authority but also familial relationship. And belief in the Son (3:23; 5:1, 5, 10, 13) is an extension of belief in God himself (4:16; 5:10).[7]

But the "single" command is, in fact, two: to believe in Jesus and to love one another. By referring to the two commands as one, John shows the indispensable connectedness between believing in Jesus and loving one another. It is not possible to do one without the other. In this way, the two commands are in effect seen as one.

The two commands treated as one recalls Jesus's answer to the question as to which commandment was the greatest in the law (Matt 22:36). Jesus answers with the two greatest commandments: to love God and to love one's neighbor (22:37–40). Yet here in 1 John 3:23, the "two commands" are to *believe* in Jesus and to love one another. What, if anything, should we make of this?

---

4. Schackenburg, *Johannine Epistles*, 188.
5. Stott, *Letters of John*, 153.
6. Lieu, *I, II, & III John*, 158.
7. Brown, *Epistles of John*, 463.

It is possible that John implies that the right way to *love* God is to *believe* in his Son. Acceptance of and faith in Christ is the mark that someone truly knows and loves the God who is revealed in Christ. And just as loving God and loving neighbor go together, so believing in Jesus and loving one another must go together.

We Live in Him and He in Us (3:24)

John concludes this section about reassurance in a relational way: "The one who keeps God's commands lives in him, and he in them" (3:24a). We have already seen that God's commands are to believe in Jesus and to love one another. The one who does so has assurance of mutual indwelling with God (see on 2:5b–6).

To live "in him" is the ultimate reassurance of right relationship with God. There is no possible closer intimacy with God available for human beings than to be in him and he in us. To share in such a relationship of mutual indwelling with God is the highest privilege we may know. It is therefore the strongest affirmation of assurance that John can offer his readers. All who believe in Jesus and love one another indwell God and are indwelt by him.

And this indwelling of God relates to our keeping his commands. Believers are not simply to perform God's will for love but to *participate* in it. On this, Macaskill comments, "Imitation of Christ in love is not a naked act of moral achievement, but a conscious and dynamic participation in God's love for the world."[8] Keeping God's command to love flows out of our mutual indwelling with him.

If our mutual indwelling with God is assured by keeping his commands, it is also confirmed in a more affective way: "And this is how we know that he lives in us: We know it by the Spirit he gave us" (3:24b). This is the first of six explicit references to the Holy Spirit in the letter (3:24; 4:2, 6, 13; 5:6, 8). The relatively few references sit in stark contrast to the major role of the Spirit in John's Gospel, as does the fact that in 1 John the Spirit is only found in contexts of discerning the truth or witnessing to the truth.[9] Nevertheless, the Spirit living in the believer *is* God living in the believer since the Spirit is the third person of the Godhead. So the Spirit's presence is direct proof (if proof were needed) that believers enjoy God's indwelling them.

John will continue in the next chapter to explore how believers may recognize the true Spirit of God. But for now, we can conclude that any evidence of the Spirit's presence in a person is proof of his or her genuine status as a

---

8. Grant Macaskill, *Union with Christ in the New Testament* (Oxford: Oxford University Press, 2013), 269.

9. Jobes, *1, 2, & 3 John*, 170–71.

believer. God lives in them as they live in him. In such a way, believers know they belong to the truth; their hearts are persuaded of their good standing before God, and they enjoy confidence in their beloved status.

LIVE the Story

Reassurance

There is nothing quite like reassurance in the face of fear or doubt. To know that you are accepted—to know that you are loved and can rest assured—gives tremendous freedom and peace. It enables us to delight in our relationship with God and frees us from the nagging feeling that things might not be quite right with him. Armed with confident assurance, we are better able to love and serve others.

Yet many believers struggle on in their Christian lives without such reassurance. They may know that their status with God is given to them through Christ, but secretly they harbor thoughts that they might be disqualified somehow. Some may even preach the assurance of salvation to others and yet suspect that they themselves will miss out. Just as assurance leads to freedom and peace, a lack of assurance can cripple believers. It can prevent them from flourishing in faith and can in fact pull them further away from a true knowledge of God as Father.

John Donne, the English poet and preacher, wrote of his struggle with assurance in his poem *A Hymn to God the Father*. He asks if God really will forgive his past sin, his current sin, and the sin he has allowed to linger. In the third stanza, Donne acknowledges a "sin of fear," referring to his lack of assurance. The poem concludes, however, with his fear alleviated. His fear "is no more" because God has sworn that "at my death thy Son shall shine as he shines now." The promise of God in Christ gives final confidence to Donne even in the face of his persistent sin. It is a beautiful poem that speaks volumes to those who, like Donne, may struggle with assurance of salvation.

A Hymn to God the Father

> Wilt thou forgive that sin where I begun,
>   Which was my sin, though it were done before?
> Wilt thou forgive that sin, through which I run,
>   And do run still, though still I do deplore?
> When thou hast done, thou hast not done,
>   For I have more.
> Wilt thou forgive that sin which I have won
>   Others to sin, and made my sin their door?

Wilt thou forgive that sin which I did shun
    A year or two, but wallow'd in, a score?
When thou hast done, thou hast not done,
    For I have more.
I have a sin of fear, that when I have spun
    My last thread, I shall perish on the shore;
But swear by thyself, that at my death thy Son
    Shall shine as he shines now, and heretofore;
And, having done that, thou hast done;
    I fear no more.
    John Donne (1572–1631)

The apostle's affirmation that "God is greater than our hearts" is a wonderful source of assurance. Just as Donne realizes in his wrestle with assurance, our confidence before God comes down to *who God is*. He is greater than our hearts. He is bigger than our subjective feelings of self-condemnation. Our status depends on his promise to us in Christ Jesus ("swear by thyself"), not on how we feel. Having come to terms with that fact, Donne can rest assured and "fear no more."

Belief and Love

The commandment that pleases God is to believe in Jesus and love one another (3:23). The pairing of these two requirements is not accidental but reflects a deep understanding of how belief and love go together.

The apostle Paul famously says that "if I have a faith that can move mountains, but do not have love, I am nothing" (1 Cor 13:2). Of course, Paul would not even suggest that love is a *substitute* for faith—faith is absolutely necessary!—but his point is that faith *without* love is not enough. He is *nothing* without love, even if he has great faith. Love is, then, the essential partner to faith.

Indeed, the constant refrain throughout 1 John is that a lack of love is evidence of a defective faith. Since love comes from God (4:7), "whoever does not love does not know God, because God is love" (4:8). We will explore the relationship between knowing God and loving others below, but here the focus is on believing in the name of Jesus and loving one another.

Just as it is not possible to know God without loving, it is not possible to believe in the name of Jesus without loving. But why is this so? In part it is because of the example that Jesus sets, as we see below at 4:9–10. To understand Jesus's death for our sins as an act of sacrificial love is to learn the true nature of love, which by its very nature compels us to reach out to others in love.

But believing in Jesus also changes our view of the world. Jesus teaches us that we are not the center of the universe. There are higher priorities than our own well-being and sense of satisfaction in life. Jesus teaches us that the kingdom of God is bigger and better than our own little kingdoms. True life, then, is to live in the kingdom of God with Jesus as our king. And since the priorities of the king involve serving others, these priorities must also become ours.

In other words, Jesus profoundly shapes our worldview, and a requirement of that Jesus-shaped worldview is that we must love one another. Once our view of life and our role in the world is seen in a Jesus-shaped way, nothing can remain the same. Instead of living for ourselves, we must live for others. Instead of being consumed by self-love, we lovingly seek the good of others. Belief in Jesus shapes our love.

There is nothing like a crisis to reveal what people really believe. The tragedy of the *Titanic* was therefore very revealing. One of the victims of the *Titanic's* catastrophic sinking was a pastor by the name of John Harper, whose story is recorded by Moody Adams in the book *The Titanic's Last Hero*.

Harper led a vibrant Baptist church in London and was traveling to Chicago to preach for several weeks at Moody Church, where his preaching the previous year had been highly successful. A widower, he was on board the *Titanic* with his six-year-old daughter Annie Jessie and sister Jessie Leitch. When the *Titanic* hit an iceberg on the night of 14 April 1912, he was able to put his daughter and sister on lifeboat eleven. Before putting his little daughter on the lifeboat, he knelt down, kissed her, and told her that she would see him again someday. With his loved ones safely away, Harper returned to the deck of the *Titanic*, yelling, "Women, children, and unsaved into the lifeboats!" As the ship began to break into two, Harper jumped into the icy, dark waters along with many others.

That night 1,528 people went into the water. John Harper was seen swimming to people in the water trying to lead them to Jesus before it was too late. He swam up to one young man who was clinging to some debris. Harper asked him if he was saved; the young man was not. He tried to lead the young man to Christ, but the man refused. So Harper took off his life jacket and threw it to the young man, saying, "Here, you need this more than I do," and he swam to other people. A few minutes later he returned to the young man, but this time was successful in leading him to Christ. Of the multitude in the water that night, only some were rescued. The young man was one of them.

In Hamilton, Ontario four years later, this survivor recounted how John Harper had led him to Christ. He saw him swimming to help other people.

And before succumbing to the frigid waters, Harper's last words were, "Believe on the name of the Lord Jesus and you will be saved."[10]

It is an amazing, little-known story about courageous faith in a moment of great crisis. Not only did John Harper's actions that night prove the depth of his belief in the name of the Lord Jesus, but his actions were marked by *love*. He saw that people needed saving—not from the waters but from their sins. He spent his last moments lovingly sharing the good news of Jesus with the lost, though he could have escaped to safety on lifeboat eleven with his beloved daughter.

Harper's worldview had been profoundly changed by belief in Jesus, and his worldview required him to love others. His example is a wonderful illustration of how believing in the name of Jesus Christ and loving others go hand in hand.

10. Moody Adams, *The Titanic's Last Hero: A Startling True Story That Can Change Your Life Forever* (Greenville, SC: Ambassador International, 2012), chapter one.

LISTEN to the Story

¹Dear friends, do not believe every spirit, but test the spirits to see whether they are from God, because many false prophets have gone out into the world. ²This is how you can recognize the Spirit of God: Every spirit that acknowledges that Jesus Christ has come in the flesh is from God, ³but every spirit that does not acknowledge Jesus is not from God. This is the spirit of the antichrist, which you have heard is coming and even now is already in the world.

⁴You, dear children, are from God and have overcome them, because the one who is in you is greater than the one who is in the world. ⁵They are from the world and therefore speak from the viewpoint of the world, and the world listens to them. ⁶We are from God, and whoever knows God listens to us; but whoever is not from God does not listen to us. This is how we recognize the Spirit of truth and the spirit of falsehood.

Listening to the Text in the Story: Deuteronomy 13:2–6; John 12:31; 14:30; 16:11; Ephesians 2:2.

Having appealed to the presence of the Spirit as an indicator of the believer's assurance (3:24), John now turns to discuss "spirits." Not every spirit is from God, so caution is required here. There is, however, a simple test to recognize the Spirit of God: proper acknowledgment of who Jesus is and where he is from. Any spirit that fails this test is not from God but is the spirit of the antichrist.

The second half of the passage addresses the fact that true believers overcome these antichrist spirits because the Spirit from God is greater than they are. In conclusion, another test is offered that involves listening to the apostolic teaching: those who listen have the Spirit of truth; those who do not listen have a spirit of falsehood.

EXPLAIN the Story

Not Every Spirit Is from God (4:1–3)

Since the indwelling Holy Spirit is one of the proofs that a believer lives in God (3:24), it is important to realize that not every "spirit" is from God and discernment is therefore required. Yarbrough points out that "spirits" (*pneumata*) are generally regarded negatively in the New Testament, being associated with evil (Matt 12:45; Luke 11:26; Acts 19:12–13), uncleanness (Mark 3:11; 5:13; Acts 8:7), false prophecy (Rev 16:13), and demons (Rev 16:14), but there are also some positive references in which "spirits" are angels sent by God (Heb 1:14).[1] John warns his readers, "Do not believe every spirit."[2] Instead, they are to "test the spirits to see whether they are from God" (4:1a).

Before telling his readers how to test the spirits, John adds they are to do so "because many false prophets have gone out into the world" (4:1b). John implicitly correlates spirits that are not from God with these false prophets. Apparently false prophets are somehow "powered" by ungodly spirits. John does not explain the nature of interaction between the spirits and false prophets, but that there is such an interaction is regarded as self-evident. The presence of false prophets clearly demonstrates the fact that there are spirits who have not come from God. These "false prophets" are the heretical teachers in view for much of the letter. They are called false prophets here "because a prophet is one who speaks in the Spirit of God, and these seducers falsely claim to be filled with the Spirit."[3]

Fortunately, there is a simple test to recognize the Spirit of God. Any spirit that acknowledges "that Jesus Christ has come in the flesh is from God, but every spirit that does not acknowledge Jesus is not from God" (4:2–3a). There is no need for alarm at the fact that John seems to refer to the Holy Spirit in the plural ("every spirit that acknowledges that Jesus Christ has come in the flesh is from God"). In 4:2a he clearly refers to *the* Spirit of God (*to pneuma tou theou*). The following phrase "every spirit that acknowledges that Jesus Christ has come in the flesh" points to the recognition of the Spirit at work in each believer. An extended paraphrase might be: "The spirit at work in the

---

1. Yarbrough, *1–3 John*, 220–21.
2. The negated present imperative (*mē panti pneumati pisteuete*, "do not believe every spirit") does *not* mean that John's readers already believed every spirit (Huffman, *Verbal Aspect Theory and the Prohibitions in the Greek New Testament*, 31–58). Some commentators make such a claim based on an inaccurate understanding of negated imperatives (e.g., Painter, *1, 2, and 3 John*, 256). Rather, the present imperative indicates a general instruction: in situations in general, they are not to believe every spirit. See Campbell, *Verbal Aspect and Non-Indicative Verbs*, 91–94.
3. Schnackenburg, *Johannine Epistles*, 199.

believer who acknowledges that Jesus Christ has come in the flesh is proved to be the Spirit from God." Just as ungodly spirits inspire the belief and confession of the false prophets (4:1), so the Spirit of God inspires the belief and confession of genuine believers.[4] As such, true confession of Christ is evidence that the "spirit" at work in a person is *the* Spirit.

Kruse rightly affirms that the Spirit's role is seen primarily as testimony to the apostolic tradition and not as a source of new revelation. Against the backdrop of secessionism that claimed inspiration from the Spirit, John "felt that it was necessary to hold together the word and the Spirit"; "it was necessary to stress the Spirit's role as witness to the truth of the gospel concerning Jesus as it was proclaimed from the beginning."[5]

The Spirit confirms the apostolic testimony about Jesus. But what exactly does it mean "that Jesus Christ has come in the flesh"? Many scholars have seen this as combatting docetism (the belief that Jesus was God but not truly human),[6] or both docetism *and* Jewish Christians who happily affirm Jesus's humanity but do not think he is a divine being.[7] According to Brown, however, the issue is more soteriological than christological so that John opposes the denial "that what Jesus was or did in the flesh was related to his being the Christ, i.e., was salvific."[8] Likewise, Schnackenburg sees here an allusion to Jesus's death, drawing on the language of Jesus's "flesh" in John 1:14 and 6:51,[9] and de Jonge points to the *atoning* death of Jesus in particular (cf. 1 John 2:2; 4:10).[10]

De Boer argues that Jesus Christ come in the flesh is "*primarily* a claim about the death of Jesus Christ and refers only *secondarily* to his humanity as such, instead of the other way around."[11] He regards Jesus's coming as his saving mission, while "in the flesh" refers to the instrumentality of his own flesh. In support of this claim, the context stresses the death of Jesus Christ (3:16; 4:7–11).[12] It is probably correct to see the death of Jesus, *and his resurrection*,[13] as at least bound up with the notion of Jesus coming in the

---

4. Kruse draws a connection here to Deut 13:2–6 in which a prophet who predicts the future or performs miraculous signs "while urging people to go after other gods must not be heeded" (see also Didache 11:7–8); Kruse, *Letters of John*, 147.

5. Kruse, *Letters of John*, 155.

6. See the introduction to 1 John.

7. Smalley, *1, 2, 3 John*, xxiii–xxvi, 223.

8. Brown, *Epistles of John*, 505.

9. Schnackenburg, *Johannine Epistles*, 201.

10. Marius de Jonge, *Jesus, Stranger from Heaven and Son of God: Jesus Christ and the Christians in Johannine Perspective* (Missoula, MT: Scholars Press, 1977), 205.

11. Martinus C. De Boer, "The Death of Jesus Christ and His Coming in the Flesh (1 John 4:2)," *NovT* 33 (1991): 330 (emphasis original).

12. Ibid., 346.

13. So Jensen, *Affirming the Resurrection*, 158–70.

flesh. Whether his death and resurrection constitute the *primary* meaning here is unimportant. Jesus's person and work must go together; his atoning death and resurrection become meaningless if he were not truly human, and denial of his saving work makes his humanity pointless. The false prophets are found false either way.

By the same token "every spirit that does not acknowledge Jesus is not from God" (4:3a). This is the simple corollary of the previous point (4:2b), but John adds more information about such a spirit: "This is the spirit of the antichrist, which you have heard is coming and even now is already in the world" (4:3b). This is the third and final time that John speaks of "the antichrist" (2:18, 22). Previously he asserted that in fact many antichrists had already come (2:18), and anyone who denied that Jesus was the Christ was such an antichrist (2:22).

In 4:3, however, the focus is on the *spirit* of the antichrist. As we saw in 4:1–2, John draws a connection between what people confess and what spirit is in them. Clearly someone who is an antichrist has an antichrist spirit. Just as anyone who denies that Jesus is the Christ is an antichrist (2:22), so any spirit that does not acknowledge Jesus is a spirit of the antichrist (4:3).

The One in You Is Greater Than the One in the World (4:4–6)

While believers are to test the spirits, they are not to fear them. John's readers are "from God" and "have overcome them" (4:4a).[14] The reason believers overcome these spirits is "because the one who is in you is greater than the one who is in the world" (4:4b). Their confidence is grounded in the "one who is in you," which must refer to the Spirit of God.

While "the one who is in the world" might seem to refer to one of the "spirits" John has just warned about (i.e., "the Spirit in you is greater than the spirit that is in the world"), Jobes correctly notes that the masculine article (*ho*) does not match the neuter noun "spirit" (*pneuma*). This "one who is in the world" is then most likely the "prince of this world," the devil (John 12:31; 14:30; 16:11).[15] Nevertheless, the devil is elsewhere known as a spirit (e.g., Eph 2:2), and so may be counted as one of the godless spirits after all.[16] John assures his readers, then, that the Spirit in them is greater than the devil.

---

14. It is possible to translate *nenikēkate autous* as "you overcome them," which points to a general state of affairs rather than an already accomplished event (i.e., "you have overcome them"; cf. Smalley, *1, 2, 3, John*, 215). See Campbell, *Basics of Verbal Aspect*, 106–7. Given that the false spirits are still a problem for John's readers, it makes sense not to read the Greek perfect as an already accomplished event.

15. Jobes, *1, 2, & 3 John*, 182.

16. Brown, *Epistles of John*, 498.

So Hilary of Arles (ca. AD 401–49) comments, "God's power to save is always much greater than the devil's power to do harm."[17]

Next John adds, "They are from the world and therefore speak from the viewpoint of the world, and the world listens to them" (4:5). While he had just been speaking of spirits and of the devil in particular, it appears now that John has switched to *people* influenced by the spirits. They are from the world and speak from the world. Given the close association between spirits and people in this passage, the abrupt switch from one to the other is not odd.

The "world" in Johannine usage normally refers to rebellious humanity (see on 2:2, 15). So these spirit-inspired, worldly people speak in accordance with the world's values (lit., "from the world," *ek tou kosmou*), and thus it is little wonder that "the world listens to them." The world listens to those who promote its values.

John and his readers, however, are "from God" (4:6a; *ek tou theou*), not the world. Just as the world listens to people from the world, so "whoever knows God listens to us." And, therefore, "whoever is not from God does not listen to us" (4:6a). The test in this half of the passage, then, involves people's response to John's teaching, which represents the apostolic witness.[18] If they "listen to us," they are from God. If they do not listen, they are from the world.

But then John brings the passage full circle by returning to the testing of spirits: "This is how we recognize the Spirit of truth and the spirit of falsehood" (4:6b). The Spirit of truth is seen at work in those who listen to people from God, while the spirit of falsehood is seen at work in those who listen to people from the world.

Putting this all together, then, we see that John's readers may "test the spirits" by their true confession of Christ and their adherence to apostolic teaching. Anyone who rejects the apostolic witness about Christ has been influenced by the spirit of falsehood, the spirit of the antichrist.

LIVE the Story

False Spirits and False Prophets

It is a sad reality that not everyone who claims to speak for God is really from him. Even in John's day, many false prophets had gone out into the world; the same is no doubt true today. They are false prophets because their

---

17. Hilary of Arles, "Introductory Commentary on 1 John," in *Patrologiae Latinae Supplementum*, ed. A. Hamman (Paris: Garnier Frères, 1958–), 3:123.

18. Dodd, *Johannine Epistles*, 100, 103–5.

accreditation is false: the spirit of the antichrist, who does not acknowledge that Jesus Christ has come in the flesh from God, is the power behind such prophets. Rather than being accredited by the true Spirit of God, these false prophets speak falsely in line with their accrediting false spirit.

In the 1980s it was estimated that around ten-thousand physicians in the United States had phony foreign medical degrees. In one case, a congressional panel was told that a broker of fraudulent diplomas, Pedro de Mesones, had accrued $1.5 million by providing these fake credentials for willing buyers. According to Congressman Claude Pepper of Florida, many American citizens may have received medical treatment from doctors and nurses who lied on their medical-school loan applications and used the money to pay a broker for fake documents rather than go to school. Pedro de Mesones, who served a three-year sentence for mail fraud and conspiracy, told the congressional panel that in three years of "expediting" medical degrees, he provided a hundred clients with false transcripts that showed they had fulfilled medical training at schools they had not attended. He admitted that "clients paid me from $5,225 to $27,000 for my services," earning the $1.5 million over three years. "I only got to keep about $500,000 of this total. The rest went for bribes and expenses."[19]

That's a scary thought! Imagine entrusting yourself to a "physician" who was no physician at all. You put your health—indeed, your life—in the hands of someone you thought you could trust, but it turns out they are no more qualified than you. Or worse, imagine entrusting the care of a loved one—a child, a spouse, an elderly parent—into the hands of someone like that. It is a reprehensible falsehood that can bring dire consequences upon innocent people.

How much worse is the false prophet? The person who claims to speak for God but is in fact a fraud can do immeasurable damage. For it is not our physical health at risk but our spiritual well-being. Just as the false physician could cause the death of a patient, so the false prophet can bring spiritual death. Anyone who comes under the spell of such a false prophet risks their eternal fate—and indeed the fate of their loved ones who may follow suit.

In John's day, it was clear that anyone who did not acknowledge that Jesus Christ came from God, in the flesh, was under the influence of a false spirit. But that test could be expanded for today's situation. A false prophet may be identified by other beliefs. Of course, someone who gets their Christology drastically wrong—such as in John's day—will reveal themselves to be false. But there are other types of false prophets too.

---

19. "10,000 Doctors Are Fakes," *The Spokesman-Review*, December 8, 1984.

For example, those who teach that God will make all his people healthy and wealthy in this life speak falsehood. They teach that if you lack health and wealth there must be something defective about your faith, since God blesses the faithful with everything they desire. This insidious lie seems ignorant of the teaching of the New Testament, which, if anything, promises *persecution* to those who desire to live a godly life in Christ Jesus (2 Tim 3:12). Yes, there are many blessings to be had in the Christian life, but there is certainly no promise from God that the faithful will be granted an easy, comfortable life. Perhaps such false prophets think that John's faith must have been defective since he spent time in exile on the isle of Patmos. Not to mention the apostle Paul with all his persecutions and sufferings. Let alone Jesus!

This is just one example of teaching and leadership that is not accredited by the true Spirit of God. It is, instead, "accredited" by a false spirit. And in keeping with all such false teachings, the prosperity gospel can destroy faith since those with genuine faith are led to question why God has allowed suffering into their lives and has not provided the prosperity that this false message promises. Conversely, those who lack genuine faith can be fooled into thinking that they are right with God because they currently enjoy good health and wealth. We must be diligent in identifying such false prophets and false teaching empowered by false spirits. The health of the church depends on it.

Overcoming the World

John encourages his readers that they are from God and have overcome these false prophets who speak from the viewpoint of the world. The world listens to the false prophets, but those who are from God listen to the truth.

John paints a stark antithesis between the viewpoint of the world and God's vision of reality. This antithesis is one that believers need to be reminded of daily. Since we live in the world (but are not *of* the world), it is our constant temptation to interpret reality according to the norms, attitudes, and values of the world. Instead, we must be reminded of God's truth—of his values and intention for humanity.

The so-called prosperity gospel is again a good example. The world desires health and wealth with freedom from suffering and pain. Thus, this false gospel is aligned to the values of the world, promising present-time deliverance from all that is wrong with the world. God's intention for us, however, is that we persevere through the world's hardships with confident reliance upon him. He does not promise health and wealth in this life; instead, the believer's experience will be marked by suffering and persecution. While God *will* one day deliver us from the sufferings of this life, the prosperity gospel claims the blessings of the future now. In this way, it misses the biblical pattern that suffering comes before glory. Like Christ we are to trust God through suffering, knowing that God will deliver his people in the end.

There are many other such examples that illustrate the stark difference between the world's perspective and God's. Another might involve leadership. All too commonly the world's perspective is that leadership is desirable in order to increase one's status and power. Positions of influence and power are often pursued for all the wrong reasons. But God's truth teaches that leadership is primarily about the *service of others*. Leadership is to be self-sacrificial, putting the interests of others ahead of one's own. Authority is given for the sake of this responsibility, not for the self-aggrandizement of the leader. The leader is not to be privileged and glorious; the leader is to be last of all.

A final example can be seen with identity. While the world chases money, success, fame, and pleasure as a means to secure an identity and some sense of meaning in life, God's truth teaches a radically different perspective. Identity is not found in such things but in knowing God and being known by him. As a child of God, loved with an everlasting love, a believer's identity is secure in Christ. We do not need the treasures of this world to increase our worth or to know who we are. We are richly blessed already in the Spirit with an eternal inheritance to come and an eternal relationship with God our heavenly Father.

These examples and more demonstrate the difference between the world's way of seeing things and God's way. Those who are from God listen to his truth and are not persuaded by false prophets. False prophets speak from the world's perspective and will entice those who enjoy the ways of the world. But those from God listen to the apostolic testimony that is empowered by the true Spirit of God.

LISTEN to the Story

⁷Dear friends, let us love one another, for love comes from God. Everyone who loves has been born of God and knows God. ⁸Whoever does not love does not know God, because God is love.

⁹This is how God showed his love among us: He sent his one and only Son into the world that we might live through him. ¹⁰This is love: not that we loved God, but that he loved us and sent his Son as an atoning sacrifice for our sins. ¹¹Dear friends, since God so loved us, we also ought to love one another. ¹²No one has ever seen God; but if we love one another, God lives in us and his love is made complete in us.

¹³This is how we know that we live in him and he in us: He has given us of his Spirit. ¹⁴And we have seen and testify that the Father has sent his Son to be the Savior of the world. ¹⁵If anyone acknowledges that Jesus is the Son of God, God lives in them and they in God. ¹⁶And so we know and rely on the love God has for us.

God is love. Whoever lives in love lives in God, and God in them. ¹⁷This is how love is made complete among us so that we will have confidence on the day of judgment: In this world we are like Jesus. ¹⁸There is no fear in love. But perfect love drives out fear, because fear has to do with punishment. The one who fears is not made perfect in love.

¹⁹We love because he first loved us. ²⁰Whoever claims to love God yet hates a brother or sister is a liar. For whoever does not love their brother and sister, whom they have seen, cannot love God, whom they have not seen. ²¹And he has given us this command: Anyone who loves God must also love their brother and sister.

Listening to the Text in the Story: Exodus 33:20; John 3:16; Ephesians 2:4–5; 5:1–2.

This long and complex passage is unified around the exhortation to love one another and is the third major section of the letter dedicated to that theme (see also 2:9–11; 3:11–18). The passage is bracketed by the first and last paragraphs, both of which begin with the exhortation "let us love" (4:7, 19) and ground this exhortation in the knowledge and love of God, respectively.

The body of the passage is structured by four "this is how . . ." statements (4:9, 10, 13, 17; *en toutō*, lit., "in this"). The first two of these deal with the love of God ("the love of God is revealed *in this*," v. 9; "*in this* is the love of God," v. 10). The third occurrence returns to the theme of assurance of being in God and vice versa (v. 13). The fourth combines the two themes of love and assurance (v. 17).

The structure, then, of the passage is as follows: introduction—let us love one another, for love comes from God (vv. 7–8); since God loved us we ought to love one another (vv. 9–12); in this we know he lives in us (vv. 13–16); in this love is made complete among us (vv. 17–18); conclusion—let us love, for he first loved us (vv. 19–21).

The overall message of the passage is an exhortation to love because love is from God. If believers truly *know* God, they will love others. If they truly *love* God, they will love others. Without love, so-called believers are shown to be false brothers and sisters and do not know or love God.

EXPLAIN the Story

Let Us Love One Another, for Love Comes from God (4:7–8)

John once again exhorts his "dear friends" (*agapētoi*) to "love one another" (*agapōmen allēlous*; 4:7a). While John has already instructed his readers to love one another several times, this is the first time he has indicated the source of love: "For love comes from God." Though John has appealed to the example of Jesus in his laying down his life for us as "how we know what love is" (3:16), even there he does not explicitly state the *source* of love. The source of all love is God.[1]

Since love comes from God, the expectation to love one another ought to be self-evident. Thus, "everyone who loves has been born of God and knows God" (4:7b). If love comes from God, then those who are "born of God" must also love. Love is the family likeness.[2]

And since love comes from God, those who love also know God. In fact "whoever does not love does not know God, because God is love" (4:8). Here

---

1. "Love originates in God and thus belongs to the divine dimension" (Smalley, *1, 2, 3 John*, 226).
2. On the theme of being born of God, see the commentary on 2:29 (cf. 3:9; 5:1, 4, 18).

John takes it a step further. Not only is God the *source* of love, but he *is* love. And in this way we see why God is the source of love: love flows out of his essential being.

To say "God is love" (see also 4:16) is to make a profound statement about the nature of God.[3] It is an absolute claim that goes well beyond treating love simply as one of God's attributes like, say, mercy or grace. God is merciful, yes, and he is gracious, to be sure. But the Bible never says, "God *is* mercy" or "God *is* grace."[4] And what is the difference between saying "God is love" and "God loves"? Dodd insightfully contrasts these two statements:

> The latter statement might stand alongside other statements, such as "God creates," "God rules," "God judges"; that is to say, it means that love is *one* of His activities. But to say "God is love" implies that *all* His activity is loving activity. If He creates, He creates in love; if He rules, He rules in love; if He judges, He judges in love. All that He does is the expression of His nature which is—to love.[5]

The statement "God *is* love" puts love on a whole different level with respect to understanding who God is. Love is so central to God's character that it is predicated of him. He *is* love. And love therefore characterizes all of his activities. God's creating, ruling, judging, revealing, instructing, blessing, disciplining, giving, rebuking, sustaining, and re-creating are all done in love. There is nothing God does that does not emanate from his loving nature.

Any view of God that does not appreciate the centrality of his love must therefore be deficient. To understand him as primarily angry or judgmental is to distort the reality. Yes, God does dispense wrath in judgment, but it is important to acknowledge that this is his "alien task" (Isa 28:21). Judgment does not define him at the core; it does not reveal his central identity. His central identity is love. Only by knowing his love can God himself be understood and known. Since love is so central to who God is, true knowledge of God simply must understand him as love. If he is not known as love, he is not known at all.

Furthermore, the person who does not love cannot know God, for to know him is to know love. The absence of love reveals a lack of knowledge of God. If God is love and if that love is known, then his love will flow through the life of the believer. To know God is to know love, and to know love is to show love. Without showing love there is no knowing love and there is no knowing God.

---

3. See Schnackenburg's excursus, "Love as the Nature of God" (*Johannine Epistles*, 210–16).
4. Though John *does* say that "God is light" (1 John 1:5) and "God is Spirit" (John 4:24).
5. Dodd, *Johannine Epistles*, 110.

Since God Loved Us We Ought to Love One Another (4:9–12)

Because God is love, love comes from God. And the preeminent expression of God's love is seen in Jesus: "This is how God showed his love among us:[6] He sent his one and only Son into the world that we might live through him" (4:9). Jesus laying down his life is "how we know what love is" (3:16), and now we see that this gift of life through the death of Jesus is the demonstration of God's love for us. God loved the world by giving his one and only Son (John 3:16).[7] Given the obvious parallel here with John 3:16, the phrase "that we might live through him" (4:9b) most likely refers to eternal life, as the former verse explicitly states.[8] Believers will live forever through Jesus Christ and what he has accomplished for us.

In this is love:[9] "Not that we loved God, but that he loved us and sent his Son as an atoning sacrifice for our sins" (4:10). While believers are expected to love God (4:21), God's love for us is prior and primary. It is *prior* in that it precedes our love for God; his action toward us in Christ is what makes it possible to be "born of God," thus enabling us to be *for* him rather than *against* him in line with the world's hostility. God's love is also *primary* in that no love for God is possible at all without the foundation of God's love for us. That is why love must be defined as *God's* love for us rather than *our* love for him. Our love will follow, but it can do only that—*follow*.

As in 2:2, Jesus is described as an atoning sacrifice, or propitiation (*hilasmos*), "for our sins" (4:10).[10] It is not simply the sending of his Son that expresses God's love; Jesus is sent for the propitiation for our sins. Correlated with the previous verse, we see that this is how eternal life is achieved for believers: by Jesus's atoning death for their sins, believers are granted eternal life rather than facing the just penalty for their sins. Here we see the love of God at its most acute point: he sent Jesus to die for us, bearing the penalty for sin himself, that we might escape its penalty and have eternal life.

Now John returns to the original exhortation: "Since God so loved us, we also ought to love one another" (4:11). The phrase "since God so loved us" literally means "since God *thus* loved us" or "since God loved us *in this manner*."[11] God's love is expressed in a deeply sacrificial way that puts the needs of others

---

6. This is the first of four "in this" statements (see the introduction to this passage).

7. As Kruse demonstrates in his helpful note on the subject, *monogenēs* is correctly rendered "one and only," not "only begotten" (*Letters of John*, 158–59).

8. Brown, *Epistles of John*, 518.

9. This is the second "in this" statement.

10. See the commentary on 2:2 for more discussion about the word *hilasmos*.

11. *ei houtōs ho theos ēgapēsen hēmas*. The word translated "so" (*houtōs*) literally means "thus" or "in this manner" (BDAG 741). Cf. John 3:16.

first. Jesus died for us, and *in this manner* God's love is revealed. As such, we also ought to love one another. As seen in 3:18, our love is also to be expressed in sacrificial action rather than only with words or speech. Yarbrough's comment is poignant: "Christ's costly propitiatory atonement uncaps an artesian well of selflessness in which believers find resources for sacrificial care for each other."[12]

The conclusion of this section includes the somewhat curious phrase "no one has ever seen God" (4:12a). Likely an allusion to Exodus 33:20 ("You cannot see my face, for no one may see me and live"), the invisibility of God raises the question of whether God can truly be known. But John resolutely answers that question in the remainder of 4:12: "But if we love one another, God lives in us and his love is made complete in us." In other words, God *can* be known, though he cannot be seen. He can be known by love. If believers show love one to another, "God lives in us." There is no closer human relationship with God than his indwelling within us (cf. 3:24). God is truly known through intimate relationship, and love for one another is the proof of his presence since he *is* love.

Furthermore, God's love is "made complete in us" when we love one another (4:12b).[13] This does not mean that his love is somehow incomplete unless believers love each other. It means, rather, that God's love comes to full fruition *in our lives* when we love others. It is the "in us" that is the emphasis here. By loving one another, God's love is manifested in us.

The two ideas found in 4:12b set the course for the following two segments: God living in us is addressed in 4:13–16, and his love being made complete is explored in 4:17–18.

In This We Know He Lives in Us (4:13–16)

Having raised the topic of God living in us, demonstrated by our love for one another (4:12), John now moves to address it more fully (4:13): "This is how[14] we know that we live in him and he in us: He has given us of his Spirit." Very similar to the parallel of 3:24, the notion of the Spirit's indwelling is again explored.

After the parallel of 3:24, John began a discussion about testing the spirits to enable his readers to confirm that it was God's Spirit who was in them (4:1–3). In 4:14–15 he cuts straight to the conclusion reached earlier: "We have seen and testify that the Father has sent his Son to be the Savior of the

---

12. Yarbrough, *1 3 John*, 240.

13. "God's love" could be rendered "our love for God" (*hē agapē autou*), but Marshall is probably correct that "when we love others, God's love for us has reached its full effect in creating the same kind of love as his in us" (*Epistles of John*, 217).

14. This is the third "in this" statement.

world. If anyone acknowledges that Jesus is the Son of God, God lives in them and they in God."[15] While the formulation is different from that of 4:1–3, the basic point is the same: the Spirit of God testifies truly as to who Jesus is.[16] The Father has sent his Son to be Savior of the world; Jesus is the Son of God.

Thus, Spirit-inspired true confession about Jesus ensures that "God lives in them and they in God" (4:15). Mutual indwelling connects 4:15 back to 4:12–13, and 4:16 connects back to the theme of love: "And so we know and rely on the love God has for us." And so we see that John has not left the overarching theme of love; mutual indwelling is part of that package.

John says we "know" and "rely on" (or "trust," *pepisteukamen*) God's love (4:16). God's love is to be known, and it is to be trusted. As Jobes comments, "Knowing that truth calls us to trust in it."[17] If it is truly known, the believer will be led to rely fully upon God's love, since his love is the foundation upon which all Christian hope is built. It is the only cause for confidence on the day of judgment and is the source of our eternal life.

John now repeats his profound statement about the nature of God: "God is love" (4:16b; cf. 4:8). And the following comment draws together all we've seen so far: "Whoever lives in love lives in God, and God in them" (4:16c; cf. 4:12b). The one who lives in love must experience mutual indwelling with God, since God *is* love.

In This Love Is Made Complete among Us (4:17–18)

The final segment of the main body of this passage (before the passage's conclusion in 4:19–21) returns to the notion of love being made complete (4:17–18; cf. 4:12b): "This is how[18] love is made complete among us so that we will have confidence on the day of judgment: In this world we are like Jesus" (4:17). While connecting to 4:12b, these verses also connect further back to the theme of assurance in 3:19–24. Confidence on "the day of judgment" (4:17a) looks forward to the believer's good standing before God on the last day, as does its parallel—setting our hearts at rest "in his presence" (3:19).

Love is made complete among us—thus offering confidence on judgment day—by being like Jesus in this world (4:17b). Identifying Jesus here is an interpretation of the context, since the text literally says, "Just as that one is,

---

15. Note the parallel of seeing and testifying in 1:2. Here in 4:14 John is much more specific about the content of the witness.
16. "Within this letter the role of the Spirit is always related to the truth about Jesus Christ" (Kruse, *Letters of John*, 163).
17. Jobes, *1, 2, & 3 John*, 197.
18. This is the fourth and final "in this" statement.

so are we in the world."[19] The interpretation is likely correct since Jesus is the one "sent into the world" by his Father (4:9).[20]

Judging by the wider context, being "like Jesus" means to demonstrate love in action.[21] This is the burden of 3:16–18: Jesus laid down his life for others, and so we ought to do the same. So again we see that love lived out is what makes the love of God complete among believers. In this instance, it is further reason for assurance in the face of God's judgment.

In this respect, "there is no fear in love" (4:18a). Believers hold no fear for the day of judgment because "perfect love drives out fear" (4:18b). While "perfect love" sounds like God's love for us,[22] here it most likely refers to our love for one another (see 4:18c).[23] It is better translated, "complete love" or "mature love" (*hē teleia agapē*), which would show its connection to believers' love being made complete (*teteleiōtai hē agapē*; 4:17). Complete love drives out fear because love gives assurance in the face of judgment (4:17), and "fear has to do with punishment" (4:18b). Since believers will not face punishment at the judgment day, there is no place for fear.

Thus John can conclude this segment with the claim that "the one who fears is not made perfect in love" (4:18c). The one who fears has not had their fear driven out by mature love, and without mature love for one another there is no ground for the confidence promised in 4:17. And so it turns out that fear in the face of judgment stands as evidence that the believer's love has yet to be made mature.

Let Us Love, for He First Loved Us (4:19–21)

The conclusion of this passage ties together the main elements of the whole. It begins with the exhortation that the passage opened with: "Let us love" (4:19). While translations generally take the verb *agapōmen* as an indicative ("we love") it is better in the context to take it as a hortatory subjunctive ("let us love").[24] Not only does this parallel the subjunctive in 4:7 (which has the exact same form), but it fits the entire thrust of the passage, which is to exhort believers to love one another.

The exhortation is grounded in God's prior and primary love for us (as it is in the introduction to the passage, 4:7–12): "Let us love, because he first loved

---

19. *kathōs ekeinos estin, kai hēmeis esmen en tō kosmō toutō.*

20. So Brown, *Epistles of John*, 529, 561. This could, however, be another instance of John's deliberate ambiguity in which he does not wish to distinguish clearly between Father and Son.

21. Brown, *Epistles of John*, 561.

22. So Yarbrough, *1–3 John*, 261–62.

23. Brown aptly comments, "There is probably continuity with the theme of love that has run through the unit: an outgoing love that comes from God, is manifested in Jesus, gives us life, and remains in us actively manifesting itself in love of others and of God" (*Epistles of John*, 530).

24. Schnackenburg, *Johannine Epistles*, 225. No doubt the presence of the pronoun *hēmeis* confuses the issue, since in English "we let us love" (*hēmeis agapōmen*) does not make sense. But this is a problem of trying to understand Greek syntax through English translation, which is never helpful. The pronoun is simply emphatic here: "Let *us* love."

us." The love of God contains within it an "ought" for its recipients: anyone who knows God's love must, in turn, love others.

This is so clearly true that the negative is also true: "Whoever claims to love God yet hates a brother or sister is a liar" (4:20a; cf. 2:9–11). God is love (4:7, 16), so the one who claims to love God (who *is* love) cannot at the same time hate. According to John, a person can only be a lover or a hater; they cannot be both. The claim, therefore, to love while also hating must be false.

In 4:20b John implies that loving someone they can see (their brother or sister) is easier than loving someone unseen (God): "Whoever does not love their brother and sister, whom they have seen, cannot love God, whom they have not seen." Not seeing God relates back to 4:12, which implies that his invisibility raises the question of whether God can be known (see the commentary on 4:12). Here the invisibility of God implies some kind of difficulty in relationship. Given this, the person who does not show love the easier way (toward people they can see) will not be able to love the harder way (toward God, who they cannot see).[25]

Finally, John concludes the passage with the fitting reminder: "He has given us this command: Anyone who loves God must also love their brother and sister" (4:21). By this stage of the argument, it is clear that this is not simply a command that can be followed by pure volition. It is actually impossible to love God without loving brother and sister. Anyone who does not love others cannot love God. In this way, the command of 4:21 is as much a statement about reality as it is an imperative. Anyone who loves God *must* also love their brother and sister.

First John 4:7–21 is the third of three major sections addressing the importance of love among believers. It is arguably the most important of the three and offers the most penetrating theological thinking about love. The love of God is the foundation, source, and motivation of all human love. God's example of love in sending his Son as a propitiation for our sins that we might live has set the example that believers must follow. Since God *is* love, it is not possible to know or love him and not love others. Knowing and loving the God who is love means that believers will by necessity relate to others in this God-like way. And it is by loving others that we know that we live in God and he in us, and may have confidence on the day of judgment.

 LIVE the Story

God Is Love

It is impossible to overestimate the significance of God's love. God *is* love, as John says (4:8). This means that love defines who God is, and it is therefore

25. Smalley, *1, 2, 3 John*, 251.

impossible to know God without understanding his love. Sadly, many people do not fully realize the extent or nature of God's love. They find themselves thinking of God more along the lines of judge, as holy, as ruler. Of course God *is* judge; he is holy; he is ruler of all. But the way John speaks about God's love puts it over everything else—God *is* love. How would our relationship with him be transformed if we came to understand more fully his character and nature as *love*?

If knowing God is to know him as love, what is the nature of this love? In 4:9–10 we read one of the clearest descriptions of this love: it is revealed by God sending his Son that we might live through him, the propitiation for our sins. This tells us that God's love is sacrificial, and it is proactive.

God's love is sacrificial. To send his Son as a propitiation for our sins is the most costly gift God could offer. God's beloved, one and only Son had enjoyed perfect harmonious relationship with his Father through all eternity. There was never a time when Father, Son, and Spirit had not lived together in perfect, fulsome relationship. For the Son to leave his heavenly place alongside the Father and to suffer in his human life, humiliating persecution, and cruel death on a cross was the most sacrificially loving act in all history. It was the sacrificial love of Jesus that led him to endure the cross, but it was also the sacrificial love of his Father who sent him to do so.

Sacrificial love is love in action. It is not mere sentiment or emotional attachment. It is love that considers the need of another and seeks to meet it, even if at great personal cost. God's love for us is exactly this kind of thing. It is not admiring sentiment or emotional attachment to his creatures; it is a deep commitment to our well-being that comes at huge cost to him. Our need was to receive life, and Jesus died to secure it. And this is all the more remarkable when we remember that prior to receiving life, our hearts were set against God—we were his enemies.

God's love is also *proactive*. It does not wait to be roused into action; proactive love takes the first step. God is not passive in any sense of the word but rather sees what needs to be done and takes the steps towards its accomplishment. The proactive nature of God's love is the very reason that our salvation is by grace. He did not wait for rebellious humanity to take the first step toward reconciliation. Indeed, as the apostle Paul says, we were spiritually dead in our transgressions and sins, unable to reach out to God and unable to please him (Eph 2:1–3). It is because of God's love for us that he made us alive with Christ (Eph 2:4–5).

Part of John's exhortation to love is the fact that God first loved us (4:19). Not only does love comes from God (4:7) and God *is* love (4:8, 16), but it is also important to note that he took the first step. He proactively sought us, came to us in Christ, and reclaimed us in love.

Love Reveals That We Know God

Since God is love and love comes from God, believers are to love one another (4:7a). Everyone who loves has been born of God and knows God (4:7b). It is important to know that God is love if we are to know God truly. But John goes further: we only really know God if we also love one another. That is, true knowledge of the God who is love is to do likewise. We simply have not genuinely apprehended the love of God if it has not caused us to likewise love. The nature of this radical, sacrificial love is *affective* and *effective*. That is, we receive it with joyful gratitude (it affects us), and it causes us to love others (it effects love). As far as John is concerned, we only truly know God's love if it has not only *affected* us, but also *effected* love from us. Thus if we fail to love, we do not know God (4:8).

Ernest Gordon spent three years in a Japanese prisoner camp during the Second World War. In his famous book *Miracle on the River Kwai*, he recounts the story of how these Scottish soldiers were forced to build a railroad through the jungle.[26] Understandably, their morale and behavior had degenerated through this experience of hardship.

Gordon tells of a remarkable incident that occurred one day while they labored on the jungle railroad. The officer in charge had become enraged upon discovering that a shovel was missing. He demanded that the missing shovel be produced. Nobody in the squadron owned up to having stolen the shovel. The officer pulled his gun and threatened to kill them all right there and then if the shovel was not recovered. The prisoners of war had no doubt that the threat would be carried out.

Then, one man stepped forward. The officer put his gun away, picked up a shovel, and beat him to death. After removing the corpse, a second count of the shovels was conducted, and it was discovered that, in fact, no shovel had been missing. There had been a miscount. An innocent man had presented himself to die for the sake of the others.

The event had a profound effect among the prisoners of the camp. Their degenerated behavior gave way to brotherhood. Each man began to respect, love, and care for one another. When at last the war came to an end, the Allies swept through the region and set the prisoners free, turning the table on their captors. Though the Japanese had been excessively cruel to these men, the former prisoners stood before them without retribution in their hearts. Instead of exacting vengeance upon their former oppressors, the men insisted that there would be no more hatred. No more killing. They recognized that what was needed was forgiveness.

This remarkable incident illustrates two points. First, the man who sacrificed himself showed genuine love toward his brothers. He laid his life down

---

26. *Miracle on the River Kwai* (Glasgow: Collins, 1965).

that they might live. No greater love has a man than he lay down his life for his friends (John 15:13), and this demonstrates the kind of love with which God loves us. It is costly, sacrificial love extended for the benefit of another. Second, the event transformed the other men who had been saved by this loving sacrifice. Sacrificial love had affected them and effected love in their hearts for one another. The love with which they were loved took effect in their own lives and led them to love in the same way, which could be seen in the forgiveness of those who had so brutally oppressed them.

When we receive the awesome, sacrificial love of God, it transforms us. We cannot go unchanged by it. This is why love is the mark of someone who truly knows God; since God so loved us, we also ought to love one another (4:11).

Love Reveals That We Live in God and He in Us

The transformative nature of God's love is such that John can claim "whoever lives in love lives in God, and God in them" (4:16c; cf. 4:12b). It is not enough simply to acknowledge that God's loves changes us, causing us to love others in the manner in which God loves. No, the one who lives (lit., "remains") in love lives in God and God in them (4:16c). Love is evidence of an actual, relational indwelling between God and his people. It is the sure confirmation that such a relationship really does exist with God. If God is love and we live in love, then we live in God.

According to John, there is simply no way to avoid the conclusion that without love we are not related to God. In the absence of love we have not been born of him, do not know him, and do not live in him. Love is an essential ingredient in the DNA of God's children. Without love we can no more be God's children than spaghetti Bolognese can exist without Bolognese sauce. Spaghetti Bolognese without Bolognese is an oxymoron, as is God's children without love.

Sadly, the history of the church is riddled with examples of people who claim to know God and serve him and yet have acted in less than loving ways toward others, even others within the church. Significant leaders within the institutional church[27] have failed the test of love in catastrophic ways. I am not talking about the occasional failure to love, which is later met with repentance and growth. I'm talking about people who have displayed deliberate, unrepentant, unloving behavior toward others.

Just as sadly, the church has been guilty of failing to address such failures of love. Peter Hollingworth was the Anglican Archbishop of Brisbane, Australia during the years 1989–91. He was the 1991 Australian of the Year. In 2001 he was appointed Governor-General of Australia, the representative of Australia's monarch, Queen Elizabeth II. In December 2001, however, claims

---

27. I use this term here to avoid claiming that such people belong to the true church of Christ.

were made that Hollingworth had overlooked church sex-abuse allegations during his time as Archbishop of Brisbane.

Hollingworth's successor in Brisbane, Archbishop Phillip Aspinall, ordered an inquiry into these allegations, and it was found that Hollingworth had allowed a known pedophile to continue working as a priest. To make matters worse, Hollingworth was forced to issue a public statement on May 8, 2003, denying allegations that he had raped a woman in the 1960s. In the wake of these scandals, on May 11, 2003 Hollingworth stood aside as Governor-General, and on May 28 his commission as Governor-General of Australia was revoked. In 2015 Hollingworth apologized to abuse victims for not pursuing their allegations more rigorously, but the damage had long been done.

There are several layers of sadness to these turns of events. First, leaders in the church committed sinful, depraved acts of abuse against innocent children. Second, the man in authority over these leaders failed to bring about justice and failed to protect those under the care of the church. Third, the church's failure to deal with sin within its ranks became a national disgrace. Fourth, the standard of ethics in secular government were seen to be higher than those within the church. It is shameful when those who claim to know God act in such unloving ways.

God lives in those who love, and he does not live in those who fail to love. A person may claim to be a follower of Christ but fail to love. Someone may even occupy a significant position of leadership within the church, but without love God is not in them. John's diagnostic for true spirituality is simple and effective: love is the key.

CHAPTER 12

1 John 5:1–12

 LISTEN to the Story

¹Everyone who believes that Jesus is the Christ is born of God, and everyone who loves the father loves his child as well. ²This is how we know that we love the children of God: by loving God and carrying out his commands. ³In fact, this is love for God: to keep his commands. And his commands are not burdensome, ⁴for everyone born of God overcomes the world. This is the victory that has overcome the world, even our faith. ⁵Who is it that overcomes the world? Only the one who believes that Jesus is the Son of God.

⁶This is the one who came by water and blood—Jesus Christ. He did not come by water only, but by water and blood. And it is the Spirit who testifies, because the Spirit is the truth. ⁷For there are three that testify: ⁸the Spirit, the water and the blood; and the three are in agreement. ⁹We accept human testimony, but God's testimony is greater because it is the testimony of God, which he has given about his Son. ¹⁰Whoever believes in the Son of God accepts this testimony. Whoever does not believe God has made him out to be a liar, because they have not believed the testimony God has given about his Son. ¹¹And this is the testimony: God has given us eternal life, and this life is in his Son. ¹²Whoever has the Son has life; whoever does not have the Son of God does not have life.

Listening to the Text in the Story: Matthew 3:13–17; Mark 1:9–11; Luke 3:21–22; John 1:32–34; 11:25; 14:6.

While several commentators take 5:1–3 or 5:1–4 with the previous passage,[1] 5:1–5 is here understood as the first part of the conclusion to the letter. There are obvious links to 4:7–21, which is why commentators include it with that passage, but there are also links to various other elements of the letter. It is in fact the most comprehensive summary of the teaching of 1 John that the letter

---

1. E.g., Jobes (4:7–5:3), Brown and Kruse (4:7–5:4a), Lieu and Smalley (4:7–5:4), and Marshall (4:13–5:4).

offers. The second part of the passage (5:6–12) also returns to a key theme of the letter but expands on it in an emphatic manner: God's testimony about his Son is absolutely critical (5:6–9). The third and final part of the passage focuses on one's response to God's testimony about his Son. The one who accepts this testimony will believe in the Son, and the one who believes has eternal life.

While there are some concluding affirmations to follow in 5:13–21, this passage is the proper conclusion of the argument of the letter. It reiterates the letter's teaching about belief that Jesus is the Christ and about being born of God, loving God and his children, keeping God's commands, and overcoming the world. It also emphasizes God's testimony by the Spirit as to who Jesus is and the eternal life he has given us.

EXPLAIN the Story

The One Who Believes Overcomes the World (5:1–5)
The conclusion begins by reiterating that "everyone who believes that Jesus is the Christ is born of God" (5:1a). The criteria of belief in Jesus's identity as the Christ is raised in 2:22 (negatively) and 4:15 (where "Son of God" is messianic). And the notion of being born of God is raised in 2:29–3:2, 3:9–10, and 4:7.[2] But here the two concepts are brought together. Belief that Jesus is the Christ is evidence that someone is born of God.

While some argue that the verb tenses of "believes" (*ho pisteuōn*) and "is born" (*gegennētai*) in 5:1a indicate that being born of God (i.e., *regeneration*) logically *precedes* faith,[3] others argue against taking the verbs in this way.[4] Both positions miss John's point, however, which is *evidential*. Belief that Jesus is the Christ is evidence of rebirth, and that is the important point for John since proper belief in Jesus is what demarcates those who belong to God and those who do not. John's concern is not to establish a theological *ordo salutis* that posits regeneration prior to faith. That does not mean that this verse opposes that theological position, but it is not what John has in view.

Furthermore, "everyone who loves the father loves his child as well" (5:1b). While "his child" could refer to Jesus (since it is literally "the one born of him," *ton gegennēmenon*; cf. 5:18), the next verse clarifies that John means

---

2. The commentary on these passages addresses what it means to be born of God.
3. E.g., John Piper, *Finally Alive: What Happens When We Are Born Again* (Ross-shire: Christian Focus, 2009), 118; Matthew Barrett, "Does Regeneration Precede Faith in 1 John?," *Mid-America Journal of Theology* 23 (2012): 5–18.
4. E.g., Brian J. Abasciano, "Does Regeneration Precede Faith? The Use of 1 John 5:1 as a Proof Text," *EvQ* 84 (2012): 307–22.

other believers.[5] Love for God is raised in 2:5, 15; 3:17(?); 4:10 (negatively), and 4:20–21. Love for others is seen in 2:9–11; 3:10–12, 16–18; 4:7, 11–12, 21. The correlation between love for God and love for others is seen in 3:16; 4:11, and 4:20–21. As indicated in that last reference, loving God *must* result in love for brothers and sisters. "Loving one another is a sign of how much we love God."[6]

While love for others is evidence of love for God, here John flips it the other way also: "This is how we know that we love the children of God: by loving God and carrying out his commands" (5:2). The kind of love for others that is required of believers is determined by love for God. Loving God and living his way is the sure sign that believers will rightly love others.[7] This is because God is love, and our love comes from him, but it is also what we need from each other. We need to be encouraged by others' love for God. Our love for him helps others to love him better. And so love for God is a key component in loving others.

Speaking of loving God and keeping his commands, John now equates these two concepts: "In fact, this is love for God: to keep his commands" (5:3a). The commands of God are previously understood as love for one another (2:7–11; 3:23; 4:21) and to believe in the name of Jesus Christ (3:23). As argued in the commentary on 3:23, believing in the name of Jesus fulfills the greatest commandment to love God with all one's heart. Consequently, the commands of God in 1 John are to love God (by trusting in Jesus) and to love one another.[8]

In this way John is able to claim that "his commands are not burdensome" (5:3b), because "everyone born of God overcomes the world" (5:4a). Someone who is truly born of God will share the family likeness and will therefore love as the Father loves. Moreover, such a person overcomes the world since love is the chief distinguishing factor between the children of God and those of the devil (3:10).

Such love is produced by genuine faith, which makes believers children of God, and is therefore "the victory that has overcome the world" (5:4b).[9] In other words, the faith of believers is what overcomes the world, and it produces love, which distinguishes believers from the world. As overcomers, those born of God are able to love as the Father loves. All of this means that we are able to keep God's commandments, which require love.

---

5. Jobes, *1, 2, & 3 John*, 208.
6. Theophylact, *Commentary on 1 John* (PG 126:57).
7. Kruse, *Letters of John*, 171–72.
8. Schnackenburg, *Johannine Epistles*, 228–29.
9. The NIV may be confusing here, using the phrase "even our faith" (*hē pistis hēmōn*) at 5:4b where the Greek clearly means that our faith *is* the victory that has overcome the world. A clearer translation would be, "This is the victory that has overcome the world—our faith."

This is the only place in the Johannine Epistles that overcoming "the world" is addressed, though the idea of overcoming occurs in two others places. In 2:13–14 the "young men" John addresses are twice said to have overcome the evil one ("I am writing to you, young men, because you have overcome the evil one"). And in 4:4 John says that believers have "overcome them," referring to the false teachers who are powered by the spirit of the antichrist (cf. 4:2–3). Overcoming "the world" is therefore the broadest sphere of overcoming; the evil one is a force within the world, and the false teachers also belong to the world.

What does it mean then to "overcome the world"? While the word "overcome" translates the Greek *nikaō*, which generally means to "conquer, overcome, prevail" (BDAG), John's meaning is not about conquering anybody. It is, rather, about successfully living God's way rather than succumbing to the whims and priorities of a rebellious world. God's way is love and requires belief that Jesus is the Son of God. By loving God and others and by believing in God's Son, believers transcend the debased values of the world.

The first half of this passage concludes by tying the theme of overcoming the world with the original notion of belief in Jesus: "Who is it that overcomes the world? Only the one who believes that Jesus is the Son of God" (5:5). This makes perfect sense given that faith *is* our victory over the world.

The Spirit, Water, and Blood Testify That Jesus Is the Son of God (5:6–9)

The second part of the letter's conclusion contains some of the most confusing and debated verses in the entire epistle. The key questions revolve around what is meant by "water" and "blood" (5:6) and what it means that water, blood, and Spirit testify in agreement (5:7–8).[10]

Before attempting to resolve these issues, however, we should note the main thrust of the passage, which will help to disentangle some of the difficulties of interpretation. The passage is clearly concerned with testimony about Jesus (5:9). There are two elements to this testimony. First, "God has given us eternal life" (5:11a), and "this life is in his Son" (5:11b). So whatever conclusions are reached about the interpretative problems of the passage, its overall meaning is not in doubt.

John states that Jesus Christ "came by water and blood" (5:6). We will not explore all of the exegetical possibilities here, but there are there main options: (1) "water and blood" refer to Jesus's baptism and crucifixion respectively; (2)

---

10. Some late manuscripts add the so-called Johannine Comma here: "In heaven: the Father, the Word, and the Holy Spirit. And these three are one. And there are three who testify on the earth." The King James Version popularized this reading, but it only appears in eight Greek manuscripts (four times as an alternate reading). All eight manuscripts date later than AD 1400. The Johannine Comma is not quoted by any of the church fathers. See Culy, *I, II, III John*, 127.

they both refer to Jesus's crucifixion, since John (alone) records the outpouring of water and blood from Jesus's side when a soldier pierced his side with a spear (John 19:34); (3) the terms refer to Jesus's birth and death.[11]

There are three main clues for sorting through the options. First, whatever the water and blood refer to, Jesus is said to have *come* through them (5:6a). Second, John stresses that Jesus came not "by water only, but by water *and blood*" (5:6b), drawing special attention to the significance of coming by blood. Third, the water and the blood testify alongside the Spirit, so the Spirit's role may help in adjudicating the matter. We will work through these three clues in turn.

First clue. What does it mean that Jesus Christ "*came* by water and blood" (5:6a)? If the water and blood refer to (1), Jesus's baptism and crucifixion, then his *coming* by these things would seem to indicate the entrance into his public ministry (baptism) and his becoming Savior of the world (crucifixion). If the water and blood refer only to (2), Jesus's crucifixion, his *coming* by them would indicate his becoming Savior of the world, though it is not clear why water is mentioned since blood alone could establish the point. If the water and blood refer to (3), Jesus's birth and death, it would establish his coming into the world and his becoming Savior. This first clue makes option (2) a little more difficult than options (1) and (3).

Second clue. Why does John draw special attention to the blood (5:6b)? If the water and blood refer to (1), Jesus's baptism and crucifixion, this would highlight the importance of Jesus's becoming Savior through his death. If the water and blood refer only to (2), Jesus's crucifixion, perhaps the emphasis on the blood infers the sacrificial nature of his death (as a blood sacrifice for sin). If the water and blood refer to (3), Jesus's birth and death, then we come to the same result as option (1)—his becoming Savior is emphasized.

Third clue. In what sense do the water and blood testify alongside the Spirit? The "Spirit is the truth" (5:6c) and is no doubt what is meant by "God's testimony" (5:9). If the Spirit offers "God's testimony," then the water and the blood may constitute a "human" testimony or they witness to Jesus's humanity. This fits all three options, though it probably fits option (3) best. If the water and blood point to Jesus's birth and death, then they powerfully testify to Jesus's genuine humanity.

However, there is one final point to consider. There is a close association of Jesus's water baptism and the Spirit in all the Gospels, and John the Baptist's (human) testimony of Jesus is that he "saw the Spirit come down from heaven

---

11. There is also a sacramental view in which water and blood refer to baptism and the Eucharist, an incarnational view in which *both* water and blood refer to Jesus's birth, and the view that equates "water" with the Holy Spirit. On the first two of these (as well as those included in the main text), see Brown, *Epistles of John*, 575–78; on the third, see Jobes, *1, 2, & 3 John*, 219–21.

as a dove and remain on him" and "I have seen and I testify that this is God's Chosen One" (John 1:32, 34). While John's Gospel does not explicitly record Jesus's baptism, John's testimony accords with the scene recorded in Matthew 3:13–17, Mark 1:9–11, and Luke 3:21–22. The baptism is also a testimony of the Spirit, since he descended on Jesus and remained on him. In this sense, Jesus's baptism represents a clear moment of "testimony," which fits the context of 1 John 5:6–9 very well.

Putting all this together suggests that option (1) is stronger than the other two. The water and blood signify Jesus's baptism and death.[12] Through these events, Jesus *comes*—he enters his ministry through baptism and he enters his role as Savior through death. He not only ministered (water), but came through baptism *and death* (blood). The water and blood testify that Jesus came to serve and die for humanity, while the Spirit testifies that he is God's divine Son.

Whoever Believes God's Testimony about His Son Has Eternal Life (5:10–12)

Now that John has established the testimony of the three witnesses to Jesus— the water, the blood, and the Spirit—he turns to apply the point. Focusing especially on God's testimony, one's response to his testimony about his Son is the decisive factor for life.

Acceptance of God's testimony about his Son—which is greater than human testimony (5:9)—is the key to the truth about Jesus: "Whoever believes in the Son of God accepts this testimony" (5:10a). One cannot believe truly in Jesus if God's testimony is unacceptable to him or her. This is the ultimate test as to who the true believer is: the one who takes God's own word for who Jesus is.

Negatively, "whoever does not believe God has made him out to be a liar, because they have not believed the testimony God has given about his Son" (5:10b). To reject the sonship of Jesus is to reject God himself, since he has testified to the sonship of Jesus by the Spirit.

While the nature of this testimony has been left vague to this point, John now defines it clearly: "And this is the testimony: God has given us eternal life, and this life is in his Son" (5:11). This is a broad summary of the matter: eternal life is found in Jesus. The one who believes the truth about the Son finds the key to eternal life. Bound up in this true belief are the various

---

12. So Yarbrough, *1–3 John*, 282–83; Kruse, *Letters of John*, 177–78; Marshall, *Epistles of John*, 231–32; Painter, *1, 2, and 3 John*, 304–6; Schnackenburg, *Johannine Epistles*, 232; Stott, *Letters of John*, 179–82; D. A. Carson, "The Three Witnesses and the Eschatology of 1 John," in *To Tell the Mystery: Essays on New Testament Eschatology in Honor of Robert H. Gundry*, ed. Thomas E. Schmidt and Moisés Silva, JSNTSup 100 (Sheffield: JSOT Press, 1994), 216–32.

elements of truth about Jesus that have been expounded throughout the letter: that Jesus's blood purifies us from all sin (1:7), that he is our advocate with the Father (2:1), that he is the propitiation for our sins (2:2; 4:10), that he is the Christ (2:22), that he destroys the devil's work (3:8), that he laid down his life for us (3:16), that he has come in the flesh (4:2), and that he is the Son of God (4:15; 5:5). These things tell us who the Son is and that eternal life is found in him.

To "have" the Son or not to have the Son is the ultimate question, for "whoever has the Son has life; whoever does not have the Son of God does not have life" (5:12). This binary choice brings supreme clarity to the whole situation. Having the Son is the essential point. This language of "having" the Son is dependent upon belief in him, as the parallel John 3:36 makes clear: "Whoever believes in the Son has eternal life, but whoever rejects the Son will not see life, for God's wrath remains on them." To believe in the Son is to "have" the Son. And to have the Son is to have eternal life since, as Stott points out, "The Son is the life (1:2; John 11:25; 14:6)."[13]

The theological conclusion to 1 John draws in the key strands of teaching in its first paragraph (5:1–5), reinforces the truth by appeal to God's testimony (5:6–9), and brings sharp clarity to the final situation: eternal life depends on whether or not one "has" the Son through belief in God's testimony (5:10–12).

 LIVE the Story

Loving God and His Children

John asserts that "everyone who loves the father loves his child as well" (5:1). The "child" of God is "everyone who believes that Jesus is the Christ" since such a person is "born of God" (5:1; see on this verse above). Thus if one loves God, one will also love those to whom God has given new birth—all genuine believers in Jesus.

The colloquial expression, "Any friend of yours is a friend of mine," bears an interesting connection to the sentiment of 5:1. The expression conveys relational strength between two people to the point that it extends to a third party, even if that person is unknown to the speaker. That is, the friendship between two people is so strong that one friend is willing to accept their friend's friend as their own friend. The saying conveys strength of friendship but also a tacit endorsement of the friend's judgment. The friend's friend is accepted on the basis of *their* friendship.

---

13. Stott, *Letters of John*, 186.

This dynamic also pertains to family relationships. A child may enjoy the benefits of his or of her parents' friendships. There is sometimes a shady side to this when, for example, a son or daughter is given preferential treatment in employment or advancement because of who his or her parents are. But there is also a wonderfully positive side to this. The strength of the parents' friendships blesses the child relationally. A family friend becomes a surrogate uncle or aunt and takes a special interest in the children of their friends.

Indeed, genuine friendship will take into account the friend's children. I am interested in my friends' children because I care about my friends. Their children are the most important people in my friends' lives, so how could I be their genuine friend without sharing an interest in their kids? Some of my friends are godparents to my children, as I am to theirs. That in itself expresses the point well: the strength of our friendship overflows to our children.

I also experienced this dynamic as a child, benefiting from the friendships between my parents and their friends. One special example is my relationship with Ross and Margie Mills, who are longtime friends of my parents. Ross knew my parents when I was born, and I got to know him, Margie, and their kids when I was a teenager. Their friendship with my parents brought them into my life, and over time they became special friends of my own. In fact, the Mills family became a second family to me when I lived at boarding school for a year. On weekends I would stay with the Mills family, and they treated me like a son. We developed our own bond, but it all began through Ross and Margie's friendship with my parents. I was drawn into their friendship and blessed by it.

In a similar fashion, to love the Father is to love his child as well. Genuine love for God will extend to those to whom he loves as children. Just as we ought to care for the children of our close friends, so we ought to care for the children of the God we claim to love. As John so often reiterates, if we fail to love our brothers and sisters we do not really know God or love him.

Overcoming the World

John says that everyone who believes that Jesus is the Christ is born of God and will love God's children (5:1), and the one who believes that Jesus is the Son of God overcomes the world (5:5). As mentioned above, overcoming the world does not mean *conquering* or *defeating* the world. It means to successfully live God's way rather than to succumb to the whims and priorities of a rebellious world.

This is a tremendously encouraging assurance that John holds out for believers in Jesus when the vicissitudes of the Christian life can be discouraging from time to time or for a season. Sometimes believers feel that they are not getting anywhere in their battle against the flesh; we struggle to be diligent in prayer, and we are often sucked into the priorities and attitudes of the world around us. The process of growth and maturity in faith is not a straight line up; it often seems to progress by two steps forward, one step back.

But John assures us that "everyone born of God overcomes the world" (5:4). Whatever our subjective experience may tell us, we will ultimately overcome. John does not mean that we will find ourselves in a state of uncompromised freedom from the trappings of the world. But neither is our overcoming purely future referring as though we will only really overcome the world at the eschaton. No, "the victory that has overcome the world" is our faith (5:4b). That is, our faith has *already* overcome the world. This is because faith in Jesus stands at odds with the default inclination of the world—to believe is to cut against the grain. If genuine faith in Jesus exists in this world, it exists *contrary* to the world—it exists in rebellion against the inclination of the world. Perhaps we could even say that faith is rebellion against a rebellious world.

While faith has already overcome the world by its very existence, it produces its fruit in our lives over time. The love that faith in Jesus brings may not instantly appear, like a magic trick. Faith grows love, just as it grows obedience, prayer, and knowledge of God. In this sense, our overcoming has begun but is not complete. While John can say that our *faith* has overcome the world, our faith-driven lives are in the process of overcoming. The reality of our Christian experience is catching up to the already-victorious reality of our faith. Our faith in Jesus brings about our new birth into God's family, and we are growing up into the family likeness like infants learning to walk.

Overcoming is assured because we *are* in God's family. We do not belong to the world any longer, and though we may walk like infants, our belonging to the family of God is fully determinative. It determines our ultimate allegiance and our ultimate destiny. We are with him; we are not with the world. No, we overcome the world.

Eternal Life Depends on the Testimony of God

God testifies that he has given us eternal life, and this life is in his Son (5:11). Eternal life in and through the Son of God is of course a major theme of 1 John, but the key thrust of 5:6–12 concerns God's *testimony* to that fact. God's testimony is greater than human testimony (5:9), and whoever believes in Jesus accepts his testimony (5:10).

Such a focus on God's testimony is an interesting feature of this part of 1 John. It speaks to the reliability of God and to the assurance that believers may have regarding eternal life. The notion of overcoming is also related to assurance (see above), but here the ground for assurance is the very witness of

God. He has given eternal life in his Son. This gift is promised, and the gift can therefore be counted on.

John Wilmot (1647–80), Earl of Rochester, was a poet at the court of King Charles II. Known for his irreverence and satire, he once penned a teasing epitaph for Charles that read,

> Here lies a great and mighty king
> Whose promise none relies on;
> He never said a foolish thing,
> Nor ever did a wise one.[14]

To which Charles replied, "This is very true: for my words are my own, and my actions are my ministers'."[15]

While the epitaph was meant in jest, it expresses a sad truism that our leaders often do not act as they speak. Charles is said to have "never said a foolish thing"—high praise, indeed—but unfortunately "nor ever did a wise one." His deeds did not live up to his words. Thus his promise "none relies on."

We may applaud noble promises offered in good faith, but if we learn that the promise-maker is unable to make good on such promises, we are no better for it. A promise becomes an empty platitude—at best it is the expression of noble intent, but the one who promised lacks the power to execute it.

King Charles's reply is equally predictable. He takes credit for his good words but blames others for his failure to enact them. It is easy to imagine a well-intentioned president expressing his desire to effect change while complaining that Congress has hamstrung his efforts.

German Chancellor Angela Merkel recently met the same kind of political resistance, even from her own ministers in the Christian Democratic Union. Her willingness to accept Syrian refugees in the wake of terrible civil war helped earn her a nomination for a Nobel Peace Prize and the distinction of being *Time's* Person of the Year. Driven by moral conviction, Merkel's open-door policy was an openhearted gesture in the face of humanitarian tragedy, but the political realities have hamstrung her efforts.

Pressure from the political right, including allies within the CDU, led her to drastically decrease the number of refugees entering Germany, signaling a compromise to critics of her open-door policy. The huge influx of refugees has been enormously unpopular in Germany, with conservative critics predicting that this issue will lead to the end of Merkel's political career.

---

14. John Wilmot, Earl of Rochester, "The King's Epitaph," cited in *The Oxford Dictionary of Quotations*, ed. Elizabeth Knowles, 5th ed. (Oxford: Oxford University Press, 2001), 302.

15. Ibid.

All too often it seems that leaders either have good will but not the power to enact it, or bad will and all too much power to enact it. God, however, testifies that his promise can be trusted. The gift of eternal life is not an empty platitude. God's intent is noble, *and* he has the power to fulfill it. Whoever believes in his Son has received God's gift of eternal life, since life is in his Son (5:11). If life is *in* Jesus, God's promise of life is offered securely because he has given us his Son. The promise of God is good and effective.

But the question is, will we take God at his word? After all, whoever believes in the Son of God accepts God's testimony, while anyone who does not believe God has made him out to be a liar (5:10). We may have become conditioned to look upon bright promises with a degree of cynicism, but we must not regard God's promise with such contempt. He is not like people who cannot keep their word. His promise is sure, and we are bound to trust him.

John's readers are in a position of having to trust in God's promise in a time of trial. That's the point of this reassurance; whatever may happen in this world, whatever sufferings, whatever trials may befall us, we know that God has given us eternal life in his Son. We can trust the gift because we can trust the giver. We can trust the promise because we can trust the one who issued it.

Whoever Has the Son Has Life

True life through the Son of God is a major theme of the letter, but here in 5:12 we find a particularly strong summary statement of it: "Whoever has the Son has life; whoever does not have the Son of God does not have life." John is fond of black-and-white dichotomies, and this is one of his starkest examples. The strength of the statement leaves no room for confusion: life is found in the Son, and without the Son there is no true life.

Such clarity stands out in today's climate. We are generally not fond of drawing sharp lines, of being defined by others, or of being put in a box. Western culture currently prefers some degree of ambiguity with various shades of gray to simple black-and-white thinking. Within the church this can be true too. Preachers who draw sharp boundaries are sometimes labeled fundamentalists, or their preaching might be characterized as hellfire and brimstone. We might prefer a message with softer edges that are less likely to cause offense.

But John will have none of that. There is a clear boundary; there is a sharp edge; there is black and white. And all of this revolves around the Son of God. The believer who has him has life—it is as simple as that. And whoever does not have him does not have life. That truth is painfully simple too.

A Wheaton College professor recently made national headlines for saying that Muslims and Christians worship the same God. The professor was put on administrative leave for her comment, and after a public and complicated resolution process she eventually left Wheaton. It has been interesting to observe how polarizing this event has become both inside and outside the church. Not surprisingly, secular commentary has championed the professor's statement and reviled Wheaton's response to it. What is more surprising is the mixed reactions from within the church. Some prominent theologians, such as Miroslav Volf, have spoken out against Wheaton in support of Dr. Hawkins. Others have supported Wheaton's action because it seems obvious that Christians and Muslims do not worship the same God.

Perhaps there is a discussion to be had about what we mean by "the same God" and what it means to "worship" such a God, especially as it pertains to mission among Muslim worshippers (cf. Acts 17:23).[16] Notwithstanding those questions, it is nevertheless clear that a Muslim—or anyone—who rejects Jesus as the Son of God cannot have the life that God offers. As politically incorrect as it may be to say such a thing, it is a direct application of 1 John 5:12. It simply is not possible to reject the Son and have life in God, no matter how devout one's worship may be. The exclusivism of the Son is central to authentic Christianity. Jesus himself taught, "I am the way and the truth and the life. No one comes to the Father except through me" (John 14:6). The church must learn again that Jesus is a divisive figure. We cannot accept him without being rejected by others. Knowing this, we should be less concerned about political correctness and more concerned with mission so that yet more people would enjoy life through having the Son.

---

16. For a variety of views on the matter among leading missiologists, see the special edition of the *Occasional Bulletin* produced by the Evangelical Missionary Society: https://www.emsweb.org/images/occasional-bulletin/special-editions/OB_SpecialEdition_2016.pdf.

1 John 5:13-21

 LISTEN to the Story

¹³I write these things to you who believe in the name of the Son of God so that you may know that you have eternal life. ¹⁴This is the confidence we have in approaching God: that if we ask anything according to his will, he hears us. ¹⁵And if we know that he hears us—whatever we ask—we know that we have what we asked of him.

¹⁶If you see any brother or sister commit a sin that does not lead to death, you should pray and God will give them life. I refer to those whose sin does not lead to death. There is a sin that leads to death. I am not saying that you should pray about that. ¹⁷All wrongdoing is sin, and there is sin that does not lead to death.

¹⁸We know that anyone born of God does not continue to sin; the One who was born of God keeps them safe, and the evil one cannot harm them. ¹⁹We know that we are children of God, and that the whole world is under the control of the evil one. ²⁰We know also that the Son of God has come and has given us understanding, so that we may know him who is true. And we are in him who is true by being in his Son Jesus Christ. He is the true God and eternal life.

²¹Dear children, keep yourselves from idols.

Listening to the Text in the Story: John 14:13–14; 20:31; 1 John 2:25; 3:14.

If the previous passage (5:1–12) is the *theological* conclusion of the letter, this passage is the *pastoral* conclusion. It consists of concluding affirmations, mostly building on theological points already discussed, though there are also some new elements introduced at this late stage.

The first paragraph deals with assurance of eternal life and confidence in approaching God, with special attention to prayer (5:13–15). A certain type of intercessory prayer becomes the focus of attention—prayer offered for someone caught in sin (5:16–17). This raises the issue of safety from sin as the children of God and the gift of understanding given by the Son of God (5:18–20). The letter ends with a single exhortation to "keep your-selves from idols" (5:21).

EXPLAIN the Story

Assurance of Eternal Life and Confidence in Approaching God (5:13–15)

The pastoral conclusion of 1 John begins with the author's final use of the "I write these things to you" phrase. John writes "to you who believe in the name of the Son of God" (5:13). Believing in the name of Jesus Christ is God's command (along with loving one another) in 3:23. He writes to those who heed this command.

John writes "so that you may know that you have eternal life" (5:13). Assurance of eternal life is one of the central themes of the letter. Jesus *is* the eternal life proclaimed by John (1:2). Eternal life is promised by God (2:25), evidenced in those who love one another (3:14), and comes to everyone who "has the Son" (5:12). That his readers *know* they have eternal life—through believing in the name of the One who *is* life—is one of John's chief concerns.

Several commentators note the striking similarities of 5:13 with the pur-pose statement of John's Gospel (20:31).[1] Both statements refer to things written, both are concerned with (eternal) life, both refer to believing, and both include the phrases "Son of God" and "in his name." But as Lieu points out, John 20:31 is written *in order* that John's readers might believe, whereas 1 John 5:13 assumes that his readers already do so; "his purpose is that they might *know* that they possess this life."[2]

Those believing in Jesus's name have confidence in approaching God (5:14a).[3] Confidence before God is also an important theme in the letter. By remaining in Jesus, believers may have confidence "at his coming" (2:28); likewise if our conscience does not condemn us (3:21) and if love is mature within us, "we may have confidence for the day of judgment" (4:17).

Such confidence before God involves knowing that "if we ask anything according to his will, he hears us" (5:14) and "we know that we have what we asked of him" (5:15). Asking God for "anything we ask" and receiving it is addressed in 3:22, but here it is qualified as "anything according to his will."[4]

---

1. E.g., Jobes, *1, 2, & 3 John*, 225; Painter, *1, 2, and 3 John*, 313–14; Smalley, *1, 2, 3 John*, 277; Lieu, *I, II, & II John*, 220–21; Yarbrough, *1–3 John*, 296.

2. Lieu, *I, II, & II John*, 220.

3. Lit., "toward God" (*pros auton*).

4. Painter, *1, 2, and 3 John*, 314.

As Christian tradition has always held, God hears our prayers and our requests are granted—*according to his will.*

Praying for Someone Caught in Sin (5:16–17)

An important type of prayer is that which intercedes for a brother or sister who is seen to "commit a sin that does not lead to death" (5:16a). We can be confident that God will give life to such a person (5:16a), but the question is, what is this "sin that does not lead to death"?[5] John now switches to that very subject by writing, "I refer to those whose sin does not lead to death. There is a sin that leads to death. . . . All wrongdoing is sin, and there is sin that does not lead to death" (5:16b–17).

This "sin that does not lead to death" could be *a* sin or just "sin," since there is no article ("a") included in the Greek expression (*hamartian mē pros thanaton*).[6] Likewise for the "sin that leads to death": it could be *a* sin, or just "sin" (*hamartia pros thanaton*).

In working this through, the first clue is found in verse 17: "All wrongdoing is sin." It is unlikely that this should be taken to mean "all wrongdoing is *a* sin," which suggests that throughout 5:16–17 John is talking about sin in general and not particular sins (or *a* particular sin).

The second clue is the phrase "leads to death" (*pros thanaton*), which occurs four times in 5:16–17 (three of the four times it is negated: "*Does not* lead to death"). This expression suggests that there is a type of sin that puts one on a path toward death—not that the sin immediately "kills" its perpetrator but that it sets a deadly direction. In 1:8, 10 John acknowledges that all people have sinned, but through confession we are forgiven and purified (1:9). If sin can be forgiven, what is the type of sin (or specific sin) that might then lead to death?

Given the thrust of the letter as a whole, it seems that the only sin that could never be forgiven is a persistent lack of belief in the one whom God has sent to die for our sins. As Kruse writes, "The sin that does lead to death is most likely that of the unbeliever."[7] Since our sins are forgiven through

---

5. The difficulty of answering this question is reflected by Schnackenburg's comment, "It might be asked whether the author should not have expressed his point differently and more clearly" (*Johannine Epistles*, 250).

6. Greek does not have an indefinite article, so when the definite article is not present other factors help to determine whether an item is definite ("the sin"), indefinite ("a sin"), or general "sin." See Wallace, *Greek Grammar*, 243–44.

7. Kruse, *Letters of John*, 194. He adds, "This explanation has the advantage of relating the matter of sins that lead and do not lead to death to the central issues being addressed by the letter" (ibid.). After Brown's lengthy consideration of the issues (612–19) he concludes, "The best solution by far is that it is the sin of the secessionists, i.e., refusing to believe that Jesus is the Christ come in the flesh" (*Epistles of John*, 636).

confession and belief in Jesus, "sin that leads to death" is sin that remains unforgiven.

The overall point is that believers may (or will) still commit sin from time to time, but this will not lead to death because their sins are forgiven. By praying for those struggling with sin, believers know that God will give them life. On the other hand, "sin that leads to death" belongs to the person who has not received God's forgiveness.

One issue remains: What does John mean by "I am not saying that you should pray about that" (5:16b)? Following his statement that "there is sin that leads to death," it could be construed to mean that John discourages prayer for people who do not believe. But this is most likely just a clarifying statement. Literally he states, "not concerning that do I say that you (may) pray." In other words, John clarifies that he is talking about prayer for those whose sin does not lead to death rather than for those whose sin does lead to death. He is not discouraging prayer for unbelievers—that's not the point.[8] His topic is prayer for believers who need it.

God Keeps His Children Safe (5:18–20)

The final section of these concluding affirmations returns to the theme of being born of God, which is also of central significance in the letter. Everyone who does what is right has been born of God (2:29) and will not continue to sin (3:9). Everyone who loves has been born of God (4:7), as has everyone who believes that Jesus is the Christ (5:1). Everyone born of God overcomes the world (5:4).

Here John says, "We know[9] that anyone born of God does not continue to sin" (5:18a). While the insertion of the word "continue" is an interpretation (lit., "does not sin," *ouch hamartanei*), it is a correct one. John has just mentioned brothers and sisters who commit sin that does not lead to death (5:16); clearly he does not now contradict himself by saying that God's children do not ever sin at all (cf. 1:8, 10). It is a question of allegiance: those born of God now belong to his family and no longer identify with the pattern of sin.[10]

The ultimate assurance is offered to those born of God: "The One who was born of God keeps them safe, and the evil one cannot harm them" (5:18b). Jesus protects the children of God.

It is possible, however, that "the one born of God" in 5:18b refers to the believer rather than to Jesus, as the phrase does in 5:18a. The best support for this reading is the presence of the word "himself" (*heauton*; translated by

8. Marshall, *Epistles of John*, 246.

9. The first in a series of three in 5:18–20, "we know" (*oidamen*) is a meta-comment, drawing attention to the proposition to follow: "*We know* that anyone born of God does not continue to sin" (Runge, *Discourse Grammar*, 101 [see the fuller description of this term in the note at 3:1]).

10. Stott, *Letters of John*, 194.

NIV as "them"): "The one who was born of God keeps *himself* safe." This, however, has the difficulty of John apparently claiming that believers can keep *themselves* safe from the evil one, which would be a foreign thought in his theology. Rather, *heautou* can be a marker of possession used in place of the possessive pronoun.[11] With this sense the phrase reads, "The One who was born of God keeps his (people) safe."

There is an obvious parallel intended here between "those born of God" and "the One who was born of God":[12] the children of God share a kinship with God's Son. And the Son himself protects and keeps God's children so that the evil one cannot harm, or literally "touch" (*haptetai*), them.

Believers' allegiance to the family of God by virtue of their rebirth disassociates them from the realm of the devil's power. John reiterates the point: "We know that we are children of God, and that the whole world is under the control of the evil one" (5:19). Literally, the whole world "lies in the evil (one)." Lying under the sway and influence of the devil, the world is no longer the home of those born of God. We have been taken out of the world and do not belong to it (cf. 2:15–17; 4:4–6). Consequently the devil has no claim to the children of God, who enjoy the protection of their older Brother.[13]

Jesus has also brought revelation: "We know also that the Son of God has come and has given us understanding, so that we may know him who is true" (5:20a). This is the only time "understanding" (*dianoia*) is mentioned in 1 John. While this may seem a new idea, it is really a recapitulation of a theme that runs throughout. John has been concerned that his readers know the truth (e.g., 2:20–21, 27; 4:6); he wants them to *understand* the realities bound up with believing in Jesus. In fact, it is Jesus himself who "has given us understanding."

The gift of understanding comes "so that we may know him who is true" (5:20a). "Him who is true" is "the true God" of 5:20c. Knowing God is also an essential theme throughout 1 John. Believers know that they know God by keeping his commandments (2:3–4). "Fathers" and "children" know him who is from the beginning (2:13–14). Everyone who loves has been born of God and knows God (4:7). The understanding brought to us in the coming of Jesus enables us to know him who is true.

---

11. BDAG 269, §3.

12. There is a difference in tense forms that keeps the referents distinct: "Anyone born of God" employs a perfect participle (*ho gegennēmenos*), while "the One who was born of God" has an aorist participle (*ho gennētheis*). If the perfect is *imperfective* in aspect (as I have argued; see my *Basics of Verbal Aspect in Biblical Greek*, 46–52), then "anyone born of God" is an "open" category: It is a general description that fits anyone past, present, or future who might become a believer. The aorist, however, indicates that Jesus *was* born of God, since the perfective aspect of the aorist indicates a summary description.

13. Bruce, *Epistles of John*, 127.

Not only do believers know God, but "we are in him who is true by being in his Son Jesus Christ" (5:20b). The idea of being "in God" or "in Jesus" is explored at several points in the letter (2:5–6, 24, 27–28; 3:6, 24; 4:13–16). While the NIV translates this phrase as "we are in him who is true *by being in his Son*," John literally says that "we are in him who is true, in his Son Jesus Christ." In other words, "by being" is added by the NIV as a way to correlate these two phrases. But there is ambiguity here. The CSB translates it as "we are in the true one—that is, in his Son Jesus Christ," while the ESV translates it as "we are in him who is true, in his Son Jesus Christ." Both translations understand the true one to be *Jesus*, while the NIV takes the true one as *God*.

Probably this ambiguity is deliberate. We have observed several instances in which it is not clear whether John refers to the Son or to the Father, and it has been suggested that such ambiguity reflects John's close identification of both persons. If that is correct, we are not meant to untangle such references. Is he talking about Jesus or the Father? The answer is yes.

The final phrase of 5:20 is also somewhat ambiguous. John writes, "He is the true God and eternal life" (5:20c). Is he speaking of the Father or the Son? On the surface, the former would be most natural. But in 1:2 John calls Jesus "the eternal life," while the Father is never so called. Could 5:20c be an explicit reference to Jesus as God?[14] It is possible. But again whether John is speaking of the Son or the Father seems deliberately vague,[15] and perhaps that's the point.

Keep Yourselves from Idols (5:21)

The final utterance of 1 John has kept commentators busy: "Dear children, keep yourselves from idols" (5:21). This is not because the instruction is difficult to understand but because it seems to come from nowhere. John does not even touch the subject of idols (in any of his writings), and there is no hint that his readers were struggling with idolatry. So this seems a bizarre way to conclude the letter.

While literal idolatry—physical images of false gods—is possibly meant, especially in the context of Asia Minor,[16] most likely idolatry is raised in direct response to mention of "the true God" of the previous phrase (5:20c). Though we are unsure whether "the true God" is a reference to the Father or the Son

---

14. Brown, Schnackenburg, Marshall, Bruce, and Yarbrough say yes, Painter says no, while Kruse remains unsure (Brown, *Epistles of John*, 625–26; Schnackenburg, *Johannine Epistles*, 262–63; Marshall, *Epistles of John*, 254–55; Bruce, *Epistles of John*, 128; Yarbrough, *1–3 John*, 320; Painter, *1, 2, and 3 John*, 326–27; Kruse, *Letters of John*, 197).

15. Dodd, *Johannine Epistles*, 140; Smalley, *1, 2, 3 John*, 295.

16. Craig S. Keener, *IVP Bible Background Commentary*, 715.

(or both), true knowledge of God is a main concern of the letter. In view of the heterodox challenge and possibly in a context of persecution,[17] John wants his readers to have confidence in their true knowledge of the true God. Anything else is ultimately idolatry.[18]

Idolatry is the worship of a false god. As such, any form of belief that leads people away from the truth is idolatry, even if it comes in a Christlike guise. Consequently, the exhortation to "keep yourselves from idols" is fitting. John's readers are to avoid false views about Jesus and errant ideas about knowing God. Jobes writes:

> Rather than an awkward and abrupt ending, 5:21 summarizes the point of the entire letter and challenges readers, both ancient and modern, to decide which god they will worship—the God who revealed himself in Jesus Christ or a false god conjured from human imagination.[19]

John's letter has laid out the truth; his readers are now equipped to put this final instruction into action.

 LIVE the Story

Confidence in Approaching God

John begins the pastoral conclusion of his letter with the theme of assurance. His readers may *know* they have eternal life because they believe in the name of the Son of God (5:13). Since assurance is a central theme of the letter, this is an appropriate way to begin John's concluding summaries.

But the special focus here is on the confidence that believers have in approaching God in prayer (5:14–15). Prayer is the ultimate expression of our access to God. The fact that the Creator of the entire universe listens to our requests and petitions is truly remarkable. Who are we that God should listen to us? And yet he does. We should stop and ponder that privilege more often—perhaps it will give us extra impetus to pray.

We know that we have access to God and that we may therefore confidently approach him in prayer. And so it seems to me that our level of confidence in prayer reflects the level of our confidence in our access to him. It is

---

17. See M. J. Edwards, "Martyrdom and the First Epistle of John," *NovT* 31 (1989): 164–71.

18. See Benjamin L. Merkle, "What Is the Meaning of 'Idols' in 1 John 5:21?" *BSac* 169 (2012): 328–40; Duane F. Watson, "'Keep Yourselves from Idols': A Socio-Rhetorical Analysis of the Exordium and Peroratio of 1 John," in *Fabrics of Discourse: Essays in Honor of Vernon K. Robbins*, ed. by David B. Gowler, L. Gregory Bloomquist, and Duane F. Watson (Harrisburg, PA: Trinity Press International, 2003), 281–302.

19. Jobes, *1, 2, & 3 John*, 244.

one thing to talk about access to God; it is another to act on it. Surely prayer is the chief way in which we act on our access.

By this I do not refer to confidence that God will grant us whatever we ask. He will do as he wills (5:14b). Instead I am referring to our confidence *to pray*—the confidence we have to bring our humble requests and petitions to him, knowing that he will not turn us away or reject us. He welcomes our coming to him, and he wants to hear our requests.

But sometimes we may struggle to really believe that God would listen to us. We so regularly fail him and don't deserve a hearing with the Almighty God of all creation. Well, it's true that we don't deserve it, but it is even more true that God grants it anyway—praise be to him! Because God has granted us access to him through Jesus, we know we can ask *anything*, and he will hear us.

I have known a few celebrities in my day. I generally feel sorry for them because everyone thinks they know the celebrity, but to the celebrity everyone they meet is a total stranger. Some celebrities are cool about that, and others not so much. Some celebrities understand what it means for a fan to meet their hero who has influenced them, inspired them, and meant the world to them—albeit all from a distance. They happily sign autographs, pose for photos, and engage in friendly chitchat.

But other celebrities seem to hate their fame. They are annoyed by their fans, who won't leave them alone. The last thing they want to do is engage in pathetic chitchat with their admirers. They wonder if fame is really worth it and would rather spend their days anonymously, perhaps on a deserted island somewhere. I can understand that attitude, though it can disappoint and hurt people whose lives genuinely have been touched by such a one.

Now imagine that in a once-in-a-lifetime opportunity, you get to meet your favorite celebrity and spend some time with him or her. Wow, what a treat! Now imagine that this celebrity takes a genuine interest in you—not just being nice, but actual interest—and befriends you. Imagine that he or she gives you their cell phone number and says you can call anytime. Imagine that your celebrity friend offers to hang out, go see a movie, or invites you to their home. Imagine that you end up having a longterm, meaningful friendship with your favorite celebrity.

You have been granted access. And access to someone like that is a privilege; lots of people would love such access, but most don't get it. Your access and friendship means you could ask your celebrity friend the kinds of questions that no one else would dream of asking. They would do you a favor. They would help you move house or be the godparent of your child.

Now imagine that you have that kind of access to the most powerful being in the universe. Imagine that he regards you as a member of his family, and you can call on him whenever you want. You can ask him for the deepest desires of your heart—things you may not say aloud to anyone else. Imagine that you have unrestricted access to him, knowing he will always listen.

Can you imagine that? I hope so, because that is what you have if you believe in the Son of God! What a remarkable privilege we have, to approach God in prayer.

Praying for Someone Caught in Sin

Our access to God in prayer is given a special focus when John raises the issue of praying for a brother or sister who commits sin (5:16). He says we should pray in such a situation because God will give the sinner life.

If confidence in prayer reflects confidence in our access to God (see above), then we might say that prayer for a brother or sister caught in sin reflects our love for them. Surely, genuine love for others ought to issue in fervent prayer for them. Yet so often we fail to pray for others as we ought. Why is that? Indeed, for some Christians it seems easier to offer practical deeds of love—expressed by action—than to sit down and pray for a loved one.

And yet there is nothing easier to do than to pray for someone. We can literally do it anywhere, anytime. We don't need to prepare, it need not take much time, and it takes virtually no energy. Not only is there nothing easier to do for them, there is nothing more powerfully helpful than prayer. The God who can do anything according to his will listens to our prayers—what can we possibly do for a friend that is more significant than that?

So therein lies the irony. There is nothing easier to do and nothing more powerfully helpful than to pray for someone in need. And yet we so often find ourselves failing to do it. Is it because we don't really believe in the power of prayer? Is it because we foolishly think that other actions will be of more benefit than prayer? Is it because we don't really care what happens to our friend?

A praying friend is a friend indeed. In her March 2013 meditation *Praying Friends*, Anne Cetas writes about the encouragement she received from her friend, Angie:

> I met my friend Angie for lunch after having not seen her for several months. At the end of our time together, she pulled out a piece of paper with notes from our previous get-together. It was a list of my prayer requests she had been praying for since then. She went through each one and asked if God had answered yet or if there were any updates. And then we talked about her prayer requests. How encouraging to have a praying friend![20]

---

20. Anne Cetas, "Praying Friends," Our Daily Bread, March 9, 2013, http://odb.org/2013/03/09/praying-friends/.

Oh, that we might be more like Angie! Let us heed John's encourage-ment and pray for our brothers and sisters in need—especially those who have sinned and require restoration. God is the one who restores, heals, and forgives. He will gladly hear our petitions on behalf of the struggling believer.

Safety from Evil

On the issue of sin and being restored to life, John assures his readers that the children of God will be kept safe from the evil one (5:18–19). By virtue of our rebirth into the family of God, believers are not under the control of the evil one, because we have been disassociated from the world, which is his domain.

In order to escape the evil one, people must be claimed by God; it is not possible otherwise. We cannot be free from the world without having been snatched from it to a better home. There is no no-man's land in between two competing domains—all territory has been claimed by one or the other. We will either be in the grip of the evil one as members of the world, or we will be free from his tyrannical reign as members of God's family.

As I write, Europe has been overwhelmed by the influx of millions of Syrian refugees. Literally millions of people—families, individuals, infants through to the elderly—have fled to escape the violent tearing apart of their cities, towns, villages, and homes. But as they escape the violent civil war tak-ing place throughout Syria, they are left homeless. They have no home waiting for them in some other place. For most, there is no family waiting to receive them, feed them, and tend to their wounds and grief. They are homeless, seeking the mercy of foreign governments for shelter and relief. They may have escaped the suffering of their natural home, but most will never know the security and comfort that most of us Westerners take for granted. They may never again call a place home.

Not so for those who belong to God. We have not only escaped the threat of the evil one by escaping from his domain but we have been scooped up into the Father's loving hands. We have been given a new home—far better than the old—which is secure, beautiful, and eternal. We are protected from the reign of evil and will never again be under its control. Thanks be to God in Christ!

Keep Yourselves from Idols

John's final, enigmatic exhortation may be succinct, but its implications reach on forever. The children of God are to keep themselves from idols (5:21). This is a fitting final note for the epistle, since so much of it has concerned false worship versus truly knowing the true God through his true Son. Idolatry is false worship that usurps God's rightful place as Lord.

Idolatry takes many forms, and in modern times it is often masked as respectable pursuits and desires. Paul says that greed is idolatry (Col 3:5), and so he recognizes humanity's capacity to worship false idols without necessarily realizing it. Most people committing the idolatry of greed do not realize they are worshipping a false god, but that is what its designation as idolatry recognizes.

So it is with many forms of idolatry today. People do not realize that they bow in worship of false gods. It might be money or material gain, as in the case of greed, or it might be pleasure, relationships, career, sports, music, sex, fame . . . and so it goes. Anything that has become the dominant desire of our hearts is an idol.

In his book *Counterfeit Gods*, Tim Keller addresses this exact issue. He defines an idol as "anything more important to you than God, anything that absorbs your heart and imagination more than God, anything you seek to give you what only God can give."[21] An idol really can be *anything*, and idolatry is ultimately a matter of the *heart*.

Keller discusses the idols of love and sex, money, success, and power. All of these are good things in and of themselves; in fact, they are gifts of God's creation. An idol is not necessarily something *bad*, but it becomes bad when it usurps God's place in our hearts. In fact, these good gifts can become downright ugly when they are not kept in their proper place. Just think how depraved sex can become when it is not respected as the gift of God for a husband and wife within the covenant of marriage. The atrocity of pornography is just one example of that.

If we are honest, we will recognize that it is not only unbelievers who commit idolatry. Christians all too often are lured away from worshipping the true God in order to fall in worship to something else. Our hearts can be enticed by the alluring false promises of counterfeit gods, as we unwittingly commit spiritual adultery.

Israel consistently struggled with idolatry in the wilderness and even in the promised land of Canaan. Perhaps their idolatry was more obvious because they worshipped physical idols made of wood and stone (or gold, in the case of the golden calf), but we have no excuse either. God clearly wants our hearts. To give our hearts to something else is to refuse his goodness and love. We know what idolatry is, and we know that we often commit it.

So, what hope is there? All is not lost. Even while John warns his readers to keep themselves from idols, he knows he is writing to people who are securely kept in the love of God. That is, the possibility of moments of temporary

---

21. Timothy Keller, *Counterfeit Gods: The Empty Promises of Money, Sex, and Power, and the Only Hope That Matters* (New York: Penguin, 2009), Kindle edition, Introduction.

idolatry does not disqualify us from membership in God's family. We will make mistakes and sin, but God forgives us through the atoning blood of Christ. Jesus's propitiatory sacrifice has already satisfied the penalty we deserve for our idolatries.

But of course, we must also banish the counterfeit gods of our hearts. Keller writes:

> The way forward, out of despair, is to discern the idols of our hearts and our culture. But that will not be enough. The only way to free ourselves from the destructive influence of counterfeit gods is to turn back to the true one. The living God, who revealed himself both at Mount Sinai and on the Cross, is the only Lord who, if you find him, can truly fulfill you, and, if you fail him, can truly forgive you.[22]

Our idolatry must be banished and replaced with worship of God our Father. He has sent his Son for this very purpose, that we might know him and love him. We will live as his children in loving adoration of our heavenly Father, knowing that he forgives our failures and has dealt with our every sin. Let us keep ourselves from idols and so reserve our affection and allegiance for him.

---

22. Keller, *Counterfeit Gods*, Kindle edition, Introduction.

Introduction to 2 John

While 1 John has a special place in my heart, I have to confess to the near neglect of 2 and 3 John. I suspect I'm not alone. In my experience, the "2" letters (2 Corinthians, 2 Thessalonians, 2 Timothy, 2 Peter, 2 John) usually suffer relative neglect compared to their "1" counterparts. They are less well known by Christians in general, less often preached, and less often studied to the same degree. Second John has the added disadvantage of being a very short letter that on the surface does not seem to add much beyond the message of its big brother, 1 John. Of course, such attitudes are unhelpful and ought to be corrected.

It is a mistake to ignore 2 John. For starters, it is in the canon. That fact alone should tell us that the early church regarded it as significant enough to warrant its designation as holy Scripture, even if that process was less straightforward than for 1 John (see below). Second, if one of the theories tentatively endorsed below is correct, 2 John originally functioned as a cover letter for 1 John. It provides a succinct overture of the latter's major themes of love and truth in keeping with that function. Third, 2 John is more than just an overture, however, as there is direct practical application of its themes with respect to hospitality. While 1 John offers abundant implications for Christian living, nothing in the letter approaches the day-to-day concrete practicality that 2 John offers with one precise punch.

Who Wrote 2 John and Why?

Authorship

Unlike 1 John, 2 John indicates both addressor and addressee, though both are rather vague: the letter is from "the elder" to "the chosen lady" and her children (v. 1). The "elder" title was evidently enough to identify the author to his original readers, and the tone of the letter suggests authority in keeping with spiritual leadership.[1] It is written by a church leader to a congregation known to him.

The first possible reference to 2 John comes from Polycarp (ca. AD 69–155), bishop of Smyrna, near the area where John lived. Prior to AD 140, he alludes to 2 John 7. The first definite quotation is of 2 John 7–8, 10, 11

---

1. Jobes, *1, 2, & 3 John*, 248.

found in Irenaeus, who refers to two letters written by "John the disciple of the Lord" (*Against Heresies* 3.16.3, 8).

According to Eusebius (ca. AD 263–340), Origen knew that 2 and 3 John were not universally regarded as genuine (*Hist. eccl.* 6.25.10). Eusebius himself claimed that they were both well known and acknowledged by most, attributing any doubt about their authorship to speculation that there might have been another author named John (6.25.10). By the fourth century, 2 and 3 John were regarded as canonical apostolic books along with 1 John.

So, while not as strong as for 1 John, the evidence of the early church points to the apostle John as the author of 2 John. While 1 John is likely a circular letter addressed to the church in and around Ephesus (see the introduction to 1 John), 2 John is apparently addressed to a single church known to the author. This relationship allows John to use the title "elder" without further qualification. And since "the elder" is technically the addressor, this commentary will use that term for the author, even though it is believed that he is the apostle John.

The Elder's Situation

If the historical evidence is correct, and there is no compelling reason to doubt it, the author's situation is addressed by what we know about the apostle John. Living in Ephesus in western Asia Minor, the elder had a ministry to a variety of churches in and around Ephesus (see the introduction to 1 John).

The Elder's Reasons for Writing

The elder writes for a surface reason, an underlying reason, and a literary reason. The surface reason for writing is to warn his readers about the deceivers who may hope to receive their hospitality. He strongly prohibits any support of the false teachers, requiring that they withhold their hospitality from them.

The underlying reason for writing is that the elder is concerned for truth and love. These twin themes (or the single theme of "truth and love") undergird the letter and are the reason that he prohibits showing hospitality to false teachers. Their theological error is so serious that their work must not be further facilitated by genuine believers. To impede false teaching is a demonstration of love toward those who are spared of the error.

The literary reason for writing (arguably) is that 2 John was intended to accompany 1 John as a cover letter (see below).

The Elder's Composition of 2 John

Second John is the second shortest letter in the New Testament (after 3 John) with only 245 words in the original Greek. Unlike 1 John, 2 John is written according to the form of a standard Greco-Roman letter. While the opening remains somewhat vague (from "the elder" to "the elect lady"), it is nevertheless according to form, as is the final greeting (v. 13). The elder expresses his desire for a face-to-face visit.

What is unusual about 2 John is the possibility that it served as a cover letter for 1 John. The evidence for this comes from Irenaeus, who at one point quotes 2 John 7–8 but seems to regard it as part of 1 John (*Against Heresies* 3.16.8). According to Painter, "it seems that the form in which Irenaeus knew 1 and 2 John did not distinguish between the two Epistles." He suggests that the reason for this is that 2 John was originally the cover letter for 1 John and that the combined form was how the letters were known to Irenaeus.[2] This may explain why 1 John lacks any formal greetings—that duty was carried by its cover letter. Furthermore, 1 John existed on its own without 2 John because John would have used it in his own church, where it did not need a cover letter.[3]

While the evidence coming from Irenaeus is slight, it is significant in the absence of any other historical evidence regarding the composition of 2 John. As such, the cover-letter theory is plausible. If the theory is accepted, it dates 2 John to the same time of composition as 1 John, likely in the early 90s. (See the introduction to 1 John for more on its date.)

The Elder's Opponents

If it is accepted that 2 John served as the cover letter for 1 John, then the opponents whom the elder warns about are the same in both letters. There is strong internal evidence for this conclusion too, as they are described as deceivers "who do not acknowledge Jesus Christ as coming in the flesh"; such a person is the antichrist (v. 7), which is exactly how John's opponents are described in 1 John (2:18–19; 4:2–3). See the introduction to 1 John for more about John's opponents.

Content of 2 John

For such a short letter, 2 John packs a lot in. The twin themes of love and truth dominate its theological content, while the instructions regarding false teachers occupy most of the second half of the letter.

---

2. Painter, *1, 2, and 3 John*, 42.
3. Ibid.

Love and Truth

Right from the opening greeting, we see love and truth in the forefront of the
elder's mind. He writes to the lady chosen by God and her children "whom I
love in the truth" (v. 1a). He quickly adds that they are loved by all who know
the truth (v. 1b). The elder says he loves them "because of the truth" that lives
in them (v. 2). Truth and love are again underscored at the end of the opening
greeting, where the elder says that God's grace, mercy, and peace "will be with
us in truth and love" (v. 3).

While the frequency of truth and love is striking in the short space of vv.
1–3, the way they are coordinated is also significant. The elder loves "in the
truth" (v. 1), and God's grace, mercy, and peace are with us "in truth and
love" (v. 3). Love and truth go together, so that the elder's love is defined by
truth, and God's blessings are mediated to us through the primary gifts of
truth and love.

The theme of truth and love (is it one theme or two?) continues into the
next section (vv. 4–6), which is bracketed by walking in the truth (v. 4) and
walking in love (v. 6). These verses are tightly coordinated in the following
way: walking in truth is what the Father has commanded (v. 4), and the command is that we love one another (v. 5), while love is walking in obedience to
his commands (v. 6a), and his command is to walk in love (v. 6b). To break
it down further: truth is command, command is love, love is command, and
command is love.

These intricately packed verses are profound in their own right, but even
more so when seen against the more lengthy exploration of truth and love in
1 John. If 2 John was written as a cover letter for 1 John (as suggested above), vv.
4–6 provide a stunning overture for two of the major themes of the longer letter.

Anti-Hospitality

Moving into the second half of 2 John, we see the elder address a practical
matter that is both pastoral and theological. And, as we will see, it is in fact
an outworking of truth and love.

The elder warns against the "many deceivers" who deny that Jesus Christ
came in the flesh; such a person is the/an antichrist (see the commentary on
v. 7 for discussion about antichrists). Truth is clearly the issue here as these
deceivers are in theological error. And the consequence of their christological
error is steep: the one who does not continue in the teaching of Christ does
not have God (v. 9a). By the same token, the one who does continue in the
teaching of Christ has the Father and the Son (v. 9b).

If any such false teacher comes their way, the elder instructs his readers to
withhold their hospitality (v. 10) because "anyone who welcomes them shares

in their wicked work" (v. 11). While such an imperative may sound harsh, indeed *un*loving to our ears, the motivation behind it is actually love. The elder firmly believes that their theological error is so significant that he does not want the deceivers' "ministry" to be facilitated (hospitality was necessary for traveling teachers; see the commentary on these verses), nor does he want his beloved readers to be put at theological risk by their teaching. At this point "the orthodoxy of the community is far more important than upholding cultural norms."[4]

The elder concludes the letter with his desire to visit and talk face to face. His love for his readers is again expressed here, as he anticipates that their being together will make their joy complete (v. 12).

Thus, the theme(s) of truth and love carries through the second half of 2 John as truth and love are applied to this pastoral situation. As such, we can say that the whole of 2 John is about truth and love.

Outline of Contents

Second John is organized into four clear sections.

Outline of 2 John

1–3	Opening Greeting
4–6	Walking in the Truth and Love
7–11	Do Not Partner in the Work of Deceivers
12–13	Closing Greeting

How Does 2 John Relate to John's Gospel and 1 John?

As with 1 John, 2 John displays echoes of the Fourth Gospel. These are not as numerous as in 1 John, which is unsurprising given the brevity of 2 John. It is also interesting to note that most of the echoes of the Gospel are simultaneously echoes of 1 John. That is, the themes in 2 John that echo John's Gospel are shared by both letters. This of course heightens the sense that they belong together.

Part of Jobes's table of similarities is reproduced here.[5]

---

4. Andrew E. Arterbury, *Entertaining Angels: Early Christian Hospitality in Its Mediterranean Setting*, New Testament Monographs 8 (Sheffield: Sheffield Phoenix Press, 2005), 119.

5. Jobes, *1, 2, & 3 John*, 25–27. The quotations of 1 and 2 John are Jobes's translations. 3 John is included in this commentary's introduction to that letter. Used with permission.

Some Similarities between John's Gospel, 1 John, and 2 John

Gospel of John	1 John	2 John
John 3:21 But whoever lives by the truth comes into the light	*1 John 1:6* If we say, "We have fellowship with him" and walk in the darkness, we lie and do not live out the truth.	*2 John 4* I rejoice greatly because I have found some of your children walking in the truth.
John 15:12 "My command is this: Love each other as I have loved you."	*1 John 3:23* And this is his command: to believe in the name of his Son, Jesus Christ, and to love one another just as he gave the command to us.	*2 John 5* And now I ask you, lady—not as writing you a new command, but [as writing a command] that we have had from the beginning—that we love one another.
John 15:7 "If you remain in me and my words remain in you, ask whatever you wish, and it will be done for you."	*1 John 3:24* And the one who keeps his commands remains in him [God], and he himself in them; and in this is way we know that he remains in us: from the Spirit, whom he gave to us.	*2 John 9* Everyone who goes beyond and does not remain in the teaching of Christ does not have Christ. The one who remains in the teaching [of Christ], this one has both the Father and the Son.
	1 John 2:18 Children, it is the last hour, and just as you heard that antichrist is coming, even now many have become antichrists, and so we know that it is the last hour.	*2 John 7* Many deceivers have gone into the world, those who do not confess Jesus Christ coming in the flesh; such a person is the deceiver and the antichrist.

Whom the Elder Addresses in the Letter

The elder writes to "the lady chosen by God and to her children" (v. 1). The two major interpretative options for identifying this "elect lady" (*eklektē kyria*) are, first, that she is an unknown individual with literal or figurative children, or, second, "she" is a congregation of believers and "her children" are its members. As argued in the commentary on v. 1, the latter is most likely.

A possible reason why the elder was not more specific in address was so that 2 John could be sent to different congregations. If it was written to be a cover letter for 1 John (see above), "the lady" could refer to any congregation to whom both letters were sent.

Whether a particular congregation is meant or multiple possible congregations, they belonged to the Johannine community in and around Ephesus in western Asia Minor. See the introduction to 1 John for more on the Johannine community and its location. If 2 John was intended to circulate along with 1 John, the elder's indications of affection for his readers would nevertheless remain genuine and well intended, since all the potential recipient congregations would have been known to him.

LISTEN to the Story

The elder,
To the lady chosen by God and to her children, whom I love in the truth—and not I only, but also all who know the truth—²because of the truth, which lives in us and will be with us forever:
³Grace, mercy and peace from God the Father and from Jesus Christ, the Father's Son, will be with us in truth and love.

Listening to the Text in the Story: 1 Corinthians 13:6; 1 Peter 1:22; 1 John 3:18; 3 John 1.

Unlike 1 John, this letter begins with a formal greeting. But like 1 John, the author is not explicitly identified and has still a rather unusual greeting in any case. The letter's author is identified as "the elder," while the recipients are "the lady chosen by God" and "her children." All of these titles require unpacking.

The elder indicates his love for the letter's recipients but quickly turns to focus on truth. His love is "in the truth," as is the love of all who know the truth, and this love is apparently issued "because of the truth, which lives in us." Truth and love come together again in the last phrase of the greeting.

EXPLAIN the Story

The Elder to the Chosen Lady and Her Children (v. 1a)

Tradition holds that "the elder," the author of 2 John, is the apostle John (see the introduction to 2 John).[1] Though the letter does not claim Johannine

---

1. Jobes offers a recent and helpful discussion of issues of authorship (*1, 2, & 3 John*, 22–23, 255–56). In short, while modern scholarship doubts the Johannine authorship of the Gospel and Letters, reasonable evidence exists that supports the tradition that John the son of Zebedee, the disciple of Jesus and an apostle, was the author of all three documents. Disputations about authorship are ultimately not decisive enough to overturn the tradition (see the introduction to 1 John).

authorship (all the Johannine Epistles are anonymous), there are striking similarities of theme, language, and theology with 1 John and John's Gospel. Written late in his life, John is an elder in years and in status. As for status, this title implies a relationship of pastoral oversight of his readers. He is *their* elder. The greeting would hardly make sense otherwise.

The elder writes "to the lady chosen by God and to her children." Who is this "elect lady" (*eklektē kyria*)? There are two major options. First, this lady is an unidentified individual who apparently has children (either literal or figurative), who are also known to the elder. Second, the "lady" is a local congregation. Her "children" are the believers who gather under her wings, as it were.

The matter was controversial in the early church, with some viewing the "elect lady" as a church (e.g., Hilary of Arles) and others a particular individual (e.g., Andreas).[2] To add to the confusion, Clement of Alexandria regarded "Eklecta" (*eklektē*) to be the name of a Babylonian woman, but whose name stood for the election of the church.[3] Others have wondered if *kyria* was meant as the proper name "Kyria."[4] Against these proper name speculations, however, Brown has shown that "Eklecta" was unknown as a name at this time, and while "Kyria" is known, the absence of the Greek article makes it unlikely that "lady" (*kyria*) is meant as a proper name.[5]

Nevertheless, it is still possible that an individual addressee is meant, even if "elect" and "lady" are not understood as proper names. In favor of an actual individual is the fact that the elder addresses her as though a person no less than six times (vv. 1, 4, 5, 10, 12, 13). If the chosen lady is *not* an individual, the elder certainly works the metaphor thoroughly through the letter. Also in favor of this reading is the fact that nowhere else in apostolic literature is a congregation personified—let alone personified as a specific gender.

In favor of the "lady" being a congregation is that while personified, there are no specific details offered as to her identity. She remains vague—personal but nondescript. Moreover, the elder sends greetings from "the children of your chosen sister" (v. 13), which sounds like another congregation.

Tradition and most of recent scholarship favor a congregation, which is well supported by the text.[6] Smalley regards the corporate reference even

---

Nevertheless, references to the author of 2 John will use the term "elder," which is the least controversial convention.

2. Gerald Bray, *Ancient Christian Commentary on Scripture: James, 1–2 Peter, 1–3 John, Jude* (Downers Grove, IL: InterVarsity Press, 2000), 231.

3. Ibid.

4. D. M. Smith, *First, Second, and Third John* (Louisville: Westminster John Knox, 1991), 163.

5. Brown, *Epistles of John*, 653.

6. Kruse, *Letters of John*, 204. So also Brown, who explores the other major interpretative possibilities before concluding thus (*Epistles of John*, 651–55).

more likely "when we recall the biblical personification of Israel as a woman or Jerusalem as the 'mother' of Israel (cf. Isa 54:1–8; Gal 4:25; Rev 12:17; 21:2) and the NT picture of the church as the 'bride' of Christ (cf. 2 Cor 11:2; Eph 5:22–32)."[7] While the "lady" is strongly and unusually personified, through this personification the elder reveals his affection for this recipient congregation (or, possibly, congregations; see the introduction to 2 John).

Love in the Truth (vv. 1b–2)

The elder speaks of his love for this chosen lady and her children. His love is "in the truth" (or, "in truth," *en alētheia*) and is shared by "all who know the truth" (v. 1b). While there is an array of meanings for "truth" in John's writings, here it most likely "signifies what is ultimately real, and in the end this means God himself, as he has been revealed in Jesus."[8]

Already, then, from the first verse of 2 John we see the intrinsic relatedness of truth and love. These twin concerns are of utmost importance in 1 John and, as will become clear, are central to 2 John also.

The elder loves the chosen lady and her children "because of the truth, which lives in us and will be with us forever" (v. 2). Again we see the intrinsic relatedness of love and truth. This truth lives or remains "in us" (cf. 1 John 1:8; 2:4; John 8:44). Truth is not conceptual only; it is embodied in the lives of John and his readers. And yet there is a conceptual component to this truth, as will be seen later in the letter (2 John 7, 9–10).

Moreover, this truth "will be with us forever." The truth is believed, embodied in believers, and remains with them for all eternity. The truth of Jesus is eternal, and those who know and believe in Jesus will eternally live in this truth.

Grace, Mercy, and Peace (v. 3)

The salutation of v. 3 is standard in many respects, holding out "grace, mercy and peace," which come "from God the Father and from Jesus Christ" (v. 3a). The elder's own stamp is placed upon this salutation, however, by drawing attention to the sonship of Jesus, "the Father's Son."

Furthermore, the elder's greeting says that grace, mercy, and peace *will be with us* in truth and love (v. 3). Clearly the emphasis on truth and love in vv. 1–2 continues here. But the focus of our attention now is the elder's statement that the gifts of grace, mercy, and peace *will be* with us.

---

7. Smalley, *1, 2, 3 John*, 306.
8. Ibid., 307.

It is normal for epistolary greetings to mention grace, mercy, and peace (especially grace and peace), but these are usually offered as a wish or prayer. For example, all of Paul's letters say "grace and peace *to you*" (he includes mercy in 1 and 2 Timothy). This is the standard way to greet one's readers—holding out the hope of grace, mercy, and peace—perhaps parallel to the modern idiom, "I hope you're well," when writing a letter or email. But in 2 John the elder does not wish or pray for these things; he emphatically states that they *will be* with us. These things are certain gifts from the Father and the Son.

While grace, mercy, and peace are on the one hand unremarkable elements within a salutation, they are not devoid of theological significance. "Grace" refers to the proactive generosity that God extends toward humanity in Christ. Our salvation is utterly dependent on the grace that comes from God the Father and from his Son.

"Mercy," likewise, is an essential ingredient of God's outreach toward us in Christ. While he is righteous in his judgments and holy in every respect, God's mercy enables sinners to stand before him as forgiven, reconciled children in his family.

Finally, "peace" comes from God in that he has reconciled us to himself. Through his grace and mercy, God has ended the hostility that once alienated us. By extending generosity to us through countless blessings and by mercifully forgiving our sins, God has brought former rebels into relationship with himself. We now experience *shalom* together.

The grace, mercy, and peace that come from Father and Son "will be with *us*." This is also the elder's own stamp on a standard Christian salutation, since most letters would offer grace, (mercy),[9] and peace to "you," not to "us."[10] But this is the elder's way of communicating the bond he shares with his readers. They are in this together, and the elder counts himself among them.

Finally, grace, mercy, and peace are accompanied by truth and love, again underscoring the significance of these themes in the letter.

The opening greeting of 2 John holds to certain epistolary norms but is remarkably distinct at the same time. With the ambiguous "elder" writing to the "chosen lady" and her children, the emphatic focus on truth and love, and the inclusion of the author with his readers as the recipients of grace, mercy, and peace, we see 2 John launched with characteristic Johannine originality along with theological and pastoral depth of concern.

---

9. Most other NT letters do not include "mercy," though it is found in 1 Tim 1:2, 2 Tim 1:2, and Jude 2.

10. See Rom 1:7; 1 Cor 1:3; 2 Cor 1:2; Gal 1:3; Eph 1:2; Phil 1:2; Col 1:2; 1 Thess 1:1; 2 Thess 1:2; 1 Tim 1:2; 2 Tim 1:2; Titus 1:4; Phlm 3; 1 Pet 1:2; 2 Pet 1:2; Jude 2.

 LIVE the Story

Love in the Eternal Truth

John's greeting proceeds with a profound intertwining of love and truth. He loves his readers in the truth, as do all who know the truth (v. 1). And this truth is embodied within believers, remaining with them forever (v. 2).

While the intertwining of love and truth is found elsewhere in the New Testament, notably in 1 John (cf. also Eph 4:15), the *embodied* nature of the truth stands out as a distinct contribution of this text. This truth "lives in us and will be with us forever" (v. 2). Such truth is not limited to head knowledge. It *indwells* us (it is "in us") and *accompanies* us (it will be "with us").

The elder speaks of this truth as though it is a substance, like oxygen, with a tangible existence. This perhaps makes most sense when we realize that the truth of which he speaks is actually the relational knowledge of God. God is *revealed* to us in Jesus. He *is* the truth. To know the truth is to have a relationship with the true God. Thus we might say that our relationship with God is spiritually "real"—it is more potent than mere abstract knowledge.

As for the intersection of love and truth, these twin features define the community of God's people. The elder loves his readers in the truth, as do all who know the truth. For the elder, truth is the feature that defines the community. It serves as a boundary marker in that those who know the truth are "in," while those who do not are not. This is the inevitable consequence of what the truth *is*. If the truth is true, relational knowledge of God through the revelation of Jesus, it *must* be such a boundary marker. Knowing God in Christ is what makes one a member of God's family and sets believers apart from the world (1 John 5:19–20).

In the first stanza of his poem *We and They*, Rudyard Kipling writes:

Father and Mother, and Me,
Sister and Auntie say
All the people like us are We,
And every one else is They.[11]

It is an insightful poem (five stanzas in all), exploring the "we" and "they" group dynamics of life. Here in this first stanza, the focus is on the family. The family belongs to a wider society it calls "we," while others are "they." The point is not about the exclusion of others, but the stanza simply acknowledges the fact that the family is defined by its belonging to a larger cultural demographic.

---

11. Rudyard Kipling, "We and They," *Debits and Credits* (New York: Macmillan, 1926).

For the elder, truth is the factor that makes believers "we" while others are "they." While his readership forms a small contingent within the wider "we" of the family of God, it is nevertheless shaped by the commitments of the wider family. Just as Kipling's family belongs to its own wider "we," so the elder and his readership belong to a wider "we," which includes all who know the truth.

If the community of God is marked out by the truth, it is characterized by love. Love is the bond that is shared within the community and binds it together. This is why the elder can say of his readers that he loves them in the truth. It is their sharing of the truth that makes them the object of his love. They are God's people together with the elder and all who know the truth, and as such love is extended to all.

Grace, Mercy, and Peace Will Be with Us

The elder's statement that grace, mercy, and peace *will be with us* is a striking element of his originality. He has converted the regular well-wishing feature of the epistolary form into an element of Christian assurance. While assurance is not otherwise a theme of 2 John, it is a major theme of 1 John. His tweaking of the greeting in 2 John 3 reflects his theological conviction that all who know the truth are and will continue to be the recipients of God's gracious bestowal.

We have already explored the significance of truth and love, but here in v. 3 we see that grace, mercy, and peace will be with us *in truth and love*. It is difficult to know exactly how to correlate these things, but if grace, mercy, and peace will be with us *in* truth and love, it seems that truth and love are together the vehicle for these other gifts.

Drawing on the comments above about truth and love, we may say that just as truth defines the community of God's people, so it defines the recipients of grace, mercy, and peace. While God does surely extend grace to *all* people in various forms (common grace), it is a special grace that believers enjoy. It is the grace that accompanies the merciful forgiveness of sins and the peace of reconciliation with God. In this respect, grace, mercy, and peace come *in* truth because truth is the boundary marker of the people of God.

And as love is the bond that exists between the members of God's community, so it is the bond that God has for his children. Grace, mercy, and peace come to us because God loves us. So we may say that truth and love are the primary features of our relationship with God. Through truth and love, grace, mercy, and peace are mediated to us.

Since we are assured of these gifts, they will continue to define and shape us. We are people who have been *graced*—we are the recipients of God's boundless generosity and kindness. He showers gifts upon us, not the least of which is our salvation by grace. This reality ought to shape our hearts and minds so that we always know that what we have, we have by God's generosity. Remembrance of grace will make us thankful.

We are people who have received *mercy*. We do not receive what we deserve, but instead enjoy God's favor in spite of our failings. The gift of mercy reminds us of who we were and what our future held apart from God's merciful intervention. It also reminds us that God's holiness and justice is met with mercy. His character is one of righteousness *and* mercy.

We are people who have been brought into *shalom* with God. He has transformed former enemies into friends and family. Our former hostility toward our Maker has been replaced with loving adoration and worship. We rest secure in our peace with him.

When we read epistolary greetings such as 2 John 3 we should not skip over them as though they are vacuous idioms, like asking "how are you?" when we do not really care to know the answer. The elder's greeting is rich with meaning and significance. Through truth and love, God the Father and his Son Jesus Christ have bestowed to us grace, mercy, and peace. These gifts are assuredly ours now and into the future and continue to shape and define us as the people God wants us to be.

LISTEN to the Story

> ⁴It has given me great joy to find some of your children walking in the truth, just as the Father commanded us. ⁵And now, dear lady, I am not writing you a new command but one we have had from the beginning. I ask that we love one another. ⁶And this is love: that we walk in obedience to his commands. As you have heard from the beginning, his command is that you walk in love.

Listening to the Text in the Story: 1 John 2:7–8; 3:23–24.

This passage is the encouraging part of the letter. The elder affirms that some of the lady's children are walking in the truth, but he follows that up with a reminder of the command they have had from the beginning to love one another. Love is then defined as walking in obedience to God's commands, which in turn is defined by love.

EXPLAIN the Story

Your Children Are Walking in the Truth (v. 4)
The elder expresses his joy to find some of the lady's children walking in the truth. His joy is great, as he says literally, "I rejoiced exceedingly" (v. 4a; *echarēn lian*). According to most translations, the elder found "*some* of your children" to be walking this way. This, however, is an interpretation of the somewhat vague phrase, "ones walking in truth out from your children" (v. 4a; *ek tōn teknōn sou peripatountas en alētheia*).[1] This means that the transla-

---

1. The NET Bible helpfully explains this in a footnote ad loc: "'Some' is not in the Greek text, but is supplied because the prepositional phrase beginning with ἐκ (*ek*) has partitive force. The partitive force of the prepositional phrase here has been taken by some interpreters to mean that the author has found some of the elect lady's children who are living according to the truth and some who are not. This is grammatically possible, but the author has merely stated that he knows of some

tion "some" should not be understood as distinguishing between "some" and "others," as though the elder thinks that some members of the congregation walk in the truth while others do not. The point is that these believers who are from the congregation are walking in the truth.

"Walking" is an ethical metaphor common in Jewish literature (and Paul) that represents one's conduct—how one carries oneself. These believers are "walking in the truth." This idea is found in 2 Kings 20:3 when Hezekiah prays, "Remember, Lord, how I have walked before you faithfully (lit. "in truth") and with wholehearted devotion and have done what is good in your eyes." In Psalm 86:11 David prays, "Teach me your way, O Lord, that I may walk in your truth" (ESV).[2] Clearly, walking in the truth has to do with faithful obedience to God's instruction.

Truth is a significant concern in John's letters, with several sections of 1 John dedicated to it. It is arguably the unifying theme of 2 John,[3] with the next segment dealing with the importance of avoiding deceivers who seek to lead them away from the truth about Christ. But truth is not simply knowledge to be understood; it must be *walked*. That is, believers are to live in accordance with the truth. The truth is to be pursued as a way of life.

These believers are walking in the truth "just as the Father commanded us" (v. 4b). The language of "command" ties verse 4 to the following two verses, as the elder explores the command(s) he has in mind. Schnackenburg rightly points out that their walking according to the command of the Father is not "meant as inner promptings but as commandments coming from outside."[4] The command of God has been *received* (*entolēn elabomen*).

Let Us Love One Another (vv. 5–6)

Now the elder asks[5] the lady "that we love one another" (v. 5b). The elder includes himself in the instruction ("we") rather than simply exhorting the congregation to love (cf. v. 3). This exhortation is not "a new command but one we have had from the beginning" (v. 5a). First John 2:7 discusses this "old" command, though in 2:8 it is also called a "new" command. As argued for 1 John 2:7–8, this apparent contradiction is no contradiction at all if

---

Christians in the church addressed who are 'walking in the truth.' He does not know for certain that all of them are, and concern over this is probably part of the motivation for writing the letter."

2. The notion of walking in the truth is also found in the Dead Sea Scrolls (1QS VIII, 4; cf. IV, 17; VII, 18).

3. Urban C. von Wahlde, "The Theological Foundation of the Presbyter's Argument in 2 Jn (2 Jn 4–6)," *ZNW* 76 (1985). 209–24.

4. Schnackenburg, *Johannine Epistles*, 282.

5. "Now I ask you" (*nyn erōtō se*) is a meta-comment, drawing attention to the proposition to follow: "*Now I ask you* that we love one another" (Runge, *Discourse Grammar*, 101 [see the fuller description of this term in the note at 1 John 3:1]).

it is understood that the command is love. Love is an old command from Moses given new expression by Jesus, which is why it can be called "old" and "new" at the same time. In 2 John 5 the focus is on the "oldness" of the love command.

Rather than stopping simply at loving one another, next the elder gives further definition to the love command. He writes: "And this is love: that we walk in obedience to his commands" (v. 6a). The elder has already acknowledged that the lady's children walk in truth, but they are also to walk according to God's commands.

However, the elder then circles back to the original point by giving further definition to God's commands: "His command is that you walk in love" (v. 6b).[6] The only other biblical instance of the expression "walk in love" is found in Ephesians 5:2 (though cf. Rom 14:15), in which Paul models Christian love on Christ's love who "gave himself up for us as a fragrant offering and sacrifice to God."

Notable in v. 6b is the deliberate switch from "commands" (plural) to "command" (singular). This phenomenon also occurs in 1 John, as observed in 1 John 3:23–24. As argued there, this is no contradiction since Jesus's "new" command of love sums up all the commands of Moses.[7]

Thus 2 John 4–6 exhibits an intentional circularity. Believers are to love one another. Love is described as walking according to God's commands. And God's command is that we walk in love. Love is obedience, and obedience is love.

LIVE the Story

There is much discussion of both truth and love in 2 John, as well as the intersection of both. What is distinct in this passage, however, is the use of the *walking* metaphor for both concepts (though it is applied to truth in 3 John 3–4). What does it mean to walk according to the truth and love?

Walking in the Truth

In the Old Testament, the metaphor of walking is often used in the sense of walking *before the Lord*. That is, it involves living in a way that is pleasing in his sight. Walking conveys conduct under God's oversight. It is not simply wandering around aimlessly; it is God-conscious living.

---

6. Yarbrough regards 2 John 6 as a "microchiasm": walk-commandment-commandment-walk (*1–3 John*, 342n8).

7. "So law and love are not incompatible; on the contrary, each involves the other" (Stott, *Letters of John*, 210).

Imagine a young boy playing in the front yard of the family home. There is a picket fence that prevents the child from running on to the busy street, and he is instructed to stay in the yard, straying no farther. Imagine that child's father sitting on the front porch, perhaps reading the newspaper but also keeping an eye on his playful son. As the son plays in the yard, he is conscious that his play is under watchful eye. He is free to have fun and play as he wishes so long as he does not climb over the fence and run onto the street. Being conscious of his father's watchful eye helps him to do the right thing and to remain safe.

As we live our lives, it is enormously helpful to remember that we live under God's watchful eye. There is no part of life that he does not see. Knowing this will help us to resist the temptation to run out on the street where we might get hit by a passing car. Knowing that we walk before the Lord is both pleasing to him and a safeguard for us.

The above illustration can also help us to see the similarities and differences between living under the law of Moses and living under the new-covenant law of love. For the former, the front yard of the family home is enclosed by a picket fence. The young boy plays in the yard freely, but the fence provides a layer of safety as it prevents the boy from running on to the busy street. In this scenario, the father is sitting on the porch, keeping a watchful eye on his son, but the son's safety is measured by whether or not he stays within the parameters of the fence. If he begins to climb over the fence, he will be in violation of this loving restriction that is in place for his own well-being.

On the other hand, under the new covenant, without the requirements of the law of Moses, there is no picket fence. The boy plays in the yard freely, as before, but he is trusted to do the right thing in the absence of a fence. The father is still sitting on the porch, keeping a watchful eye, but now the son's safety is not measured by whether or not he climbs over the fence. There is no fence. Nevertheless, the instructions are more or less the same: he is to stay in the yard; he may not run on to the street.

In this way the New Testament can show strong parallels between the old and new covenants without putting Christians under the old. In Christ the fence has been removed (Eph 2:14–15), meaning that other children in the neighborhood can come and play in the yard. The gentiles are now welcome alongside the descendants of Abraham. But even without the law, we are still required to stay within the parameters of the yard. We are still to live in accordance with God's truth and instruction, characterized by love for him and for our neighbor.

Indeed, in Christ we have the Spirit of God living in us. This is another major difference between the new and the old covenants. The Spirit teaches and enables us to play within the yard. While a fence is an external boundary marker, the Spirit is internal; he lives in us, teaching us, directing us, and empowering us. It is as though the young boy playing in the yard has grown up a little; perhaps now a teenager, he does not need a fence to keep him safe. He knows the dangers of the street and is able to avoid them without external restrictions.

This is, in effect, Paul's argument in Galatians 3:23–25: the law was a guardian or babysitter (*paidagōgos*) until Christ came. Now we no longer need a babysitter. But just because the babysitter is now gone, this does not mean that believers can just do whatever we want. On the contrary, it is now our responsibility to discern what it means to live God's way in the world. We are to walk in the truth as we learn it from God himself.

We walk in the truth by consciously living in accordance to God's instruction, knowing that we do so before his watchful eye. The truth sets parameters by which we may live; it teaches us what is good, and it warns us of dangers that must be avoided. The truth instructs us to live in a way that is consistent with God's nature and character. It teaches us to reject false truths about him and to identify the idolatries of the world.

Walking in Love

Given the elder's intentional circularity in 2 John 4–6, it is clear that walking in the truth will lead to walking in love, for God's command is that we love one another. Since there has already been plenty of discussion in this commentary of the command to love one another, we will focus on *walking* in love.

If walking in the truth sets helpful parameters for living before God, walking in love characterizes such living. It is one thing to stay off the street while playing in the front yard, but what if the boy has a mean spirit as he plays with his little sister? He might be safe from oncoming traffic, but he is still not doing the right thing. The watchful father will encourage him to be kind to his sister because that's how he is to treat other members of the family. The son knows his father's love for him and knows that the father also loves his sister. To be a good son and brother, he needs to love.

As the neighbors see the children playing in the yard, the way they treat each other will become known. It's one thing for the children to remain safe, staying within the parameters of the yard, but it is another thing to play well together. If the children constantly bicker and fight with each other, how does that reflect on the household? The family will become known as good rule keepers but not very nice. They don't even treat their own family members well—how will they treat others?

Yet more importantly, what does the behavior of the children say about the nature of their Father? Sure, kids will be kids, and even with the most gracious, loving parents, kids can still be punks sometimes. But constantly harsh and unloving relationships between siblings are something else. Perhaps love is not being modeled to them? Maybe they have not received parental love themselves? Perhaps their parents are mean-spirited too?

On the other hand, children who play together with love, respect, and fidelity will make their household stand out like lights in the neighborhood. The unmistakable character of love reflects well on the children's father and says a lot about the nature of the family. It will be one of those families that other kids love to hang around—especially those kids who lack love in their own homes. The loving family will be all the more impressive when they extend their love to other kids. Playing in the yard is a joy for all, and no one is rejected. They are even invited inside to share a feast together. What a delight that family will be to their neighbors!

Without walking in love, we risk becoming Pharisees. They were consistently concerned about righteousness, but they frequently failed to love. Without walking in love, we will be seen as bickering siblings, reflecting poorly on our Father in heaven. By contrast, Jesus lived in perfect righteousness, but he did not fail to show compassion to those around him. He held truth and love together in perfect harmony. Likewise, as God's children we must strive for the same harmony. Let us walk in the truth. Let us walk in love.

LISTEN to the Story

⁷I say this because many deceivers, who do not acknowledge Jesus Christ as coming in the flesh, have gone out into the world. Any such person is the deceiver and the antichrist. ⁸Watch out that you do not lose what we have worked for, but that you may be rewarded fully. ⁹Anyone who runs ahead and does not continue in the teaching of Christ does not have God; whoever continues in the teaching has both the Father and the Son. ¹⁰If anyone comes to you and does not bring this teaching, do not take them into your house or welcome them. ¹¹Anyone who welcomes them shares in their wicked work.

¹²I have much to write to you, but I do not want to use paper and ink. Instead, I hope to visit you and talk with you face to face, so that our joy may be complete.

¹³The children of your sister, who is chosen by God, send their greetings.

Listening to the Text in the Story: Matthew 24:11; Ephesians 4:14; 1 John 4:2–3.

If the previous passage was the encouraging part of 2 John, this is the warning section. The elder warns the chosen lady about deceivers and antichrists who have not continued in the teaching of Christ. Such people do not have God and should not be welcomed by genuine believers.

The elder concludes the letter by expressing his desire to speak with his readers face to face and passes on the greetings of the chosen lady's "nieces and nephews."

 ## EXPLAIN the Story

Watch Out for Deceivers (vv. 7–8)

While genuine believers will walk in the truth and live according to the obedience of love, many deceivers have gone out into the world (v. 7a). Concern about deceivers is a major theme of 1 John (2:26; 3:7; 4:6) and is the major issue addressed in this second half of 2 John.

These deceivers "do not acknowledge Jesus Christ as coming in the flesh" (v. 7b). This expression is obviously parallel to 1 John 4:2: "Every spirit that acknowledges that Jesus Christ has come in the flesh is from God." However, scholars debate the significance of the different tenses used in the two verses—2 John 7 has Jesus "coming in the flesh" (using the present participle *erchomenon*) while 1 John 4:2 says "has come in the flesh" (using the perfect participle *elēlythota*)—some suggesting two different "comings" of Jesus. Jensen, however, has demonstrated that it is misguided to build such interpretations on the different tenses.[1] Recent research has shown that the present and perfect tenses are very often used in parallel,[2] and thus Jensen concludes, "There is no real difference between the confessions of 1 John 4:2 and 2 John 7."[3]

The deceivers seem to tap into the idea that Jesus was divine but not fully human. It is generally understood to represent a form of early Gnosticism, which regarded flesh as evil. A specific type of gnostic belief, docetism, regarded Jesus as only *appearing* to be human. It is possible then that these deceivers were early docetists. However, as Jobes suggests, the broader concern is salvific: "While sound Christology certainly insists on the physical incarnation of Christ as fully human, Christ's full humanity was necessary *because of* his role in God's plan of salvation as the atoning sacrifice for sin."[4]

Such a deceiver is also regarded an antichrist (v. 7b). Again, "antichrist" is a concept raised in 1 John (2:18, 22; 4:3), and Lieu points out that "it would be difficult to understand [this verse's] intention without reference to the passage in 1 John."[5] In that letter, the antichrist is not a single individual but is "whoever denies that Jesus is the Christ" (1 John 2:22). Such a person is "powered" by "the spirit of the antichrist," which "does not acknowledge Jesus" (1 John 4:3).

The elder's readers are to watch out for these deceivers, and in particular they are to make sure they "do not lose what we have worked for, but that you may be rewarded fully" (2 John 8). It is not clear what the elder means by

---

1. Matthew D. Jensen, "Jesus 'Coming' in the Flesh: 2 John 7 and Verbal Aspect," *NovT* 56 (2014): 310–22.

2. Constantine R. Campbell, *Verbal Aspect, the Indicative Mood, and Narrative: Soundings in the Greek of the New Testament*, SBG 13 (New York: Peter Lang, 2007), 161–211; idem, *Verbal Aspect and Non-Indicative Verbs. Further Soundings in the Greek of the New Testament*, SBG 15 (New York: Peter Lang, 2008), 24–29.

3. Jensen, "Jesus 'Coming' in the Flesh," 322.

4. Jobes, *1, 2, & 3 John*, 265 (emphasis original).

5. Lieu, *I, II, & III John*, 252.

"what we have worked for" and whether the "we" here means the elder and his associates or includes his readers.[6] Probably it is the latter. Most likely the elder is referring to the maturity and standing of this Christian community. They have been built up in the true faith, and the elder does not want to see their progress annulled by falling under the spell of deceivers. Polycarp of Smyrna encourages his readers thus:

> Let us be zealous for that which is good, refraining from occasions of scandal and from false brothers and those who hypocritically bear the name of the Lord, deceiving empty-headed people.[7]

Rather than lose "what we have worked for," the elder wants his readers to be "rewarded fully" (v. 8b). While this could refer to some kind of heavenly treasure (cf. Matt 6:20; Mark 10:21; Luke 12:33), in the immediate context the most likely "reward" is God himself: "Whoever continues in the teaching has both the Father and the Son" (v. 9b).

The One Who Continues in the Teaching of Christ Has the Father and the Son (v. 9)

Anyone who "runs ahead and does not continue in the teaching of Christ does not have God" (v. 9a). Running ahead (*ho proagōn*) should be interpreted as synonymous with failing to remain in the teaching of Christ. Yarbrough writes that it means "to represent Christ in ways that are inconsistent and irreconcilable with established apostolic recollections that crystallized in Christian congregations over a period of a half century or so."[8] Running ahead means that a person has left behind the teaching that should be kept. It is an image of someone running headlong into trouble or going off the edge of a cliff.

Such a person does not continue in the teaching of Christ (*tē didachē tou Christou*). This could mean Christ's teaching (subjective genitive) or teaching about Christ (objective genitive). The latter is more likely given the context.[9] The elder has just described the deceivers as people "who do not acknowledge Jesus Christ as coming in the flesh" (v. 7), so we know their error is

---

6. Apparently some scribes also felt the tension of this question, amending the text to "what *you* have worked for." Some manuscripts read "*we* do not lose what *we* have worked for" (we, we), some read "*you* do not lose what *you* have worked for" (you, you), and yet others read "*you* do not lose what *we* have worked for" (you, we). The first reading (we, we) is unlikely due to the weight of manuscript evidence. The second reading (you, you) is possible, but the third (you, we) is most likely. See Culy, *I, II, III John*, 148–49.

7. Polycarp, "The Letter of Polycarp, Bishop of Smyrna, to the Philippians," in *Early Christian Fathers*, ed. Cyril Richardson, vol. 1 of *The Library of Christian Classics*, ed. J. Baillie et al. (Philadelphia: Westminster, 1953–66), 134.

8. Yarbrough, *1–3 John*, 350.

9. Culy, *I, II, III John*, 150.

christological; they have a wrong understanding of who Jesus is. Because of this, the RSV helpfully translates this portion of v. 9 as anyone "who goes ahead and does not abide in the doctrine of Christ."

The consequence of leaving behind the true teaching about Christ is that such a person "does not have God" (v. 9a). The ultimate penalty for straying from the truth is lack of relationship with God himself. This is in perfect keeping with the elder's theology: to deny Jesus is to deny Father and Son (1 John 2:22–23), but to believe in the name of Jesus Christ is to ensure that God lives in him or her, those born of God (1 John 3:23–24; 4:15; 5:1).

On the other hand, "whoever continues in the teaching has both the Father and the Son" (v. 9b). Those who remain in the truth are rewarded with true relationship with God. And as we have just seen, if we have the Son we have the Father, and vice versa. They are a package deal. Notice also the reciprocal parallel of *not having God* and *having the Father and the Son*. It would seem that "God" is understood here as equivalent to "Father and Son," which partially conveys the elder's implicit Trinitarianism.

The contrasting positions in v. 9 are known today as apostasy and perseverance. *Apostasy* is the abandonment of right belief. It is not a momentary lapse in judgment or a temporary failure. It is the sustained, persistent rejection of the truth. It is running ahead, leaving behind the teaching about Christ. On the other hand, *perseverance* refers to theological fidelity over the long haul. In spite of momentary lapses or temporary mistakes and failures, the perseverance of believers shows that they are indeed true believers. Their sustained commitment to the truth about Christ demonstrates the caliber of their commitment.

Do Not Welcome False Teachers (vv. 10–11)

Rather than leaving his instruction abstract, the elder directs his readers about what to do if and when a deceiver comes across their path. If anyone comes "and does not bring this teaching, do not take them into your house or welcome them" (10). The "house" (*oikia*) most likely means a personal dwelling, though some commentators take it to mean the house in which the church would meet for worship.[10] According to this reading, the prohibition forbids welcome into the congregation rather than private hospitality. Against this view, however, is the fact that "house" church meetings in the New Testament are indicated by a different word (*oikos*; Rom 16:5; 1 Cor 16:19; Col 4:15; Phlm 2).[11] Most likely, the elder therefore prohibits the extension of private hospitality to false teachers.

---

10. E.g., Smalley, *1, 2, 3 John*, 321; Stott, *Letters of John*, 214; Brown, *Epistles of John*, 676.

11. Smalley acknowledges this point but opts for a congregational reading nonetheless (*1, 2, 3 John*, 321).

This command highlights the severity of danger these deceivers represent. The elder does not want the faithful to show Christian hospitality to false teachers; the risk is far too great for that. It ought to be immediately clear who such people are and that their presence is life threatening from a spiritual perspective.

The elder even goes so far as to say that "anyone who welcomes them shares in their wicked work" (v. 11). While this may seem overly harsh to modern ears, it makes perfect sense in the ancient world. The offer of greeting to visitors and receiving them into one's house would have meant giving them lodging. In the ancient world, rented accommodation was often unreliable and even precarious, which meant that most people would rely on the hospitality of others when they traveled.[12] Indeed, "early Christians often hosted traveling missionaries who spread the gospel (e.g., Lk. 9.1–6; 10.1–18; *Did.* 11–12; Ignatius, *Eph.* 7.1; 9.1; Hermas, *Mand.* 11.12)."[13] That is the situation envisaged here: the elder imagines visiting teachers who require lodging from "other believers."

Lieu draws attention to the significance of hospitality in the early Christian movement. It "established or reinforced bonds between different communities," so that welcoming strangers is a theme in New Testament letters (Rom 12:13; Heb 13:2).[14] According to Malina, hospitality was the "means of which an outsider's status is changed from stranger to guest."[15] To offer hospitality to false teachers would establish "a relationship of acknowledgment and acceptance; such a relationship is formed not merely with the person but with what they represent."[16] In other words, hospitality would approximate endorsement. In fact, Keener observes in the Dead Sea Scrolls that someone who provided for an apostate person was regarded an apostate sympathizer and would be expelled from the Qumran community.[17]

The elder's instruction to refuse this need means that visiting false teachers would not be able to remain in that location. They would be forced to move on. Moreover, false teachers would be unendorsed by genuine believers who refuse to welcome them. In this way, we can see why the elder would say that greeting such visitors would approximate sharing in their wicked work; it would give them the opportunity and endorsement to conduct their

---

12. Abraham J. Malherbe, "Hospitality and Inhospitality in the Church," in *Social Aspects of the Early Church*, 2nd ed. (Philadelphia: Fortress, 1983), 94–96.

13. Arterbury, *Entertaining Angels*, 119.

14. Lieu, *I, II, & III John*, 261.

15. Bruce J. Malina, "The Received View and What It Cannot Do: III John and Hospitality," *Semeia* 35 (1986): 181–82.

16. Lieu, *I, II, & III John*, 262.

17. Keener, *IVP Bible Background Commentary*, 717.

"ministry" unabated. On the other hand, the refusal of hospitality would hinder their ability to cause damage among genuine believers. Thus, while seemingly unloving, the elder's instruction is given out of pastoral concern for the faithful.

Closing Greetings (vv. 12–13)

The closing of 2 John is quite personal, as the elder indicates he has much to write but hopes instead to see his readers personally (v. 12). He does not want to communicate everything through "paper and ink" (lit., "papyrus and ink") but hopes to visit them so that they can talk "face to face" (lit., "mouth to mouth"; *stoma pros stoma*). In this way "our joy may be complete."

Finally, the elder passes on the greetings of "the children of your sister, who is chosen by God" (v. 13). If the elect lady of verse 1 is a congregation and her children are its members, then it follows that her "sister" is another congregation. Her "children" then are the members of this congregation, and it is they who send greetings to their "cousins." This fellow congregation is mostly likely one to which the elder himself belongs or at least is one that he has recently spent time with.

The close of 2 John reminds us that the elder is not issuing warning and instruction simply out of duty or responsibility. He writes to fellow believers for whom he has a strong bond of affection. He writes out of love and genuine concern for their welfare. He longs to see them again that their mutual joy might be complete.

LIVE the Story

We have already addressed some of the implications surrounding deceivers and antichrists (see on 1 John 2:22; 4:3). Here we need to explore the importance of continuing in the teaching about Christ (v. 9) and what we are to make of the elder's "anti-hospitality" instruction (vv. 10–11).

Continuing in the Teaching about Christ

The elder warns his readers about running ahead and not continuing in the teaching of Christ. First, the running-ahead metaphor is striking. It evokes a picture of someone impatiently rushing forward. It is easy to imagine someone who does not like the pace kept by the group and thus surges on ahead alone. Perhaps such impatience is mixed with pride, as the culprit enjoys being ahead of the pack.

But what is wrong with pushing ahead? Shouldn't Christians *want* to grow, develop, and mature? Why shouldn't we surge forward?

The point at which the deceiver and antichrist fail is not from urgency to grow and mature. It is from an urgency to leave behind the established understanding of who Jesus is. The deceiver surges forward in order to leave something behind, and what's left behind is not immaturity; what's left behind is orthodox belief.

The truth is that we never graduate from studying the revelation of God through his Son. Jesus Christ come in the flesh is the first *and* the last point of Christian theology, not to mention all the points in between. The incarnate Son of God is the alpha and omega, the beginning and the end. It is all about him.

Real growth in Christian theology does not leave the truth about Jesus behind. Rather, genuine theological growth goes *deeper* into Jesus. This is much like Paul's message to the Colossians, who may have been tempted to leave behind the message they first heard in order to find deeper spiritual fulfilment. But rather than being taken captive by hollow philosophy and human tradition, Paul exhorts the Colossians to continue to live *in Christ*, rooted and built up *in him*, just as they first received Christ Jesus as Lord (Col 2:6–8). The Jesus they *received* is the one into whom they were to grow up. They were to go deeper *into* Jesus, not away from him.

Curiosity, they say, killed the cat. Personally I am quite fond of curiosity. But as the proverb warns, it can lead to danger. There is nothing wrong with theological curiosity, but there are dangers to avoid. We can profitably learn new things about theology, the Bible, and Jesus himself. A desire to learn and understand is healthy in this respect. We can even profit from studying ideas that are, to put it bluntly, heterodox. The study of incorrect doctrine can help us to better understand orthodoxy, and it can refine and sharpen our thinking.

However, a preoccupation with heterodoxy can quickly become unhealthy. It can unsettle established faith, and it can wreak havoc with our core convictions. We need to proceed with care. Without wanting to banish a healthy dose of curiosity and theological inquiry, it seems wise to remind ourselves of the gospel we first heard. We need to keep going in the direction that was first set for us. We need to learn Jesus more deeply. And by having the Son, we have the Father also.

And What about Anti-Hospitality?

When the elder warns his readers against welcoming false teachers (vv. 10–11), it is essential to remember the historical context regarding hospitality. To welcome a false teacher or to give them lodging was to endorse them and their message. For the elder, such an endorsement would be tantamount to partnering in their false ministry. He clearly cannot tolerate such a mistake, given the potential danger to the church.

But what does this mean for us today? The elder wants his readers to refuse false teachers entry into their homes (v. 10); should we think similarly? On the basis of this verse, some Christians have refused to enter into discussion with Jehovah's Witnesses or Mormons who have landed on their doorstep. Regarding such groups as heterodox, these Christians do not welcome their evangelists and will not engage them in conversation. But is this really what the elder is addressing?

Times have changed, and it is difficult to imagine that having a conversation on one's doorstep would be tantamount to partnership in heterodox ministry. Visiting Mormon missionaries are not dependent on our hospitality; they already have somewhere to stay. Usually they live locally, but in any case a hotel is an acceptable solution for travelers, which was not normally the case in the first century.

I would argue that a conversation (or debate!) on your doorstep is perfectly appropriate. It is not an endorsement, and it does not support an alternate message. In fact, it might be an opportunity to try to win someone over to our way of thinking.

When my wife and I were newly married, we had a number of such visitors to our door. We had a few fruitful conversations with Mormons and Jehovah's Witnesses. In fact, in both cases we had the same missionaries visit a few weeks in a row so that we could continue the conversation. We invited them inside and offered them tea and coffee. Of course, we hoped to see them converted, while they wanted to convert us. But in the process, both parties grew in our understanding of each other, and my wife and I became more solidly convicted of the truth of the gospel.

In light of the changed cultural situation, a better application of the elder's warning would be to think of ways we might accidentally endorse unhelpful messages. That's not likely to happen through hospitality, but perhaps there are other ways we might make a parallel error. Maybe you've "liked" a group on Facebook that really shouldn't have your endorsement. Perhaps by buying certain products—books or music, for example—we have given financial support to an organization that engages in false teaching. Maybe someone has lacked the theological smarts to recognize false teaching and has inadvertently given their approval to a dodgy church near their friend's house.

The take-home message is that we must not be complicit in the ministry of a false gospel. Ecumenical conversation is one thing, but partnership in the spread of heterodox views about Jesus is another. We should be on our guard against accidental endorsement of a message that can actually do people harm. We need to continue in the teaching of Christ ourselves so that we might be equipped to spot danger when it approaches and know to walk the other way.

Introduction to 3 John

If 2 John suffers neglect because of its "2" status and its brevity (see the introduction to 2 John), 3 John has the toughest gig in the New Testament: it is the only "3" book in the entire Bible, *and* it is the shortest book in the Bible.

But it would be a mistake to ignore 3 John. First, it is in the canon. Second, like 2 John it directly applies the twin Johannine themes of truth and love with respect to hospitality. Third, 3 John offers practical application with respect to leadership. It will sometimes be necessary to "call out" a bad leader like Diotrephes. And, conversely, it is fitting to endorse good models for others to emulate, as the elder puts forward Demetrius for Gaius's benefit. Like 2 John, 3 John offers the kind of concrete practicality that is not found in the lofty 1 John. All three letters go together and complement each other for our encouragement.

Who Wrote 3 John and Why?

Authorship

The addressor of 3 John is "the elder," apparently indicating the same author as 2 John. The two letters also share virtually the same opening and closing formulas and other similarities. These striking similarities have caused most scholars to conclude that they came from the same author.[1] Unlike 1 and 2 John, however, 3 John is written to an individual, Gaius (see below for more about him). This fact alone makes 3 John the most personal of the Johannine Epistles.

The third letter attributed to John enjoys less historical attestation than 1 or 2 John. There is no explicit mention of it until the third century and no clear citation from it until the fourth century.[2] Origen of Alexandria (AD 185–254) attested the existence of the letter but acknowledged that 2 and 3 John were not universally regarded as genuine (so Eusebius, *Hist. eccl.* 6.25.10). Eusebius (ca. AD 263–340) said both letters were well known but acknowledged that some doubted their authenticity (*Hist. eccl.* 6.25.10). Jerome (ca. AD 347–420) regarded all three letters as written by John the

---

1. Brown, *Epistles of John*, 15.
2. Dodd, *Johannine Epistles*, xv.

apostle but recorded that some attributed 2 and 3 John to a certain John the Presbyter (*Vir. ill.* 9.18). Yet by this time the three letters were already regarded as canonical, in part thanks to the authority of Athanasius.[3]

The authenticity of 3 John, however, is best tethered to its relationship to 2 John and in turn 2 John's relationship to 1 John. If the three letters are accepted together as from a single author, we can enjoy fair confidence in the traditional claim of their Johannine authorship.

The Elder's Situation

According to the only historical evidence we have, the apostle John lived in Ephesus in western Asia Minor following the Jewish rebellion in AD 66 (see the introduction to 1 John). Second and 3 John reveal that he had relationships with multiple congregations, suggesting that his ministry was spread through the region in and around Ephesus and across (possibly several) different house churches in that area.

The Elder's Reasons for Writing

The elder writes to commend and exhort his dear friend, Gaius. Gaius apparently belonged to a different congregation from the elder, but the elder planned to visit him and his other friends there.

He commends Gaius for the love he has shown by way of his hospitality toward visiting missionaries. Such hospitality is praised as partnership in the work of the truth. The elder also informs Gaius about the negative example of Diotrephes and exhorts him not to imitate what is evil but what is good. Demetrius is instead put forward as a positive model to emulate.

The letter is written in anticipation of the elder's visit. He planned to see Gaius and to speak to his church. The elder will call attention to the bad leadership and unloving example of Diotrephes when he comes. It is possible that he expected Gaius to share the letter with other members of the congregation to draw attention to Diotrephes's bad behavior in preparation for the elder's arrival.[4]

The Elder's Composition of 3 John

At just 218 words in the original Greek, 3 John is the shortest book in the New Testament. The original letter would have fit on a single piece of papyrus, the most common writing material in the first century. Third John has several features expected of a typical Greco-Roman letter and is closer in form

---

3. Dodd, *Johannine Epistles*, xv.
4. Smalley, *1, 2, 3 John*, 359.

and structure to other ancient personal notes than any other New Testament book.[5]

Some scholars regard 3 John as a letter of recommendation, since the elder commends a certain Demetrius in v. 12. But it is unlikely that this is the main purpose of the letter. While there is a clear commendation of Demetrius in v. 12, the overall message of 3 John does not revolve around it (see the commentary on v. 12).

The Elder's Opponent

The elder writes in clear opposition to the character Diotrephes (vv. 9–11). Nothing is known about him except what the elder indicates. Diotrephes "loves to be first" and will not welcome the elder and his group (v. 9). He has also been spreading "malicious nonsense" about the elder's group (v. 10a). Furthermore, Diotrephes has been unwelcoming toward other believers and even goes so far as to reject members of the church who want to welcome others (v. 10).

There have been various scholarly proposals about Diotrephes's identity.[6] Zahn and Harnack saw him as a monarchical bishop. Bauer believed the struggle between the elder and Diotrephes was theological, with the latter teaching heresy in the form of docetism. Käsemann reversed this, with Diotrephes as the orthodox bishop excommunicating the heretical elder (!). Price speculated that it was all a misunderstanding.[7] Abraham Malherbe has convincingly argued, however, that the struggle between the elder and Diotrephes was more likely personal than theological.[8]

It is possible that Diotrephes was the leader of the house church that the elder sought to visit or was its host (but not necessarily its leader). Either way, it is clear that he wielded the power to put people out of the church (v. 10).

Content of 3 John

Though the shortest book in the New Testament, 3 John has a rich and edifying message. Addressed to the individual, Gaius (see below), the main themes revolve around truth and love, as we see also in 2 John. As in that letter, these themes are expressed in relation to hospitality.

---

5. Jobes, *1, 2, & 3 John*, 282.

6. As summarized by Painter, *1, 2, and 3 John*, 362–63.

7. Robert M. Price, "The Sitz-Im-Leben of Third John: A New Reconstruction," *EvQ* 61 (1989): 109–19.

8. Abraham J. Malherbe, "The Inhospitality of Diotrephes," in *God's Christ and His People: Studies in Honour of Nils Alstrup Dahl*, ed. Jacob Jervell and Wayne A. Meeks (Oslo: Universitetsforlaget, 1977), 222–32.

Walking in the Truth

The elder first expresses his "love in the truth" for Gaius (cf. 2 John 1) and describes his prayers for him (vv. 1–2). The next two verses focus on the elder's joy that Gaius is walking in the truth. Other believers have told the elder about Gaius's faithfulness to the truth (v. 3). The elder expresses his joy in hearing that his children are walking in the truth.

Truth is a major concern of all three of John's letters. The specific language of "walking in the truth" is featured in 2 and 3 John. The Jewish metaphor of "walking" represents one's life conduct, and "walking in the truth" has to do with faithful obedience to God's instruction (see the commentary on 2 John 4 and 3 John 3–4). To see believers walking in obedience to the truth gives the elder great joy (v. 4).

Hospitality

The elder praises Gaius for taking good care of the "brothers and sisters" who were strangers to him (v. 5). These guests have reported Gaius's love, and now the elder requests that Gaius send them on their way in a manner that is worthy of God (v. 6). The elder indicates that these people are missionaries who went out "for the sake of the Name," and believers ought to show hospitality to such people in partnership for the truth, especially since they receive no help from the pagans (v. 7). Gaius's hospitality is a tangible expression of his love as well as his commitment to the truth. On the other hand, the elder has himself experienced *in*hospitality from a certain Diotrephes. Nothing is known about this figure except what the elder tells us (see above).

Gaius and Diotrephes thus provide positive and negative examples (respectively) of Christian hospitality extended to traveling teachers or prophets in the early church (cf. Luke 9:1–6; 10:1–18; Did. 11–12; Ign. *Eph.* 7.1; 9.1; Hermas. Mand. 11.12).[9] These missionaries have been sent out by the elder to deliver their teaching to believers in a different Christian community and would have expected to receive accommodation from the recipients of their ministry. Third John, along with 2 John, therefore reinforces the prominence of this missionary-hospitality practice in the first century.[10]

Imitating the Good

Diotrephes represents an attitude that is opposite to the love in the truth that the elder exhorts. Gaius is not to imitate evil but what is good, since those who do good are from God (v. 11). Though Gaius has already been praised

---

9. Arterbury, *Entertaining Angels*, 120.
10. Ibid., 120–21.

for his faithfulness and love (vv. 5–6), the elder does not assume that he has arrived. There is yet a place for imitating the good and growing in it, especially when negative examples present themselves, such as Diotrephes. There is always the potential threat of steering into a bad direction, and this must be diligently avoided. The elder holds up Demetrius to counteract the possible negative influence of Diotrephes. Unlike the latter, Demetrius is well spoken of by everyone—even by the truth itself (v. 12).

Outline of Contents

Third John is structured in four clear sections.

Outline of 3 John

1–4	Opening Greeting
5–10	Hospitality—Positive and Negative
11–12	Imitate What Is Good
13–14	Closing Greetings

How Does 3 John Relate to 1 and 2 John?

There is relatively little overlap between 1 John and 3 John. The latter shows no direct evidence of schism, no christological error or antichrist, and no call to love one another.[11] And yet those are the major themes of 1 John, and they resonate with 2 John also, thus creating a natural affinity between the first two letters.

While 3 John may not share in that affinity between 1 and 2 John, it does bear some connection to 2 John, including the author's title, "the elder," and the language and form of the opening and closing greetings. While some have posited that the letter mentioned in 3 John 9 was actually 2 John, the reference is too vague to make such a conclusion.[12]

The most interesting connection between 2 John and 3 John relates to the issue of hospitality. While 2 John prohibits its readers from extending hospitality to the deceivers and antichrists, 3 John records an incident in which the elder is himself denied hospitality. Some have speculated that Diotrephes, who loves to be first (v. 9), refused to welcome the elder as an unhappy response to 2 John. Perhaps finding the elder's prohibition of hospitality offensive, he decided to give him a taste of his own medicine. While this would explain

---

11. Painter, *1, 2, and 3 John*, 361–62.
12. Peter-Ben Smit, "A Note on the Relationship between II and III John," *BN* 123.3 (2004): 93–101.

why both letters share the motif of hospitality, the proposal is entirely speculative, without the support of any direct evidence from the letter itself.

Some Similarities between John's Gospel and 1–3 John[13]

Gospel of John	1 John	2 John	3 John
John 3:21 But whoever lives by the **truth** comes into the light	*1 John 1:6* If we say, "We have fellowship with him" and walk in the darkness, we lie and do not do the **truth**.	*2 John 4* I rejoice greatly because I have found some of your children walking in the **truth**.	*3 John 3* I rejoice greatly when brothers come and tell of your **truth**—how you are walking in the truth.

Whom the Elder Addresses in the Letter

Unlike 1 and 2 John, 3 John is addressed to an individual—Gaius. This common Roman name appears five times in the New Testament, referring to at least three different men. While one ancient tradition puts Gaius of Derbe (Acts 20:4) as the addressee of 3 John, whom John apparently installed as the first bishop of Pergamum, most scholars think that the Gaius of 3 John is an otherwise unknown church figure (see the commentary on v. 1).

What we can know for certain is that the elder regards Gaius with affection; he loves him (v. 1), prays for him (v. 2), and regards him as one of his spiritual children (v. 4). The elder is concerned for Gaius's spiritual health (vv. 11–12) and looks forward to seeing his dear friend (vv. 5, 11) face to face (v. 14). Gaius apparently belonged to a different congregation than the elder, but it was one that was known to him and that he planned to visit (vv. 10, 14).

---

13. This portion is reproduced from Jobes's chart (*1, 2, & 3 John*, 25–27). The quotations from the letters are Jobes's own translations (bold original). Used with permission.

LISTEN to the Story

> ¹The elder,
> To my dear friend Gaius, whom I love in the truth.
> ²Dear friend, I pray that you may enjoy good health and that all may go well with you, even as your soul is getting along well. ³It gave me great joy when some believers came and testified about your faithfulness to the truth, telling how you continue to walk in it. ⁴I have no greater joy than to hear that my children are walking in the truth.

Listening to the Text in the Story: Colossians 2:1–5; 2 John 4.

In this third letter of John (the second addressed from "the elder"), we see him address an individual for the first time rather than a congregation. He writes to Gaius, a dear friend, who evidently belonged to a congregation other than John's but who had shown hospitality to some believers known to John (vv. 5–8).

Even in his personal correspondence, we see John's characteristic concerns come to the fore—truth and love, in particular. This is evident from the beginning of the letter, as we see in the greeting of vv. 1–4.

EXPLAIN the Story

From the Elder to Gaius, a Dearly Loved Friend (vv. 1–2)

Third John is addressed from "the elder," who is clearly the author of 1 and 2 John.[1] The thematic parallels between all three letters are strong. The shared linguistic features of vocabulary, style, and phrasing all point to a single author, even as the audience changes from a congregation in 1 and 2 John to an individual in 3 John.

---

1. See the introduction to 3 John for discussion of these matters.

The elder writes to Gaius. A common Roman name meaning "rejoicing," it occurs five times in the New Testament (Acts 19:29; 20:4; Rom 16:23; 1 Cor 1:14; 3 John 1), probably referring to at least three different men: Gaius of Corinth (Rom 16:23; 1 Cor 1:14); Gaius of Macedonia (Acts 19:29); and Gaius of Derbe (Acts 20:4). According to a tradition dating to the fourth century (*Apostolic Constitutions* 7.46.9), the apostle John installed Gaius of Derbe (Acts 20:4) as the first bishop of Pergamum in Asia Minor, and he is the addressee of 3 John.[2] The tradition is possibly correct, but due to a lack of earlier evidence, the general consensus among modern commentators is that the Gaius of 3 John is probably not the man from Derbe but an otherwise unknown church figure.[3]

Gaius is the elder's "dear friend," literally, "beloved Gaius" (*Gaiō tō agapētō*). The elder loves him "in the truth" (v. 1). Even here, in the opening description of his dear friend, the elder combines the themes of love and truth. The elder's love for Gaius is not undefined or lacking in content. It is defined by truth, just as truth is also to be defined by love, according to the apostle.

As is customary in the greetings of ancient letters, a prayer is offered for the recipient. The elder prays that Gaius might enjoy good health and "that all may go well with you" (v. 2).[4] But his prayer is not only concerned with Gaius's way in the material world; he also considers how his soul is getting along. Thus the elder shows concern for Gaius's spiritual, as well as physical, situation.

Gaius Has Been Faithful to the Truth (vv. 3–4)

Moving on from his prayer for Gaius, the elder now praises him for his faithfulness. He says that he rejoiced "when some believers (lit., "brothers") came and testified about your faithfulness to the truth, telling how you walk in it" (3). These believers seem to have been travelers known to the elder, who had enjoyed Gaius's hospitality (vv. 5–8). They testified to his "faithfulness to the truth" (v. 3a). Faithfulness to the truth appears to refer to Gaius's conduct, since the following clause elaborates, "telling how you continue to walk in it" (v. 3b). Truth does not exist solely in the realm of abstract ideas or intellectual commitments; it must be lived out (see on 2 John 4). Gaius's walking in the truth is the way in which he was faithful to the truth. He demonstrated "wholehearted allegiance to God's truth as manifested in concrete actions to specific individuals."[5]

---

2. Jobes, *1, 2, & 3 John*, 289.

3. Dodd, *Johannine Epistles*, 156; Brown, *Epistles of John*, 702–3; Smalley, *1, 2, 3 John*, 344; Stott, *Letters of John*, 221–22; Yarbrough, *1–3 John*, 363.

4. Marshall raises the possibility that Gaius was not in the best of health, but there is little support for this conjecture (*Epistles of John*, 83, 89).

5. Thompson, *1–3 John*, 161.

Gaius's faithfulness prompts a general statement from the elder: "I have no greater joy than to hear that my children are walking in the truth" (v. 4). This comment reveals the elder's pastoral heart: he is given great joy to see other believers live in faithfulness to the truth (cf. 2 John 4). That he *hears* such news reveals that his concern extends beyond his immediate community. Believers living elsewhere are on the elder's pastoral radar.

We also see that the elder regards Gaius as one of his "children." This characteristic Johannine term of endearment for believers under John's pastoral oversight is seen throughout 1 and 2 John. While it implies that Gaius was younger than the elder, the main import of the term is its expression of fatherly care for a spiritual disciple.

In this opening greeting of 3 John, we see the Johannine concern for love and truth in action. The elder regards his friend Gaius with love in the truth, praying for his physical and spiritual well-being. Gaius is faithful to the truth, walking in it while demonstrating love to brothers and sisters previously unknown to him. Such faithfulness to the truth, expressed by love, prompts the elder's exceeding joy.

 LIVE the Story

Rejoicing in How Others Walk

The significance of walking in the truth is explored at 2 John 4. And while 2 John 4 also mentions the elder's great joy at finding that people are walking according to the truth, here in 3 John 4 the elder adds that he has "no greater joy" than to hear that his children are walking in the truth.

The elder's great joy demonstrates his true other-person centeredness. Gaius was not a part of the elder's daily life (cf. v. 3), yet the report of his fidelity to the truth elicits the elder's deep joy. He is overjoyed to hear that a brother is doing well spiritually.

I wonder how often we might share the elder's joy for such a reason. Do we rejoice to see our brothers and sisters' progress in their spiritual maturity? In my own pastoral experience, I have no trouble rejoicing when someone I am currently invested in is walking in the truth. I have a vested interested in the members of my home-group Bible study, for instance. And I am delighted to see my seminary students grow or to witness the progress of those who listen to my preaching. But to be honest, those to whom I am not directly ministering are simply not on my radar most of the time.

I suspect I'm not alone. Pastors have enough to deal with in the day-to-day demands of their ministry that it is easy to forget about believers in other places. Perhaps we will shoot off a quick thanksgiving when we read an encouraging prayer letter or see a heartening Facebook status. But do we experience *exceeding joy* at this kind of good news?

The elder is not the only New Testament example of this kind of pastoral concern for people at a distance. Paul's letters reveal an excellent example of a pastor who is consumed with love and care for his brothers and sisters in far-flung places. He is even devoted to saints he has not ever met in person (Col 2:1–5). Peter and James show similar commitment.

But what is the underlying factor here? Perhaps it can best be described as an overarching desire for God's glory. Those whose pastoral concern is wide and deep share a genuine conviction that Jesus Christ really is the center of everything. To see God glorified is the strongest driving force they know. This is certainly the impression we get from John's letters, not to mention those of Paul. The centrality of Jesus Christ powerfully shapes their thinking, attitudes, and pastoral love for others.

When the elder expresses exceeding joy at Gaius's faithfulness to the truth, his joy is produced by a love for God that has bred a love for others. It does not matter that they are currently separated from one another, for the elder is not solely concerned with the immediate and proximate. His vision is larger than that, and so is his heart.

LISTEN to the Story

> ⁵Dear friend, you are faithful in what you are doing for the brothers and sisters, even though they are strangers to you. ⁶They have told the church about your love. Please send them on their way in a manner that honors God. ⁷It was for the sake of the Name that they went out, receiving no help from the pagans. ⁸We ought therefore to show hospitality to such people so that we may work together for the truth.
>
> ⁹I wrote to the church, but Diotrephes, who loves to be first, will not welcome us. ¹⁰So when I come, I will call attention to what he is doing, spreading malicious nonsense about us. Not satisfied with that, he even refuses to welcome other believers. He also stops those who want to do so and puts them out of the church.

Listening to the Text in the Story: Matthew 10:40; John 1:12; 2:23; 3:18; 20:31; Acts 5:41; Romans 1:5; 1 John 2:12.

This passage constitutes the main body of 3 John. Its two segments contrast a positive example of loving hospitality (vv. 5–8) with a negative example of unfriendly rejection (vv. 9–10).

In the first segment, Gaius is again praised for his faithfulness. This time the elder expands on Gaius's demonstration of hospitality to previously unknown believers. He is encouraged to send off these brothers and sisters in a way that honors God. The elder makes a general point out of the importance of hospitality as an expression of partnership in the truth.

In the second segment, the elder expresses his disappointment with Diotrephes, who refused to welcome the elder and his group. When the elder visits the church in question, he plans to expose Diotrephes's malicious activities and unwelcoming attitude.

EXPLAIN the Story

Gaius's Hospitality Expresses Partnership in the Truth (vv. 5–8)

The elder again praises Gaius for his faithful care of visiting strangers, who have reported Gaius's love to the church (vv. 5–6a). These were not just any visiting strangers—they were "the brothers and sisters" (v. 5). This group was apparently known to the elder, who seems to be a member of the church from which they went out and to which they report. They left the elder's church in some kind of missionary capacity—"for the sake of the Name" (v. 7a).

While Jesus is not named anywhere in 3 John, it is most likely that "the Name" for whose sake these missionaries went out is to be understood as the name of Jesus. Painter points to Acts 5:41 and Romans 1:5 as clear examples of "the name" referring to Jesus.[1] The phrase is also used in 1 John 2:12, but it is left undefined. Moreover, as Painter points out, believing "in the name of Jesus" is a frequent refrain throughout John's Gospel (1:12; 2:23; 3:18; 20:31).[2]

Working for the "name" of Jesus, these missionaries received no help from the pagans (v. 7b),[3] who may have opposed them and their message. At the very least, they did not offer care for these traveling missionaries. It is for this reason that the elder offers the general exhortation that "we ought therefore to show hospitality to such people" (v. 8a). Since their labor "for the sake of the Name" apparently excludes such missionaries from assistance from nonbelievers, it is naturally the responsibility of other believers to address their needs.

Gaius is to "send them on their way in a manner that honors God" (v. 6). Literally, this is a send-off that is "worthy of God" (*axiōs tou theou*). Perhaps his manner is to resemble "how Gaius would have sent God on if God had stopped at his home for hospitality."[4] If so, according to Arterbury the elder "appears to be drawing upon the rich Mediterranean tradition of an incognito god who seeks hospitality from human hosts."[5] Perhaps more significantly, the exhortation echoes Jesus's instructions that hosts should welcome his disciples as though they were welcoming him (e.g., Matt 10:40).[6]

1. Painter, *1, 2, and 3 John*, 371–72.
2. Ibid., 372.
3. Lit., "nations" (*ethnikōn*), used by extension to refer to unbelievers in line with its Old Testament use for peoples outside God's chosen nation, Israel.
4. Arterbury, *Entertaining Angels*, 121.
5. Ibid.
6. Ibid.

3 John 5-10   219

Hospitality was an important social feature of the ancient Mediterranean world that "established or reinforced bonds between different communities,"[7] and was the "means of which an outsider's status is changed from stranger to guest."[8] Moreover, in showing hospitality to traveling missionaries, believers "may work together for the truth" (v. 8b). Literally, this is "in order that we might become fellow workers in the truth." Hospitality is not seen merely as a mundane responsibility, nor is its significance exhausted by viewing it as love in action. Hospitality is in fact *partnership in the truth*. By providing for their material needs, believers become coworkers alongside traveling missionaries.

We can see why, then, the elder puts such a high premium on the service of hospitality. In this ancient context travelers depended on reliable hospitality. Most inns served as brothels, ruling them out for Jews and Christians.[9] Without hospitality, missionaries were not able to do their work. But with their material needs met, missionaries were enabled to travel and conduct their ministry. So hospitality became partnership in missionary work in a very tangible sense.

But Diotrephes Shows Anti-Hospitality (vv. 9–10)

In stark contrast to Gaius's hospitality is the negative example of Diotrephes, who "will not welcome us" (v. 9).[10] We don't know who Diotrephes was, nor why he opposed the elder. The only explanation offered is that he "loves to be first" (v. 9). Perhaps he viewed the elder as a threat to his own authority and status in his congregation,[11] but it is impossible to say with certainty. There is no indication that the issue was theological. Whatever the case, Diotrephes publicly dishonored the believers he turned away, and he dishonored the elder, since the "matrix for the dispute is in the honor-culture of the first-century Mediterranean world."[12]

It is clear from the elder's descriptions that Diotrephes enjoyed some kind of leadership within the congregation, but we do not know in what capacity. Dodd offers three main possibilities: he was either (1) an acknowledged bishop of the church; (2) one of several presbyters who through force of

---

7. Lieu, *I, II, & III John*, 261.

8. Malina, "The Received View," 181–82. For more on the importance of hospitality in the ancient world, see the commentary on 2 John 10–11.

9. Keener, *IVP Bible Background Commentary*, 719.

10. Translations that read "does not accept our authority" (e.g., ESV, NRSV) have been shown to be incorrect. The meaning of the Greek verb is to *receive* or to *welcome* (so NIV, CSB). See Margaret M. Mitchell, "'Diotrephes Does Not Receive Us': The Lexicographal and Social Context of 3 John 9-10," *JBL* 117 (1998): 299–320.

11. D. Edmond Hiebert, "An Exposition of 3 John 5-10," *BSac* 144 (1987): 204–5.

12. Barth Lynn Campbell, "Honor, Hospitality and Haughtiness: The Contention for Leadership in 3 John," *EvQ* 77 (2005): 338.

character came to dominate; or (3) a layman who had usurped leadership.[13] Dodd explores all three possibilities, but there is no way to decide between them.[14] See the introduction to 3 John for more on Diotrephes's identity.

The elder indicates that he wrote to the church and will visit (vv. 9, 10a). Despite not being welcomed by Diotrephes, he plans to call attention to this leader's actions, which include "spreading malicious nonsense about us" (v. 10a). Refusing to welcome the elder was accompanied by slanderous lies. But Diotrephes's culpability went beyond his treatment of the elder; he "even refuses to welcome other believers" (v. 10b). It is clear that Diotrephes lacked love for others, and in this way he did the exact opposite of what the elder calls for among the fellowship of believers. He stopped those who wanted to join the congregation, and he put out of the church those who wanted to welcome them (v. 10c).

Diotrephes, it turns out, is the perfect negative example of the elder's concerns. Love and truth are what the elder cares most about in this letter, but Diotrephes embodied the opposite of both. He opposed other believers and spoke falsely about them. The only thing he loved was to be first. Gaius, on the other hand, exhibited love in abundance, walked in the truth, and was a partner in the truth.

 LIVE the Story

Partnering with Missionaries

The elder regards hospitality as an expression of partnership in the truth (v. 8). The significance of hospitality is explored at 2 John 10–11 where it is negatively applied. The elder's readers are not to show hospitality to deceivers and antichrists because it constitutes a sharing in their wicked work. Here, Gaius's hospitality to those who went out "for the sake of the Name" (v. 7) made him their partner in their missionary endeavor.

As suggested at 2 John 10–11, the modern application of such concern for missionary hospitality may need to be widened, since hospitality today does not mean what it once did. While it may indeed be very useful to house-visiting missionaries, there are several other ways that believers today can become partners in mission.

The most obvious way to partner in missionary work is to take part in it ourselves. But this is not really what the elder is driving at in 3 John; his immediate concern is that Gaius would be a partner to those who are doing the missionary work. It is the kind of partnership that supports mission rather

---

13. Dodd, *Johannine Epistles*, 162.
14. Dodd, *Johannine Epistles*, 162–64.

than doing the work personally. Of course, believers ought to consider doing missionary work, but let us here think more about *supporting* mission, since that is the elder's burden.

The next most obvious way to partner in missionary work is to offer financial support. For millions of Christians, financial support of missions is simply part of their giving budget. But for others, this kind of giving is not a priority. Sadly, missionaries are often pressed to raise the needed support, but this need not be the case. In 2004 K. P. Yohannan cited the statistic that the average American Christian gives only one penny a day to global missions.[15] One penny a day! Surely we can do better than that.

The author, publisher, and missions promoter Gordon Lindsay once wrote:

> The main hindrance to world evangelization has not been for the want of devoted missionaries, nor is it the lack for trained nationals, which was a serious problem for many years. The hour has come when we have an eager army of gospel soldiers ready to launch out in faith and preach the apostolic gospel. And they are doing it! Nor is there any lack of people responding to the message. Any missionary will tell you that almost every place an evangelistic effort is attempted, hundreds and in many cases even thousands will respond. Where then is the lack? It is in the lack of necessary financial assistance that often is not available at the moment the Spirit of God moves in a community.[16]

It is clear to Paul that in the matter of giving and receiving, the Philippians made themselves genuine partners with him in the work of proclaiming the gospel (Phil 4:14–19). He anticipates that their generosity will lead to God adding "credit" to their account (v. 17). Perhaps one reason that more Christians do not give to mission work is that they do not realize that their financial support constitutes genuine partnership in the work. If we could see such giving less as "supporting those who do mission" and more as "partnering with them in mission," we may be better motivated to do our part.

Another obvious way to partner in mission work is to pray. In his book *On This Day in Christian History*, Robert J. Morgan recounts the incredible history of a one-hundred-year prayer meeting that spawned remarkable mission activity:

> In 1722 Count Nikolaus Ludwig von Zinzendorf, troubled by the suffering of Christian exiles from Bohemia and Moravia, allowed them

15. K. P. Yohannan, *Revolution in World Missions* (Carrollton: GFA Books, 2004), 142.
16. Gordon Lindsay, *God's 20th Century Barnabas* (Dallas: Christ for the Nations, 1982), 235.

to establish a community on his estate in Germany. The center became known as Herrnhut, meaning "Under the Lord's Watch." It grew quickly, and so did its appreciation for the power of prayer.

On August 27, 1727 24 men and 24 women covenanted to spend an hour each day in scheduled prayer, praying in sequence around the clock. Soon others joined the prayer chain. Days passed, then months. Unceasing prayer rose to God 24 hours a day as someone—at least one—was engaged in intercessory prayer each hour of every day. The intercessors met weekly for encouragement and to read letters and messages from their brothers in different places. A decade passed, the prayer chain continuing nonstop. Then another decade. It was a prayer meeting that lasted over 100 years.

Undoubtedly this prayer chain helped birth Protestant missions. Zinzendorf, 27, suggested the possibility of attempting to reach others for Christ in the West Indies, Greenland, Turkey, and Lapland. Twenty-six Moravians stepped forward. The first missionaries, Leonard Dober and David Nitschmann, were commissioned during an unforgettable service on August 18, 1732, during which 100 hymns were sung. During the first two years, 22 missionaries perished and two more were imprisoned, but others took their places. In all 70 Moravian missionaries flowed from the 600 inhabitants of Herrnhut, a feat unparalleled in missionary history.

By the time William Carey became the "Father of Modern Missions" over 300 Moravian missionaries had already gone to the ends of the earth. And that's not all. The Moravian fervor sparked the conversions of John and Charles Wesley and indirectly ignited the Great Awakening that swept through Europe and America.

The prayer meeting lasted 100 years. The results will last for eternity.[17]

In whatever ways we can, Christians ought to partner in missionary work whether through prayer, giving, hospitality, or by other means. It is working together for the truth with those who go out for the sake of the Name.

Showing Hospitality

While the elder's chief concern regarding Gaius's hospitality is his partnership in missionary work, it nevertheless raises the topic of hospitality more generally. In her book *Making Room: Recovering Hospitality as a Christian Tradition*, Christine Pohl calls the church to regain its calling to and vision for hospitality. By drawing on Scripture and early-church practice, Pohl asserts

---

17. Robert J. Morgan, *On This Day in Christian History: 365 Amazing and Inspiring Stories about Saints, Martyrs and Heroes* (Nashville: Thomas Nelson, 1997), Kindle edition, August 27.

that "hospitality is basic to who we are as followers of Jesus" and "every aspect of our lives can be touched by its practice."[18]

These days, we often limit our understanding of hospitality to having people come to our homes for dinner. But for the early church, hospitality was much broader than pleasant dinners with friends. It included meals, yes, but also accommodation and taking care of a traveler's every material need. For many believers today, that kind of care is normally only reserved for family and close friends. The challenge for us, then, is to recapture a vision of hospitality that pushes beyond our comfort zones. Would we be willing to accommodate a stranger whom we meet at church? What about a homeless person? What about a refugee family? And would we be willing to host such people for longer than a few nights? How about a few weeks? How about a few months?

Pohl recognizes that some believers today may be daunted by the prospect of assuming some personal responsibility for hospitality to strangers because we have become dependent on large-scale institutions and specialists in almost every area of life.[19] And though institutions do important work, "hospitality requires both personal and communal commitment, and settings which combine aspects of public and private life."[20] She explores how to prepare our various "hospitable places," such as our homes, our churches, intentional communities, and social services, to become comfortable settings for human flourishing, shelter, and sanctuary.[21] "In such places life is celebrated, yet the environment also has room for brokenness and deep disappointments. Such places make faith and a hospitable way of life seem natural, not forced."[22]

But the first step in making a place for hospitality is to make room in our hearts. Pohl comments, "Welcome begins with dispositions characterized by love and generosity."[23] While our capacity for hospitality will vary at different times in our lives, we may always seek a humble attitude of generous, outreaching love toward others.

Hospitality in all its forms ought to flow from Christians as an acknowledgment of God's hospitality toward us. We were not "good guests," but he took us in and lavished us with love, mercy, and abundant provisions. He has even gone so far as to make us members of his family. Those of us who wrestle with an unwillingness to show the same sort of loving kindness to

---

18. Christine D. Pohl, *Making Room: Recovering Hospitality as a Christian Tradition* (Grand Rapids: Eerdmans, 1999), 150.

19. Ibid., 151.

20. Ibid.

21. Ibid., 152–69.

22. Ibid., 152.

23. Ibid.

others ought to pray that God will soften our hearts, remind us of what we have received from him, and teach us to love as he loves.

Calling Out a Bad Leader

The elder says he will call attention to the deeds of Diotrephes, who had been spreading about malicious nonsense, refused to welcome believers, and cast out of the church those who wanted to offer them a welcome (vv. 9–10). Clearly Diotrephes was a bad apple. And what's worse, he seemed to be a leader in his congregation. Burge writes:

> Conflict is no stranger to the church. Strong persons like Diotrephes often become leaders and teachers. In fact, they are generally invited and encouraged in those roles and quickly enjoy a wide following. But what happens when the views of people like this conflict with pastoral leadership? Perhaps it is not disagreement about views at all but a conflict of personalities, some form of competition, or even a loss of respect for each other. In some cases (rare ones, we hope), such lay leaders pose an overwhelming threat to pastoral authority. I have known cases where a "Diotrephes" has successfully worked to remove a pastor or where such a person has actually split the church in two, sometimes making an irreparable fracture within the congregation and sometimes leading parishioners out to form a second congregation.[24]

The elder recognizes the damage that a person like Diotrephes can do to a community of believers, and he is prepared to call a spade a spade. But sometimes Christians today can be too nice. And for all the right reasons: we want to be loving, accepting, tolerant, and patient with people, right? After all, we are all sinners struggling with our own issues. If someone like Diotrephes has a humility problem, well, we've all been there. So he's not the most welcoming guy in the world—but all of us need to learn how to accept others in love; it doesn't come naturally to most people. Let's just give Diotrephes a break, shall we?

But that's not the elder's attitude. On the one hand, he consistently exhorts believers to love one another, which no doubt includes bearing with one another's burdens and weaknesses. But on the other hand, he thinks that Diotrephes must be rebuked and the whole congregation needs to know what he has been doing.

The elder's attitude toward Diotrephes does not contradict his own mandate to love. Rather, Diotrephes must be opposed *because of* love. His actions are so dangerous that he puts the congregation at spiritual risk. He does not

---

24. Burge, *Letters of John*, 251.

seem to embody love for God, which is meant to issue in love for God's children. And someone who does not love God and/or God's children has no business leading God's people. He will lead them in the wrong direction, and he will warp their knowledge of God. It is his love for his brothers and sisters in Christ that compels the elder to act against this bad leader.

Bede the Venerable puts the matter well:

> It is true that we must do nothing to stir up the tongues of accusers, lest they should perish on our account. Likewise we must patiently endure those who attack us because of their own wickedness, so that we may become better people. Nevertheless there are times when we have to protest, because those who spread evil stories about us may corrupt the minds of innocent people who otherwise would have heard nothing but good about us. This is why John objects to his accuser.[25]

The elder's example challenges us to reassess what love might look like within church leadership. Being "nice" to everyone all the time will not always be the most loving disposition. On occasion we must exercise tough love. We must confront the bully; we must remove the immoral leader; we must rebuke the bad influence. Genuine love for God's people demands tough actions such as these on occasion. Of course, we ought to carry out tough love with grace and humility, but we also need a sturdy backbone. Pray the Lord will strengthen us when the time comes.

---

25. Bede, "On 3 John," in *Patrologiae Latinae Supplementum*, ed. A. Hamman (Paris: Garnier Frères, 1958–), 93:124.

CHAPTER 19

3 John 11–14

 LISTEN to the Story

> [11]Dear friend, do not imitate what is evil but what is good. Anyone who does what is good is from God. Anyone who does what is evil has not seen God. [12]Demetrius is well spoken of by everyone—and even by the truth itself. We also speak well of him, and you know that our testimony is true.
>
> [13]I have much to write you, but I do not want to do so with pen and ink. [14]I hope to see you soon, and we will talk face to face.
>
> Peace to you. The friends here send their greetings. Greet the friends there by name.[1]

Listening to the Text in the Story: Ephesians 5:1; 1 John 3:6, 9–10; 4:3, 7, 8, 20; 2 John 12.

In this last section of the letter, the elder offers a final exhortation, speaks of Demetrius's good reputation, and then signs off.

 EXPLAIN the Story

Do Not Imitate What Is Evil But What Is Good (vv. 11–12)

With the third address to Gaius as his "dear friend," the elder begins to conclude his letter with the instruction to imitate (*mimeomai*) what is good, not what is evil (v. 11a). Gaius is to emulate and follow the good, making it his model.[2] Perhaps that is why he mentions Demetrius in v. 12—to offer a model for Gaius to emulate in contrast to the pernicious Diotrephes.

Imitation of the good is not an empty platitude. The elder writes, "Anyone who does what is good is from God" (11b). Only a person who comes from God produces true "goodness." Such a notion has strong parallels in

---

1. In some versions, v. 14b appears as v. 15.
2. BDAG 651.

1 John (e.g., 3:9–10; 4:7). On the other hand, "anyone who does what is evil has not seen God" (11c), which also finds parallels in 1 John (3:6, 9–10; 4:3, 8, 20). Acts of good and evil are symptomatic of one's spiritual condition. Since God is the source of all that is good, those who truly belong to him will emulate his goodness. But without God, it is only possible to produce works of evil.

Demetrius is offered as someone who imitates what is good. According to Smalley, there is no reason to associate him with the Demetrius of Acts 19:23–41 or the Demas (possibly a contracted form of "Demetrius") in Colossians 4:14, Philemon 24, or 2 Timothy 4:10.[3] The fourth-century tradition that John made Demetrius the bishop of Philadelphia (*Apostolic Constitutions* 7.46.9) is not necessarily reliable. What we know about this Demetrius comes only from 3 John.

He was well spoken of by everyone, "even by the truth itself" (v. 12a). He enjoyed a healthy reputation with others, and the testimony of "the truth" about Demetrius probably means that he was on the right side of the truth. That is, he upheld the true apostolic teaching and walked in it (cf. v. 4).

It is difficult to know why Demetrius—who is not mentioned anywhere else in John's letters—now occupies the elder's attention. Perhaps he was simply a model for Gaius to follow (as suggested above), or perhaps he was one of the believers to whom Gaius showed hospitality. Some have even suggested that 3 John is in fact a letter of recommendation for Demetrius.[4]

The third option is unlikely, at least as an explanation of the overall purpose of the letter. While letters of recommendation played an important networking role in ancient society, Lieu points to recognized vocabulary for such purposes that is not found in 3 John.[5] Furthermore, the overall shape of the letter does not support a purpose centered on Demetrius, unless the elder's recommendation is deliberately subtle.

The second option would perhaps make better sense than the first due to the elder's personal affirmation of Demetrius's reputation: "We also speak well of him, and you know that our testimony is true" (v. 12b). This emphasis would hardly be necessary following the general endorsement of v. 12a if the sole purpose was to commend Demetrius as a model to emulate. But if Demetrius was in Gaius's company as the elder writes, then his personal affirmation is offered by way of reassurance about these "strangers" for whom Gaius was caring.

---

3. Smalley, *1, 2, 3 John*, 346.
4. E.g., Keener, *IVP Bible Background Commentary*, 718, 719.
5. Lieu, *I, II, & III John*, 280–81. See also Luca Marulli, "A Letter of Recommendation? A Closer Look at Third John's 'Rhetorical' Argumentation," *Bib* 90 (2009): 203–23.

Closing Greetings (vv. 13–14)

The elder's concluding remarks indicate that he has more to say to Gaius but would prefer to see him in order to talk face to face rather than to do so "with pen and ink" (vv. 13–14a).[6] These comments are nearly identical to the closing remarks of 2 John 12: "I have much to write to you, but I do not want to use paper and ink. Instead, I hope to visit you and talk with you face to face, so that our joy may be complete." Though the ideas in 3 John 13–14a and 2 John 12 are basically identical, they are worded differently in the original Greek. This means that one was not simply copied from the other, even while the meaning of both is virtually the same. Both those facts strongly point to common authorship since the parallel meaning suggests they came from the same mind, while the different wording indicates that it is not simply copied by an imitator.

The elder wishes Gaius "peace," a common Hebraic and Semitic greeting,[7] and extends the greetings of "the friends" (v. 14b). He asks Gaius to "greet the friends there by name" (v. 14c). This indicates that the elder was known to the congregation of which Gaius was a part. The church he plans to visit (v. 10) was one he already knows.

As we have seen in 2 John, the closing of 3 John reinforces the bonds of fellowship between the elder and his addressee. His desire is for Gaius to live according to the good. The elder hopes to be reunited with Gaius shortly, and wishes him peace in the meantime.

LIVE the Story

Not Imitating the Bad

It is no accident that the elder's exhortation to imitate what is good, not evil (v. 11), follows immediately after his discussion of the pompous Diotrephes (vv. 9–10). He implicitly acknowledges that people like Diotrephes can negatively influence those around them, and Gaius must avoid being so influenced.

Imitation is a powerful factor of human development. We can't help but be influenced by those around us—in positive and negative ways. Often this occurs without us even realizing that it's happening. And, indeed, it can even happen when we *know* that a person is a bad example. Such knowledge does not necessarily protect us from negative influences because we often cannot help but be shaped by those around us.

---

6. The pen is a reed pen (*kalamos*); BDAG 502.
7. Bruce, *Epistles of John*, 156.

As Paul says, quoting the Greek poet Menander, "Bad company corrupts good character" (1 Cor 15:33). Likewise Proverbs 22:24–25 warns:

Do not make friends with a hot-tempered person,
    do not associate with one easily angered,
or you may learn their ways
    and get yourself ensnared.

If we take these warnings seriously, we will acknowledge that the regular presence of bad influences in our lives is unhealthy for our spiritual well-being. It is foolhardy simply to dismiss the warnings on the grounds that we know better than to let bad influences change us. Even the most discerning believers can be unwittingly shaped and influenced in unhelpful ways.

Admittedly, we do not always have the ability to choose our company. I doubt that Proverbs—or Paul for that matter—would endorse estrangement from family members, colleagues, or neighbors on the basis that bad company corrupts good character—except perhaps in rare, extreme cases. Additionally, we would not want these warnings to prevent us from associating with those who need to experience the life and light of Christ. Again, Paul would hardly endorse avoiding unbelievers for the sake of keeping ourselves from negative influences. Instead, such people need *our* positive influence in their lives. They need the gospel. They need Jesus. And so we ought to be willing to do life with them, even at the risk of unhelpful influence on us. Notwithstanding those considerations, the basic principle is nevertheless sound: bad company corrupts good character. Believers need to avoid bad influences so far as we are able and so far as is wise.

Imitating the Good

With bad examples like Diotrephes around, it is important that believers model themselves on those who do good. Imitation is a powerful factor for learning and growth, and so it is the tool that the elder endorses: Gaius should imitate what is good (v. 11).

But imitation is not always intentional, which is why Diotrephes was so dangerous. Even if others knew that he was not setting a good example, over time Diotrephes would still influence and shape them. And as the leader of the congregation, he would shape its culture. We often cannot help but be influenced by those around us, and consequently we may end up imitating what is evil. The elder exhorts Gaius to choose imitation of the good over imitation of evil, tacitly acknowledging that it is possible to go either way.

It is vital to have good role models in our midst. Paul understood this when he encouraged the Corinthian congregation to follow him as he followed

Christ (1 Cor 11:1). We need good models to imitate. It is a major part of how we learn and mature, so we ought to take care to choose our models carefully.

Believers need role models at each stage of their growth. When I first became a Christian, I was deeply influenced by the leaders of my church and Bible-study group. Another friend discipled me as we met each week for a couple of hours of one-on-one Bible study and encouragement. I looked up to all of these men and women and imitated them in various ways. When I went to seminary, I entered a new stage of my Christian growth and found other models, some of whom were my instructors. And now as a divinity-school professor myself, I look to yet other models. At each stage, I have needed and benefited from the wise examples whom God put in my life.

But also at each stage of my Christian growth, there have been others who might have been a negative influence on me, as I'm sure would be the case for most people. Perhaps a bad influence comes in the form of a colleague with a temper problem, or a narcissistic student, or a neighbor with a foul mouth. As much as I loved my unbelieving jazz-musician buddies when I was in music school, there were some attitudes and practices that rubbed off on me in unhelpful ways.

Our task is to think carefully about the influence that others might have on us. There will always be good and bad models to imitate, so we need to be discerning. Let us consciously and deliberately seek out those who do what is good and imitate them. Let us also identify those whose example we ought to avoid. Pray that God would help us to reject negative influences and resist the imitation of evil.

Scripture Index

Subject Index

is evidence, 113
exhortation to, 142
with expiation, 53
for the Father, 78–79
for God, 67
of God, 64–66
God is, 143–44
lack of, 106
and light, 70
makes us His, 101–3
offers life, 116–18
one another, 72, 114, 193–94
as sacrifice, 121–22, 149
source of, 142–43
theme of, 2, 10–11, 178–80, 214
and truth, 187, 189
walking in, 60, 64
for the world, 78–79
marriage, view on, 120
mercy, 187, 190–91
Merkel, Angela, 162
Messiah, Jesus is the, 9
missions, support of, 221
Muratorian Canon, 5
murder, is hate in action, 118
murderer, 116, 119
Muslims, and Christians, 163–64
obedience, 57, 193
Old Testament, references to, 2
opponents, John's, 8
orthodoxy, better understand, 204
outline: of 1 John, 14
of 3 John, 211
overcoming, the world, 160–61
partnering, with missionaries, 220–22
Passover lamb, 51
peace, 187, 190–91
perfectionism, 40, 43, 109–10
Perpetua, 107
persecution, 31, 139; context of, 171
perseverance, 201
Philby, Kim, 96
pornography, struggles with, 43
prayer, 165, 167
approaching God in, 171
for believers, 168
is offered, 214
power of, 222
praying: for someone, 167–68

for someone caught in sin, 173
proclamation: is continued, 34–35
importance of, 30–31
is a joy, 32–33
Promise Keepers, 120
propitiation, 50–54; and expiation, 62–63
for our sins, 144, 149, 159
the word, 12
purification: acts of, 103
from unrighteousness, 40
purpose, for John's writing, 47–48
reason, appeal to, 27
reassurance: comes in two, 126
in the face of fear, 129
the ultimate, 128
reconciliation, with God, 84
regeneration, and faith, 154
relationship: growing in our, 98
truth and, 94
remaining, in him, 59, 98
in the Son, 94
resurrection: is key, 92
links to the, 25
right, everyone who does right, 100
righteousness, of Jesus, 49
sacrifice: atoning, 144
Jesus's, 39
is love, 121–24
of a spotless animal, 49–50
salvation, plan of, 199
savior, role as, 158
scapegoat, 52
secret sin, 45–46
secularism, rise of, 30
seed, referring to, 105–7, 116
sin: atoning sacrifice for, 199
avoidance of, 48
in believers, 109
casual attitude towards, 60
comfortable with, 44–46
confession of, 34, 39–40
and forgiveness, 11–12
that leads to death, 167–68
living according to, 37
pattern of, 168
purifies us from, 38–39
secret, 45–46
today, 43
sinlessness, 109–10
sinning, keeps on, 103, 109

Author Index